Discovery at Rosetta

Discovery

at

Rosetta

Jonathan Downs

CONSTABLE • LONDON

Constable & Robinson Ltd
3 The Lanchesters
162 Fulham Palace Road
London W6 9ER
www.constablerobinson.com

This edition published by Constable,
an imprint of Constable & Robinson, 2008

A copy of the British Library Cataloguing in Publication
Data is available from the British Library

ISBN: 978-1-84529-579-0

Printed and bound in the EU

1 3 5 7 9 10 8 6 4 2

Mixed Sources
Product group from well-managed
forests and other controlled sources
www.fsc.org Cert no. SA-COC-1565
© 1996 Forest Stewardship Council

For my father

Contents

Acknowledgements

There are numerous people without whose generous assistance this book would never have been possible. At the British Museum I would like to thank Dr Patricia Usick, Honorary Archivist, and Dr Richard Parkinson, Keeper of the Department of Ancient Egypt and Sudan; I would also like to thank Adrian James, Chief Librarian of the Society of Antiquaries of London; Dr Frances Willmoth at the library of Jesus College, Cambridge; Dr Brian Muhs at the University of Leiden; the Beinecke Rare Book and Manuscript Library at Yale University and the Philomathean Society of the University of Pennsylvania.

I would like to thank Roland Pintat of the Bibliothèque nationale de France for his tireless patience; thanks also to Yves Laissus for his help regarding the savants; but in particular I would like to thank Marie-Claire Cuvillier, Secrétaire générale of the Société française d'égyptologie, for providing me so readily with her generous support, research assistance, and the work of the esteemed Jean Leclant.

I would also like to thank Anne Yannoulis for the diaries of her ancestor Major T. Marmaduke Wybourn – and Elizabeth Imlay, for publishing his story in *Sea-Soldier*, which led to the production of this book.

Thanks also to Peter Furtado, Charlotte Crow, and Sheila Corr of *History Today*; Rob Gray, House and Collections Manager of the National Trust property Kingston Lacy; Middle East specialist Dr Manouchehr Moshtagh Khorasani; historian John Norris; Trudy Foster of the Jersey Heritage Trust; L/Sgt Gorman of the Scots Guards archives; authors Paul Strathern, Dorothy King, and William St Clair. Thanks also to Leo Hollis at Constable & Robinson and Dr David Dalby, founder of the Linguasphere Observatory, l'Observatoire Linguistique, for their continual help and support. Finally, more than I could ever convey, to my wife, Alison, who made it all possible.

J.D., 2008

Illustrations

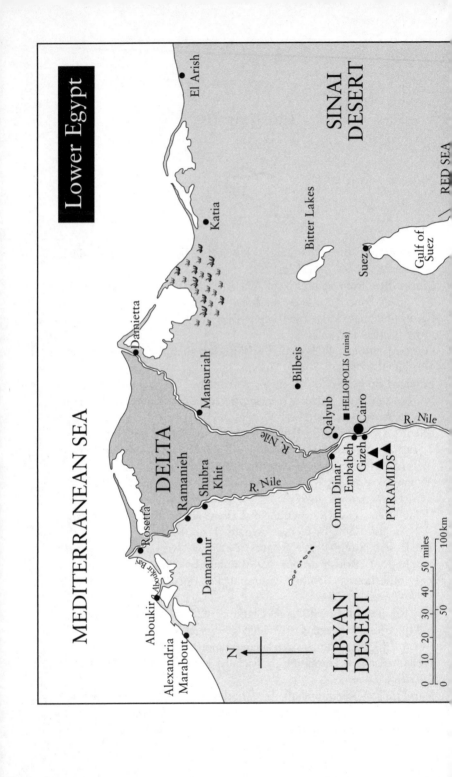

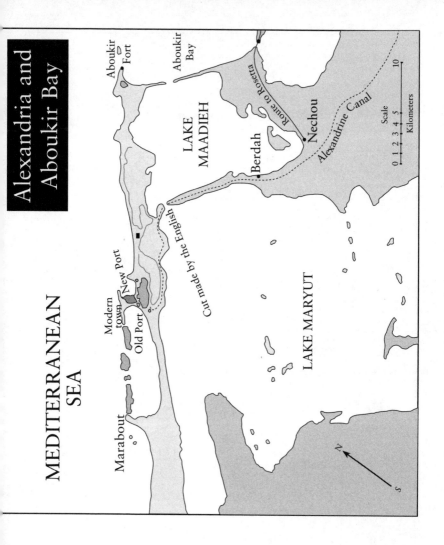

From an original map by savant Édouard de Villiers du Terrage, showing the
cuts through the Alexandrine Canal, which flooded the once dried-up plain of
Lake Maryut with the waters of Lake Maadieh, isolating French Alexandria during
the Anglo-Turkish siege of 1801.

FRANCE

DALMATI

Genoa

Marseilles
Toulon

CORSICA
Ajaccio

Civita
Vecchia •Rome

ADRIATIC SEA

SARDINIA

Naples

ITALY

Messina

SICILY
Syracuse

MALTA

MEDITER

The Voyage to Egypt,
May–July 1798

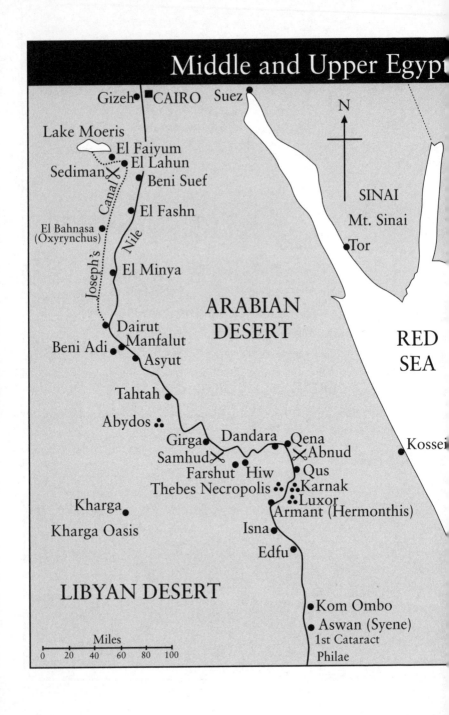

Middle and Upper Egypt

Gizeh • ■CAIRO Suez•

N

Lake Moeris
El Faiyum
El Lahun
Sediman ✕
Beni Suef

Canal

SINAI
Mt. Sinai

El Fashn

Tor

El Bahnasa
(Oxyrynchus)

Nile

Joseph's

El Minya

ARABIAN
DESERT

RED
SEA

Dairut
Manfalut
Beni Adi •
Asyut

Tahtah

Abydos ∴

Girga Dandara Qena
Samhud ✕   ✕Abnud
Farshut Hiw   Qus
Thebes Necropolis ∴ •∴Karnak
                      ∴Luxor
Kharga •   Armant (Hermonthis)
Kharga Oasis   Isna•

Kossei

Edfu•

LIBYAN DESERT

•Kom Ombo
• Aswan (Syene)
1st Cataract
Philae

Miles
0 20 40 60 80 100

Introduction

The Sword and the Stone

Somewhere out to sea, bearing down furiously upon the sweltering coast of Egypt, came an invasion fleet sent by the greatest power in the East. Crammed aboard the plunging decks, clutching musket, pistol and razor-sharp *yataghan* sword, were 15,000 Ottoman Turks bent on revenge: after Bonaparte's slaughter of their countrymen in Palestine and his desecration of the Holy Land, they were coming for French blood.

The attack due at any moment, *chef de brigade* Dhautpoul, battalion commander of the engineers in the Delta, ordered Lieutenant Pierre François Xavier Bouchard to repair and re-inforce the crumbling outer wall of Fort Julien, on the shores of the west branch of the Nile. The ancient stone castle stood just to the north of a small, palm-lined port called Al-Rashid – known to Europeans as 'Rosetta'. As others anxiously scanned the horizon for signs of Turkish sail, Bouchard hurriedly organized his platoon and labourers. Little did he realize, in the midst of their frantic efforts, that he was about to make an extraordinary discovery – a discovery that would open the floodgates of history, reviving the gods of the Nile after two thousand years of their patient, megalithic meditation. Bouchard's engineers would unwittingly provide the key to the greatest mystery of this most ancient of antique lands.

Cooled by the sea breeze and tormented by the tempting blue waters of the Nile before them, the sweating engineers waited, ready on the guy-ropes. Bouchard gave the order: the ropes tautened and the sledge-hammers swung. Within moments the ramshackle wall came crashing down, great blocks of stone tumbling in a stinging hail of fragments and choking clouds of ochre dust. Work stopped abruptly. There, barely visible among the sand and rubble of the foundations, was an unusual chunk of dark, chiselled rock. Eager for reward, labourers shovelled aside the loose debris as the hitherto unknown lieutenant of engineers moved quickly through the small crowd which had begun to gather. He knelt and brushed away the dust to reveal at first a smooth surface; until, beneath his fingers, he felt the delicate indentations of a tightly compacted inscription.

Bouchard had found the Rosetta Stone.

The Rosetta Stone is arguably the most important Egyptian artefact ever discovered. Without it, Egypt would have stayed a silent civilization, the hieroglyphs inscribed upon its tombs, temples, monuments and memorials remaining so much elegant and artistic incomprehensibility. The sacred writing of the Egyptian priesthood had resisted the enquiries of the profane since its first institution; with the passing of the pharaohs and the slow dwindling death of their religion, the arcane script seemed destined never to reveal its secrets – until that hot day on the shores of the Nile.

What Bouchard had found was a large, irregular-shaped slab of hard, dark rock, the major portion of a broken stele (an inscribed stone),[1] often incorrectly described as granite or basalt but considered by the British Museum to be granodiorite, not black, but grey, shot with traces of pink. It is 112.3 cm high, 75.7 cm wide, 28.4 cm thick, and weighs approximately 762 kg – over three-quarters of a ton.[2] On its smooth, polished face, was a declaration, intricately carved in three different scripts arranged in three horizontal bands, Greek at the bottom; popularly spoken, or 'demotic' Egyptian across the centre; and, at the top, a mere fourteen incomplete lines of the tantalizing and indecipherable ancient Egyptian hieroglyphics. It was recognized that the Greek, though ancient, was a known language and could be translated; if it could be correlated to the hieroglyphs, the stone would become a linguistic key, a key to the written records across the whole of the Nile kingdom. It would reveal the history of a world lost to humanity, enabling ancient Egypt to tell its tale, the secrets of the priests to be finally decoded. At last, the stones would speak.

On 1 July 1798, barely a year before the find, General Napoleon Bonaparte had assembled an army of nearly 40,000 men and landed on the Egyptian coast. In the space of just three and a half weeks he captured Alexandria, Rosetta and marched into Cairo, having defeated Mameluke forces at the Battle of the Pyramids. However, Bonaparte had determined this was to be no ordinary conquest or military occupation: it was an adventure into uncharted territory, no less than the voyages of Columbus or Cook across alien seas. The future emperor of France had brought with him the specialists who would record the grand opening of Egypt to the West.

This was carried out by 167 scholars and scientists, members of the Commission of the Sciences and Arts, from engineers and astronomers, to geographers, botanists and artists. These 'savants' performed more than an inventory of a new colony, or a second Domesday Book for an enquiring conqueror; they revealed the scattered titanic remnants of a lost civilization, their exhaustive efforts an expression of that insatiable eighteenth-century appetite for discovery, a thirst for knowledge which had raged through the cultural centres and societies of Europe for decades. Although there had been published works throughout the centuries concerning the nature of Egypt, there had never before been a like enterprise: this was to be the first modern archaeological expedition of its kind.

However, after three years of isolated occupation, Bonaparte's oriental dreams were finally crushed in 1801. In March of that year, the British executed a daring assault on the heavily defended beaches of Aboukir on the Mediterranean coast, as an allied Ottoman army marched across the desert border from Syria.

The news sent shock-waves down to Cairo. General Abdallah Menou, now commander-in-chief of the French forces, marched north from the capital four days later with only half his army, the savants and their precious collections of artefacts soon to follow. Arrogant and blustering, Menou was no leader of men. His pompous administrative notes and lecturing tone inspired indignation among his peers and ribald jokes among the ranks. Within ten days of leaving Cairo, he had lost the Battle of Canopus to Sir Ralph Abercromby, retreated to Alexandria and slammed the gates. By the end of April, Rosetta was taken by the Anglo-Turkish allies and Alexandria was surrounded, cut off and besieged. After the fall of Cairo in June, the siege of Alexandria was the last action of the French forces in Egypt. In September 1801, it was all over.

What the British army had not fully anticipated was that the French expeditionary force had amassed the largest collection of Egyptian artefacts ever seen, ranging from captured butter-flies to colossal granite statuary and sarcophagi, in total amounting to over 50 tons of relics. Applying the law of arms, Britain demanded the treasures of Egypt be handed over – particularly the Rosetta Stone, whose fame had been trumpeted across Europe since its discovery two years earlier. Had the artefacts been left to France, Britain's mortal enemy, there would have been no guarantee that British scholars would ever have been able to see or study them again; there were no common agreements to share such works of art, no international committees or foundations to house them for the benefit of all peoples: possession was imperative.

As far as the British army was concerned these massive trophies were to be seized from a vanquished foe for the glory of King George. They were spoils of war, and the celebrated Rosetta Stone was their crowning glory. At last, here would be evidence to a fearful populace that Bonaparte could be defeated – as Nelson had hounded him at sea, so too could the scarlet line of battle drive him from his conquests on land. The matter proved not as simple as the army had hoped.

In February 1802, after the exhausting desert campaign that saw the end of French colonial aspirations in the Middle East, a captured French frigate, HMS *L'Egyptienne*, sailed into Portsmouth harbour to unload its weary occupants. The frigate was itself a grand prize of the Royal Navy, taken from the port of Alexandria. Along with several storm-tossed officers of the general staff, there was a colonel of the 3rd Foot Guards, Tomkyns Hilgrove Turner, later knight of the realm and attached to the royal household. In his charge, in the creaking hold of the *L'Egyptienne*, buffeted by the baggage and belongings of his fellow officers, was a very precious cargo: the massive chiselled relic uncovered by Bouchard.

How precisely the Rosetta Stone came to Britain aboard HMS *L'Egyptienne* remained something of a mystery. More mysterious still is Turner's heroic tale of how he personally had seized the Rosetta Stone from the outraged French commander and carried it off in triumph with the aid of a squad of artillerymen. Despite the overwhelming interest in the stone and the Egypt affair, his dramatic account did not appear in print until eight years later, in a letter addressed to the Society of Antiquaries of London.[3] In it, Turner cites no witnesses to his actions, other than respectful mention of Lord Hutchinson, his commander-in-chief. The only man to shine in the affair, according to Turner, was Turner himself.

However, the renowned traveller, scholar, antiquary and mineralogist, the Reverend Edward Daniel Clarke, happened to be in Alexandria with Turner in September 1801, and told a very different story. His multi-volume memoirs, *Travels in Various Countries of Europe, Asia and Africa*,[4] was published shortly after the emergence of Turner's statement. In it there is a different detailed account of the hand-over of the stone – as if in direct response to Turner's claim.

Upon their arrival in Alexandria just after the French surrendered to the besieging British and Turkish forces, Clarke and his student companion, John Cripps, had met up with William Richard Hamilton, the diplomatic envoy and personal secretary of His Majesty's Ambassador to Constantinople, Lord Elgin. With the formal capitulation of the French there came the awkward problem of taking charge of the great collection of antiquities. Responding to the British commander's requests for assistance, Clarke, Cripps and Hamilton were entrusted with this task. In his account of 1810, Turner does not mention them.

In order to execute their new commission, the trio of Englishmen had to liaise directly with the French savants – into whose care and protection the stone had originally fallen and who had undertaken the first attempts at translating its ancient inscription. According to the memoirs of Edward Daniel Clarke, the stone was not 'captured' as Turner claimed, but handed over secretively to Cripps, Hamilton and himself in the quiet backstreets of Alexandria, by an unnamed French officer, a member of the savants' Institut d'Égypte. Turner, wrote Clarke, was not present. The mystery deepened in the 1950s with the discovery of a document among the personal papers of an officer of Marines, Major T. Marmaduke Wybourn, who had served in the Egypt campaign during the siege of Alexandria. The document is a list of some twenty artefacts proudly entitled 'Relicts bro.t down from Egypt, and now in the British

Museum, by me, in the Madras, 50 guns'. Item 8 on the mundane list of treasures is readily identifiable:

> 8. *A stone with three inscriptions, hieroglyphics, Gothic and Greek, black granite from Rosetta.*

Wybourn's list seemed to cast as much doubt upon Turner's claims as Clarke had done in his memoirs – this list suggested the stone sailed to England aboard HMS *Madras*, not HMS *L'Egyptienne*.

Of the other witnesses to these events, John Cripps evidently left journal entries to his elder tutor, Clarke, and focused on other aspects of antiquities in his later years, content with his mentor's account; William Richard Hamilton, in his own report of the period, entitled *Aegyptiaca*, is restrained, self-effacing, his words treading diplomatically. He does not mention Turner by name, nor any heroic actions – and certainly not Turner's capture of the stone.

Despite this discrepancy, history tends to credit Turner with the stone's recovery, accepting his version of events and his warrior's assertion that it was a military trophy, a triumph of British arms. However, it was Clarke, Cripps and Hamilton who helped Turner secure those objects now standing in the Egyptian collection of the British Museum – and more besides.

There was no grand surrender of magnificent art treasures to a gracious victor by a humbled enemy. Instead, the surrender of Alexandria was only the first act in a drama that was to last another two weeks, its final stages climaxing in the greatest scavenger hunt of the day, a chase through the labyrinthine byways and backwaters of Alexandria, at one point led by Alexandrian informants to the stinking hold of a half-crippled hulk used as a hospital ship. Clarke, Cripps and Hamilton encountered an Aladdin's cave of treasures, the like of which they had never seen before, all carefully concealed within the ancient capital, their efforts continually frustrated by the blustering evasion of the eccentric *général en chef*, the notorious Jacques 'Abdallah Pasha' Menou. Of all the pieces, Menou fought the most tenacious struggle over the Rosetta Stone.

Caught amid the thrashings of the two opposing army commanders, the dour, gruff and impatient General Sir John Hely-Hutchinson on the one hand, and the maddening Menou on the other, the French savants and English scholars co-operated as well as they could in the difficult circumstances. Abused, arrested, and threatened by their own forces, the savants had been abandoned by Menou; with nowhere to turn, their only allies were the English scholars. Though first perceived as the enemy, Clarke, Cripps and Hamilton pleaded with Hutchinson on their behalf, saving many of their invaluable collections from the clutches of the British military.

It is possible that this mutual understanding lies at the heart of the successful British recovery of the Rosetta Stone. History owes the men of the Institut d'Égypte more than a passing comment or footnote that they gave birth to the explosion that became Egyptology: if Turner is to be believed, the stone was wrested from the grip of a crass and arrogant enemy who, in his thoughtless rage, tried to damage the arte-fact at its point of capture. However, if Clarke is to be believed, the recovery of the relic owes as much to scholar-ship and science as the sword – for it would appear that the French savants had tried not simply to surrender it, but also to preserve it. Using the accounts of William Richard Hamilton, the French savants themselves, the correspondence of General Jacques Abdallah Menou, and the detailed memoirs of Edward Daniel Clarke, Colonel Turner's statement will be tested and contrasted to uncover how, and by whose hand, Britain acquired the Rosetta Stone.

The truth lies hidden somewhere between Clarke, Turner and the savants. To find it involves a journey with the greatest general of the age, Napoleon Bonaparte, who in 1798 was bent on oriental conquest and immortal glory. For the Mameluke horsemen of Egypt the journey was to prove an appalling encounter with a drilled, disciplined and professional army, and an occupying force of alien political and religious ideals. For the French soldier, it was hoped to be a great adventure in a mystic land – a land known to him chiefly through Holy Scripture, rich with golden treasures and painted palaces, soaring towers and turrets. For the extraordinary men of the Commission of the Sciences and Arts it would be the opportunity of a lifetime: to explore the lost world on the Nile.

1

Egypt: The Lost World

Egypt has entranced the world for millennia, acquiring an almost mythical status. Its cryptic inscriptions, colossal temples and monuments led historians and philosophers to believe that here was formed the first civilization of man, here was the source of all knowledge – and here could be found the answers to imponderable universal mysteries. There are few places on earth that have inspired the same romantic associations as the lost world on the Nile – its exotic qualities heightened for many by the threatening, inexorable creep of the desert, gods and goddesses swallowed by seas of shifting sands, consuming the vanities of long-dead kings.

It is understandably difficult for us to appreciate that even to our classical forebears in Greece, Persia or Rome, Egypt was already considered an ancient land. It was believed to be the oldest nation in the world, though this was debated, some believing the same of Phrygia, the realm of King Midas in Asia Minor. According to Herodotus, writing in the fifth century BC, there was an attempt to resolve this question in the reign of the Pharaoh Psammetichus,[1] who conducted a bizarre experiment to discover the truth of man's origins: he ordered two newborn infants be given to a shepherd and reared among his flocks, and that they should live beyond the reach of any human voice until they could speak.

It was Psammetichus' belief that, with no modern tongue to imitate, their first utterance would stem from the root language of all mankind. In the event, reports Herodotus, on one of the daily visits of the shepherd (who kept his charges alone in a hut, far removed from his own home) the two-year-old children cried out for *bekos* – which was identified as a Phrygian word for bread. Therefore, they concluded, the Phrygian nation must be older than the Egyptian. Herodotus comments on the Greek version of the tale which included other 'absurdities', but goes on to say this was what he had been told by the learned Egyptian priests of Heliopolis, whose word was certainly to be trusted.

Despite the evidence of the Phrygian infants, Egypt has the longest continuous written history of any nation on earth. The Turin Canon, written in the thirteenth century BC, provides king lists that identify Menes as the first ruler of the first dynasty of Upper and Lower Egypt in roughly 3100 BC. The Palermo Stone, an Egyptian stele fragment in Sicily since 1866, bears king lists that predate Menes considerably, indicating pre-dynastic rule of Egyptian pharaohs as long ago as 4400 BC. Even discounting these unconfirmed pre-dynastic kings, from Menes to the present, Egypt has historical records of some kind for at least 5,000 years.

The perception of this great-grandfather of the ancient world has varied from civilization to civilization, but we owe much of our inherited interpretation of Egyptian culture to the Greeks. Its deep-rooted religious system with its colossal monuments and temples of a scale beyond even their own drew Greek adventurers, philosophers and merchants to Egyptian shores from the earliest days. Herodotus devoted a significant portion of his great *Histories* to descriptions of Egypt's secular and religious practices, its history and geography. 'It has very many remarkable features and has produced more monuments which beggar belief than anywhere else in the world.'[2] Egyptians pursued customs that Herodotus described as 'opposite to other nations' – their sexual politics (women sold goods in the market while men did the weaving at home), their sailing methods, their dress, their writing – all was different, upside-down, or backward compared with the Greek.[3]

Greek mercenaries had fought against the Persians in the army of the Pharaoh Amasis (569–526 BC) and Greek merchants inhabited settlements in the Nile Delta, in particular Naucratis and later Alexandria. To Greek philosophers and commentators, Egypt was an ancient and venerable civilization entirely independent of their own cultural traditions – with an alien script of animals and objects which, being familiar, tantalized in its defiance of understanding. Egypt was as mysterious then as it later was to the first European explorers of the eighteenth and nineteenth centuries.

The Egyptian influence is evident in Greek science and art: Greek thinkers looked upon Egypt as the ancient source of wisdom and religious devotion and reflected this in their architecture and statuary. The Greek historian Diodorus Siculus, writing in the first century BC, described instances of Greek scholars travelling to Egypt to study – perhaps much in the same way as the Grand Tourists of the eighteenth century looked upon Italy and Greece. Pythagoras and Plato both travelled to Egypt, the latter allegedly to become initiated into the arcane Egyptian mystery schools. Plato ascribed the invention of numbers, arithmetic, astronomy and, above all, writing, to an ancient Egyptian deity he called 'Theuth', identified with the sacred ibis. This is also an Egyptian tradition, that the ibis-headed 'Thoth' was the god of science who created hieroglyphs and more. Although Pliny mentions Accadian cuneiform and Diodorus Siculus speaks of Ethiopian hieroglyphic writing, it was generally accepted that the Egyptian hieroglyph was the oldest in the world.

There are those who would compare the two cultures of Greece and Egypt to two ends of a spectrum – the Greek, of 'scientific' and rational thought, in opposition to the Egyptian, of myth and magic. In Egypt, logical experimentation was entwined with theology, involving their complex pantheon of gods – in contrast to Greece, where philosophers such as Socrates and Plato made deductive reasoning their aim and proved concepts by argument alone – justice was justice, irrespective of the nature of Zeus or Poseidon.

However, to understand Egypt required an understanding of the hieroglyphs, and this was where the Greeks fell short. Unable to decipher the inscriptions and thereby interpret the culture, this impenetrability served only to make Egypt still more exotic, particularly as these symbols were carved on temples large enough for a thousand sons of Zeus. The priests of Egypt were not about to divulge their secret.

The greatest obstacle to the translation of hieroglyphs by the Greeks was their assumption that Egyptian thinking was much as their own. By the fifth century BC, Greek religious beliefs had for some time been viewed by philosophers more as allegories than literal truths, and they mistakenly applied this same allegorical yardstick to Egyptian mythology and its sacred inscriptions. Diodorus Siculus devoted much of his *Historic Library* to the study of Egypt; he stated plainly that Egyptian writing did not use syllables as in other languages, but instead conveyed its meanings through the significance of the objects depicted and their figurative meaning. According to his confident assertion, the hieroglyphic image of a serpent or hawk would indicate not a sound or a character within a word, but a quality or intent, such as stealth or speed. This approach affected all subsequent European attitudes to Egypt: for centuries it was seen as a land that communicated not by letter but by mystic symbol.[4]

In the third century AD these views eventually resulted in Plotinus' foundation of a new school of 'mystic' Platonic

philosophy. This doctrine was to shape western European attitudes to Egypt – and to hieroglyphs – for the next 1,500 years.
In this Neoplatonism of Plotinus, hieroglyphic images were
seen as occult, esoteric symbols that could reveal the truth of
all things only to the initiated philosopher. As a script they
became part of a philosophical movement which, with the
growth of alchemy in the Middle Ages and Renaissance, saw
the study of Egypt transformed into more an exercise in meta-
physics and mysticism than history. Thus to subsequent
generations Egypt became the gateway to ancient wisdom, its
portals and mysteries guarded by occult images carved in stone.
For many this attitude persists today.

The struggles of the medieval and Renaissance thinkers to
uncover the meaning of hieroglyphs seemed secondary to their
interest in using Egyptian script and motifs as iconic symbols of
mystic philosophy. The study of alchemy, in its lowest form the
pursuit of turning base metal into gold, was at its highest a study
of disciplines to transcend the physical world in search of divine
enlightenment. In this search, the supposed Egyptian mysteries
once more played their part, with hieroglyphs relegated to the
role of symbols laden within hidden meaning. However, in the
sixteenth and seventeenth centuries the study of hieroglyphs
increasingly became more a matter of science than philosophy,
and this led to the first appearance of an Egyptian script in Europe.
The wealthy noble Roman traveller and collector Pietro della Valle
(1586–1652) spent twelve years touring the Mediterranean and
the Near and Middle East. As well as an extensive collection of
antiquities, he returned with documents from Egypt that included
rare manuscripts detailing Coptic grammar and vocabulary.

Coptic was a form of the ancient spoken tongue of Pharaonic
Egypt, but was not devised as a written language until the
second century AD, using a combination of Greek letters and
new characters to convey particular Egyptian sounds not
expressed by the Greek alphabet.[5] Della Valle's manuscripts

formed the foundation of new European studies in Coptic, an introduction to which was published by the great Jesuit thinker and Renaissance scholar Athanasius Kircher in 1636. This became the first sample of an Egyptian language published in a European tongue. Consequently, Kircher's introduction to Coptic is regarded as one of the first works of egyptology – it was followed in 1644 by the publication of Della Valle's Coptic grammar keys and vocabulary. A contemporary of Galileo, and a student of the hermetic philosophy so popular in the Renaissance, Kircher produced landmark works in Egyptology, proclaiming his belief in the holistic nature of Egyptian religion and script – the most accurate assessment of hieroglyphics before their eventual translation.

In the eighteenth century, the emphasis shifted to the practical and tangible pursuits of archaeology. Rome became the natural centre for these new studies, and researchers and amateur antiquaries flocked to the old capital. The 1700s were to witness no less than the birth of both a new type of science, and a new type of scientist.

By the end of the 1700s, the 'antiquary', a dedicated collector of antiquities, had become something of a professional historical detective. This was a far cry from the misguided enthusiast of the previous century, who had sought strange objects to fill his often valueless cabinet of curiosities – coins arranged according to colour, or size, the unidentifiable detritus of dubious period laid next to the occasional rare artefact, the collector unaware of the true nature of his collection. By contrast, British antiquarian researchers of the eighteenth century were used regularly in great topographical and sociological surveys as far-reaching as the Domesday Book; they could analyse ancient road networks or river courses, and determine through excavation the shifting patterns of the social and economic welfare of people, and the evolution of the landscape. Antiquarianism was more than the birth of modern archaeology – it was the application of a new way of looking at history, through studied, detailed observation and comparison, rather than solely by reference to classical authorities.

Previously, the social status of antiquaries had been uncertain: by nature the antiquary concentrated on his chosen subject often to the exclusion of all else, whereas the educated gentleman did not – he had a broad, useful, general knowledge. Although the sciences became more defined in the latter half of the eighteenth century, history, aesthetics and art came to blend with the rise of the wealthy connoisseur. Soon there was no stopping the tidal wave of excitement for antiquity within the moneyed classes: to have an interest in the aesthetic quality of the past and the beauty of bygone civilizations was soon accepted as part of a cultured gentleman's education.

Important research findings were often reported to the gatherings of the august Royal Society. Here, at the 'invisible college' of natural philosophers, all 'physico-mathematicall and experimentall learning' was to be pursued. The majority of members of this learned society and others were keen amateurs who grew to become dedicated collectors. Some of their artefacts would later adorn the new British Museum, founded primarily to house a collection of more than 71,000 objects willed to the nation by the great naturalist and antiquary Sir Hans Sloane, upon his death in 1753. Sloane, the archetypal gentleman scientist of his age, was president of both the Royal College of Physicians and the Royal Society. Many of his acquaintances gathered pieces for him on their travels and his collection swelled accordingly – although his bequest included over 150 Egyptian objects, they were not colossal statuary or refined sculpture, but small curiosities, collected arbitrarily rather than with any archaeological intent.

The popular reawakening of interest in antiquity was fuelled by excavations at Herculaneum, which began in 1738, and

Pompeii, in 1748. The works attracted swarms of enthusiasts who travelled to Italy to study and, above all, collect antiquities. A fire had been kindled in cultural circles across northern Europe, and these collectors looked south to the Mediterranean. Travel to France and Italy had been an essential part of upper-class education since the 1500s, when it had become fashionable for young aristocrats to visit Paris, Venice, Florence and Rome as the pinnacle of their classical education. Edward De Vere, the 17th Earl of Oxford, one of several candidates for the authorship of Shakespeare's works, was often called the 'Italian Earl' owing to his extraordinary classical knowledge and the tastes he acquired during his travels. Over the next two hundred years this fascination for the ancient world increased dramatically. The neoclassical movement in art in the eighteenth century generated an ever-increasing interest in classical antiquity, its artists expressing a love for classical harmony and proportion – characteristics most visible in the surviving architecture of Rome and Greece.

Although Italy was key to the Grand Tour, adventurous travellers went further afield. Archaeologists and antiquaries, explorers and travellers eventually forced a path to the more ancient Greek remains of Athens and the islands – few would venture to the Asiatic interior of the Ottoman Empire or even Cyprus or Alexandria, as these involved longer sea-journeys. The rewards of such voyages were made evident when William Lethieullier returned from Turkey and Egypt in 1756, bringing with him the first mummy to be displayed in the British Museum.

The attitude of many north Europeans to the Asian or African landscape of antiquity is exemplified in a letter from Alexandria by Charles Sloane to his brother: he wrote with some distaste of 'the barbarians' who inhabited the country, continuing to do what they had done for ages, namely, to 'destroy everything of antiquity remaining'.[6] For this very reason, archaeological collecting was seen by antiquaries as preservation rather than random looting or theft. With their own reawakening to a classical past, the intellectual European elite eventually came to feel they had a greater claim to antiquity than the inhabitants surrounded by it – inhabitants who, in allowing their great artistic achievements to fall into ruin or be consumed by the deserts, displayed what was interpreted as a mystifying cultural apathy. Many travellers distinguished ancient Greeks and ancient Egyptians from their modern descendants, who seemed corrupt and benighted to the touring aesthetes, who worshipped the faded fantasy of the former but despised and distrusted the latter.

There was little doubt that North Africa west of Alexandria was dangerous. Thomas Shaw, a chaplain in Algiers and later Regius Professor of Greek at Oxford, made a tour of Egypt, Sinai and Cyprus in 1721. On occasions he headed into the wilder interior of 'Barbary' and subsequently, in 1738, wrote his famous *Travels or Observations relating to several parts of Barbary and the Levant*. James Bruce became another famous traveller and tourist; in the second half of the eighteenth century he explored Spain, Portugal and Italy and was later appointed consul in Algiers in 1763. He spent a year on an archaeological tour of North Africa, in the process sketching the Roman ruins of Carthage. Although Egypt was still terra incognita, Bruce made an attempt to penetrate the interior but suffered horrendous privations and ordeals: he endured shipwreck, robbery, capture and five months' imprisonment at the hands of natives on the edge of the Nubian desert, before making it finally to the upper reaches of the Nile.

This was far from tourism in any sense of the word – this was exploration. Few travellers attempted it, most keeping to Italy, Greece and Spain, though even this was still not for the faint-hearted. Travel was difficult enough in mainland Europe with its treacherous, ill-kept roads, exhausting coach travel and sites often accessible only to the hardiest of adventurers. Egypt offered little of the restorative comforts of Rome or the opulent salons of royal Naples, but was ruled by destructive savages of an alien culture and religion. As if this were not reason enough to avoid it, Egypt was set within the equally menacing Ottoman Empire, a monstrous force crouched on the shores of Asia, which only a century earlier had sent its invading hordes as far as the gates of Vienna. To the Grand Tourist Egypt was a lost world, the romance of its setting tainted by its barbarous keepers, the glories of its past fallen into ruin, its shattered remains lying scattered in the sands, neglected, unappreciated. How the land of the pharaohs had sunk into such a state is a story of gradual decline rather than cataclysmic destruction: Horus, the one-eyed god who had first unified the Nile kingdoms, must have wept the tears of heaven to see his Eden so despoiled.

Egypt's fall is a chronicle of the ebb and flow of foreign empires, dated by many from the invasion of the Assyrians under Esarhaddon in 671 BC, centuries before the full flowering of Greece or Rome. A Levantine revolt against Esarhaddon's father, King Sennacherib, had been supported by Egyptian and Nubian forces, and to safeguard against future attack, the Assyrians marched on the Nile and captured Memphis. Years later Esarhaddon's son, Ashurbanipal, finished the work, sacking Thebes and installing puppet kings, effectively marking the end of Egyptian rule over its own land. Its independence was not fully to return until the twentieth century, 2,500 years later.

The Assyrian Empire collapsed in 612 BC, and the long-reigning Pharaoh Psamtek I, once Ashurbanipal's vassal, reconquered the country in a resurgence of Egyptian nationalism that flourished for a brief time in the hope of resurrecting the ancient past. However, Egypt fell once again, but to a new force from the East, the Persian Empire, under King Cambyses in 525 BC. This, the subjugation under the Achaemenid Persians, is considered the most bleak episode of Egypt's history. The Greeks, who had developed strong trading links with Egypt, had mustered mercenary troops to fight alongside the Pharaoh Amasis, but had failed to stem the tide of the Persian advance – the Greeks would meet this enemy time and again over the ensuing decades at the Battles of Marathon, Thermopylae, Salamis and Plataea.

Egypt erupted with isolated rebellion against the tyrannical Persian administration only a few years later, sufficiently weakening the empire's grip to such an extent that, when Alexander the Great landed in 332 BC, he smashed the remnants of Persian dominance in Egypt with ease. Alexander was hailed as a liberator, and had himself crowned pharaoh in the Temple of Ptah at Memphis, revered by the Egyptians as the divine son of Amun himself. His new Mediterranean port capital of Alexandria was later to become the most important city in the eastern Mediterranean, second only to Byzantium.

In contrast to the powerful effect he had on the nation, the great deliverer Alexander spent only one year in Egypt. Having founded his new capital and instituted a provincial government administration, which wisely respected Egyptian customs and religious observance, he was able to use Egypt's wealth to fund his campaigns and his ultimate goal, the annihilation of the Persian Empire. Only one year after his arrival, he took his forces and headed to Phoenicia, never to return. After Alexander's death in Babylon eight years later, in 323 BC, the largest empire ever known was soon to crack and finally shatter into separate pieces, descending into a Macedonian war on an international scale.

Ptolemy, one of Alexander's generals, was appointed satrap of Egypt, and after the Wars of the Succession won independence for his new state, crowning himself king in 305 BC and taking the name of Ptolemy I 'Soter' (Saviour). His dynasty was to last nearly 300 years, until the death of the fabled Cleopatra, last Queen of Egypt, in 30 BC. It was during the rule of these Greek pharaohs that the Rosetta Stone was created.

With the death of Cleopatra, Egypt came formally under the yoke of Rome's new empire and its new First Consul, Augustus, and would remain so for the next 700 years. Rome understood that religion would play a key role in its wealthy new province of Ægyptus, arguably more so than in any of its other conquests. Although, like Alexander before them, the Romans did not interfere with the complexities of Egyptian religious practices, the influx of foreign invaders had an inevitable impact on the Egyptian priesthood: after Alexander, the Ptolemies had successively 'Hellenized' the Egyptian gods, associating their own Greek gods with those of Egypt; thus the multi-faceted Hermes, the messenger and herald of the divine, was associated with Thoth, the bringer of wisdom and divine knowledge. This dilution of Egyptian deities and reassignment of their divine duties was continued with the importation of Roman gods and their particular functions; as a result many temple ruins in Egypt are more Roman or Ptolemaic Greek than Pharaonic Egyptian. In this fashion the power of the priesthood slowly dwindled through the centuries, its gods fading as surely as their images would soon be swallowed by the sands. But the greatest threat to over 3,000 years of Egyptian tradition came not from the invader's sword but from Christianity.

After the destruction of Jerusalem in AD 70 by the Romans, Alexandria became the new capital of Judaism and Jewish culture in the Mediterranean; with this new wave of immigration came an influx of Christians. There was little sustained resistance to this new faith from the Egyptian priesthood, and it has been argued that the old priesthood's long history of collaboration with the Greek and Roman administrations had left it impotent and incapable of defending what popular authority it had left. It was this period of religious flux in the first and second centuries that saw the development of the Coptic language – the ancient

Egyptian tongue rendered into Greco-Egyptian characters. In Coptic, the two cultures of Greece and Egypt had blended linguistically, forming a religious bridge, in that the new script was adopted by early evangelists and became the liturgical language of Christian Egypt.[7]

In AD 324, the Emperor Constantine moved the capital of the Roman Empire, building his new city in the wealthy trading port of Byzantium,[8] which duly became Constantinople, retaining this name until the twentieth century. With the tolerance of Christianity by Constantine and its eventual adoption across the empire, paganism in Egypt slowly died out over the course of the fourth century – although the cult of Isis still had its followers among Egyptians into the fifth century. Many of Egypt's temples were either converted to churches or abandoned. These events saw the end of the old priesthood and the use of hieroglyphs; henceforward the sacred inscriptions carved from the Delta to the cataracts of southern Egypt would remain a mute reminder of a lost civilization. Yet the most lasting change was still to come.

In the year 622, the Prophet Mohammed fled persecution from Mecca to Medina, and a new religious revolution was soon to take form. Egypt's complex mixture of Judaism, Christianity, vestigial cults and Gnosticism was to be inundated by a new tide of religious doctrine, one which would dominate the nation and the region to the present day – Islam.

Umar, second of the four chosen caliphs who succeeded Mohammed, sent an army of 4,000 into Egypt in the year 639. The following year a second army of some 12,000 joined them and defeated the Christian armies of Constantinople's 'Byzantine' Empire. The great trading empire was beset by Bulgars and Slavs to the north and Turks to the east, and made several failed attempts to recapture Egypt, the final bid made in 654. This invasion force too was defeated, setting the seal on the religious destiny of Egypt.

Over the following decades of fighting with the Byzantines, the new caliph put an end to nearly 1,000 years of Greco-Roman rule in Egypt and colonized the country. Egypt slowly became a Muslim nation, and in the eighth century, Arabic was adopted as the official language. The world of Islam eventually spread from Cordoba in Spain across North Africa to Baghdad; the new capital of Cairo was founded in the tenth century, and later adorned by the Al-Azhar Mosque, rivalling the seats of learning in Moorish Spain and the Baghdad House of Wisdom. However, the constant wars of succession and the struggle for power within Egypt had introduced an unforeseen change – an alien population had grown, swelling the ranks of armies on all sides. These warriors eventually became powerful enough to rule the Nile Valley and reach out beyond Sinai to defeat the Mongols. They were the Mamelukes.

The Mamelukes were originally enslaved soldiers, mainly Turkish non-Muslims captured or bought from poor families north of the Black Sea in south-western Russia and the Caucasus. Despite being considered the lowest of the military castes, they often became fiercely loyal to their tribal sheikh, much more so than to the sultan or caliph; their horsemanship and skill on the battlefield was an awesome spectacle, their courage and unflinching obedience similar to the Norse 'Varangian Guard' of the Byzantine emperors and dread Myrmidons of Xerxes.

Mamelukes were first used as troops by the Abbassid Arab armies in the eighth century, but were used with increasing frequency in Egypt until they came to be the largest military force in the country. They rose up in revolt, trying to establish Egypt as their own province, defending it against the Christian forces of Louis IX on the Seventh Crusade, capturing Louis and defeating the crusaders. By 1250 the Mamelukes rose to true independent power after bloody murders of succession within their own ranks.

As the Mamelukes rose in number in Egypt, the expanding enemy of the Byzantines, the Seljuk Turks, spread from the East into much of modern-day Turkey. In the eleventh century they established the Sultanate of Rum, occupying the lands once held by the Byzantine Romans. This eventually crumbled before the onslaught of the Mongol invasion of the mid-thirteenth century.[9] With the weakening power of the sultanate one of the surviving beyliks,[10] under Osman I, declared independence from the old sultan in 1299, and united other beys under his banner. Eventually, Osman, or Ottoman, forces spread across Asia Minor and, under Mehmed II, overwhelmed Constantine's old Byzantine capital in 1453. Here was born the Ottoman Empire, ruled from the Sublime Porte at Constantinople, later known as Istanbul.[11] At its height the Ottoman borders stretched from Vienna down to Yemen, across North Africa and down into Egypt. It was the greatest power in the Mediterranean, not fading until the end of the First World War.

Having established dominance in the eastern Mediterranean, and faced with the constant rebellion of the Mamelukes, Sultan Selim I invaded Egypt in 1517, and made it a vassal state of the Ottoman Empire, putting an end to Mameluke independence. It was to be ruled by a pasha in the name of the sultan, and the beys and sheikhs would at last bow to the Sublime Porte of Constantinople. Over the next 200 years the Mameluke influence in Egypt rendered Ottoman control almost impossible. When the pashas tried to quash the Mameluke practice of mass extortion, soldiers ran riot in open revolt or drove the pasha out of the capital. The Mamelukes were so unruly that on one occasion they returned a new pasha sent by the Porte on the grounds he would not pay them a gratuity and was therefore not wanted – they sent him home with a request for a replacement. The Ottomans changed their Egyptian pasha nearly every year, making continuous rule difficult, thus allowing the corrupt and despotic Mameluke beys to carry on their politics of assassination and usurpation unchecked – in Egypt the political pole was not so much greasy as bloody.

Insurrection followed insurrection, culminating, in the late 1700s, with the final stages of Mameluke rule before the French occupation. Ali Bey, in the appointed position of Sheikh al-Balad, had gained such power in Egypt and was considered so untrustworthy by the sultan that the Porte sent orders to Egypt for his execution. Ali intercepted these orders and succeeded in convincing his fellow beys that the Porte wished all of their deaths as well, and raised them to rebellion under his leadership. In 1769 Ali declared Egypt an independent state, seized control of much of the southern reaches of the Ottoman Empire and proclaimed himself sultan, in direct competition to Constantinople. In 1772 the Ottomans were forced to reconquer Egypt. Ali met the imperial army in a decisive battle, but was abandoned by two chieftains, Murad and Ibrahim Bey, who switched their allegiance to the sultan to safeguard their own positions.

However, they would both be a thorn in the side of the sultan for some time to come, contending with Ismail Bey for control of the province. By 1786 their constant revolt had grown too much for the Ottomans, and the Sublime Porte sent an expeditionary force to Egypt to restore imperial rule, defeating Murad Bey, who fled with Ibrahim southwards to Upper Egypt. In 1791 Ismail, who had been appointed Sheikh al-Balad, died during a plague epidemic. Though no doubt reluctant to do so, the Ottomans sent for Murad and Ibrahim to return to Cairo and govern jointly in the posts of Sheikh al-Balad and Amir al-Hajj under the new Ottoman pasha. It was these same two faithfuls who were to face Bonaparte at the Battle of the Pyramids.

Egypt had been battered by invasion and counter-invasion, raiding armies and long-lived empires, its forgotten past graven in its temples and on the faces of its most visible guardians. In

1798, when self-serving Mameluke beys squabbled over title and luxury while their troops trampled upon an oppressed population, a new invader was set to liberate the people: in a land where knowledge, experiment and understanding had once been the cultural hallmark of its civilization, rediscovery and recognition was at hand. Yet this liberation would come at a price – Egypt would soon learn a new expression of doom, already echoing across Europe: *Bonaparte is coming.*

2

A Raging Continent: Europe at War

In 1789, when the financial crisis facing Louis XVI demanded the reconvening of the three Estates General, the crowned heads of Europe watched with alarm as the Commons of the Third Estate, the people, proclaimed themselves the new governing National Assembly of France. Although they invited the nobility and clergy to join the new body, they declared they would govern with or without them. Louis hoped that locking the assembly rooms of the Salle des États would somehow staunch the flow of opposition to his management of France's bankrupt state coffers. Undaunted by this measure, the Assembly members moved into a nearby indoor tennis court to proceed with the business of the day, and swore not to leave the hall until they had agreed a new constitution. Within a week of the 'Tennis Court Oath' on 20 June 1789, this body became the National Constituent Assembly. Three weeks later, a Paris mob stormed the Bastille. The French Revolution had begun.

The ensuing 'world war' would establish new borders, create new nations, and lead eventually to the struggling rebirth of the most ancient: indirectly, Egypt would be awakened by the flaming torches of the Paris mob. At the outset, the revolution appeared to be a French problem alone. However, as events escalated within the French capital, it became clear that the same could happen to the other royal domains of Europe: only thirteen years earlier Britain's colonies in America had declared themselves independent and risen up in successful armed rebellion. Everywhere, a new liberalism breathed uprising, sedition and revolt.

The unthinkable fall of the French monarchy had been caused by a deadly contagion which had to be stopped; European states saw that war with this new revolutionary government was inevitable – with the overthrow of Louis and the nation in disarray, there was no better time to pounce. In June 1791, after two years of impotent uncertainty, and wary of accepting offers of help from other European leaders, nearly all of whom were his potential enemies, Louis XVI attempted to flee to the royalist stronghold of Montmédy, with his Queen, Marie-Antoinette and their children. Disguising themselves as the retinue of a Russian noblewoman, played by the dauphin's governess, the king acting as her butler, the queen one of her maids, they were discovered and arrested by an observant checkpoint guard in Varennes – tradition would have it the king was recognized from his profile on a coin, but other stories speak of an illustrated handbill. They were taken back to Paris and placed under guard.

After the threats of Austria and Prussia to invade France and 'punish' any person or town resisting their course to rescue the king and re-establish the monarchy, Louis's position grew increasingly hazardous. With the uprising of royalist supporters in the Vendée region it was clear the king provided a focus for national discontent and the prospect of counter-revolution was a serious threat. Accused of secret collusion with Austria and Prussia, Louis XVI was condemned to death by the Paris Convention on 17 January 1793. He went to the guillotine on the 21st. His Austrian Queen, Marie-Antoinette, followed soon after.

There was a collective shudder throughout the courts of Europe. In Britain, there was outrage, not just among the aristocracy and bourgeoisie – the common mob surrounded the coach of George III, howling for war and demanding action: at last, there would be war with France. Europe united in its opposition to the new revolutionary state and the resulting alliances brought an end to allegiances that had lasted for most of the century – Sweden now allied with its old enemy Russia, as did Prussia with its enemy Austria, and the maritime nations of Holland, Naples, Sardinia, Spain and Portugal sided with Britain. On the Continent, France faced this new coalition of enemies alone, dealing its diplomacy with musket and cannon. Shifting through different phases and temporary armistices, the 'Great French War' was to last until the Battle of Waterloo in 1815, twenty-two years later.

The invasion of Egypt was not one of the grand ambitions of Napoleon Bonaparte from his first days as a young officer. It was not his own plan, although he put his full weight behind it. On the surface, it seemed a strange distraction from the European war, but was part of a general strategy in the fight against Britain. Each step of its execution would be taken on a trembling web of fragile diplomacy, each move jeopardizing a delicate balance.

After its first faltering steps in 1792 the new revolutionary army became a successful and efficient fighting force.[1] Desertions of conscripted troops from the first great levy in 1793 left behind a hard kernel of dedicated Jacobin republicans, often vastly superior in number to anything fielded by the enemy. The first objectives of this military machine in the Revolutionary Wars were Prussia and the Holy Roman Empire of Austria under the Habsburgs, the greatest power on the Continent. These wars lasted from 1792 to 1802, culminating in the Egypt campaign and the Treaty of Amiens. The first phase of the contest was the War of the First Coalition, led by a loose conglomerate of nations which banded together to defeat the new revolutionary government in their midst.

This anti-French league was a new phenomenon in Europe. Austria, France and England had been the three great superpowers of the 1700s, since the Peace of Westphalia in 1648, bound in a cold war of mutual distrust; the revolution had changed everything, and later the invasion of Egypt would change the balance of power still further. In the War of the First Coalition French conquests expanded with an impressive rate of success, each triumph bringing more gold to the empty state coffers, each victory strengthening the rule of the government. It would not be long before this political influence was wielded by one officer of artillery in particular, who would rise rapidly to prominence.

Some commentators have observed that Bonaparte was more a statesman blessed with a genius for tactics than a commander with a gift for politics. He learned to manipulate both the military and the state with skill, ever able to take advantage of circumstance whether in the staterooms of Paris or on the field of battle – this was highlighted most dramatically by the Egypt campaign. The 'myth' of Bonaparte did not develop in posthumous hindsight, gathering momentum by an ongoing historical analysis of his achievements – it was very much in existence during his lifetime. At his peak he was the invincible hero of the new France, an example that one could rise, through sheer talent, virtually to rule the world.

Corsican by birth, but of noble Italian blood – a connection he despised – he later changed his Italianate name 'Napoleone di Buonaparte' to the simpler French 'Napoléon Bonaparte'.[2] Commissioned at sixteen as a Second Lieutenant in the artillery, the most technical branch of the army, he made the gargantuan leap during his time on Corsica to lieutenant colonel of a corps of volunteers supporting the Jacobin faction in the complex revolutionary nationalist struggle on the island, which resulted eventually in his flight to France with his family in 1793.

Through the influence of the revolutionary Montagnard politician and diplomat Antoine Saliceti, Bonaparte was given command of an artillery unit at the protracted siege of Toulon, the Mediterranean French port that had been occupied by British forces supporting a royalist insurrection against the republic. After capturing the heights overlooking the harbour he ranged his guns to fire on the enemy ships, forcing the British troops to evacuate. Wounded in the action, he was promoted to the rank of brigadier general. He was twenty-four years of age.

Bonaparte was soon to become more than a general, but a political force. His launch to power and fame came with the events of 13 Vendémiaire 1795.[3] Some 30,000 men, re-armed units of the royalist faction which had rebelled in the Vendée and been crushed by the republican forces of General Hoche, broke their peace agreement and returned to attack the Convention government, marching on Paris. The protection of the state was unwisely given to the General of the Interior, one Jacques-François Menou, Baron de Boussay.[4] With a peculiar taste of things to come, Menou bungled his mission to disarm the insurgents in the Le Pellitier area of Paris, and was sacked from his new post in favour of General Paul François Jean Nicolas, Vicomte de Barras.[5] Bonaparte was ordered to support the new general – but Bonaparte was of sufficient reputation that he refused, agreeing to participate only if he could have independent authority. The unpopular Convention, which had vowed not to leave its assembly room until it had resolved the crisis, acquiesced to his demand, fearful lest the capital become the scene of yet another revolution, possibly bloodier than the first, fought on this occasion not by mobs but by armies.

Bonaparte acted quickly: in the middle of the night, without Barras's intervention, he ordered cannon to be dragged into the streets by the cavalry. By dawn he had personally established devastating fields of fire and had the guns loaded with grapeshot. When the first royalist attack came early that morning, his cannon shredded the rebel ranks with volley after volley, supported by the massed musket fire of the 'patriot battalions'. The royalists fled in the face of a final republican charge. It was the end of the royalist threat – though declared by many to be a massacre. There was no doubt that Bonaparte had single-handedly saved the revolution.

With the support of Barras, who subsequently rose to power in the new Directory government which had replaced the Convention, Bonaparte became a political figure, a focal point for the people. After his invasion of Italy in 1796 and his defeat of both Sardinian and Austrian forces, no politician in France could afford to ignore him. Crushing the Austrians in Italy and driving them northwards until he threatened the borders of the Austrian homeland, he had forced the greatest power in Europe to sue for peace. Bonaparte seemed invincible.

After the settlement with Austria in 1797, the First Coalition crumbled, leaving only Great Britain to stand against France. The other states had met the French in the field, and suffered defeat, but, owing to Britain's island position, France would never face British armies in the same manner, fighting on the borders of their own country – France would first have to destroy the Royal Navy. Despite great victories on land, France could not equal this success at sea; the French navy had largely been confined to ports by British blockades.

France opened its war with Britain in 1793 severely out-numbered at sea, with barely half the strength of Britain. Since then the gap had widened, Britain embarking on an arming programme that gave her almost unquestioned maritime supremacy. In the eighteenth century, the ship of the line[6] was a mobile artillery regiment, controlling the highways of inter-national trade, and Britain did this with a terrible efficiency, threatening French economic survival. France had lost many of her naval officers in the revolution, and the ranks were denuded of experienced hands. By contrast, British seamen and gunners were considered some of the finest in Europe – professional, harshly disciplined, their expert commanders experienced and aggressive, spurring their crews on with the lure of prize money, calling on an ancient heritage fostered by men like Hawkins and Drake centuries earlier.

Although France was outnumbered at sea she could call on potential allies and still pose a threat, particularly in the Mediterranean. The Spanish Bourbon rulers were of French descent, and Britain was very much aware of the danger posed by a Franco-Spanish alliance which would give France access to Spain's sizeable fleet. Not only this but France could turn to the Ottoman Empire for support in the eastern Mediterranean – the Sublime Porte had enjoyed close ties with France since the sixteenth century, and had sought French military assistance to modernize the Turkish army. But until an agreement with Spain or a concerted effort against the British in the Levant could be achieved, France had to find a way to defeat Britain without direct naval confrontation.

Many plans were considered, including support of an uprising in Ireland, combined with dreams of fomenting English discontent to provoke a similar revolution in England. With this objective, General Hoche led 15,000 men in a small invasion fleet to the Irish coast, there to support the uprising of the United Irishmen under Wolfe Tone in December 1796. But, as with the Spanish Armada, the weather proved an English ally and forced the storm-battered French ships to withdraw. The English Revolution never happened, though outbursts did occur, but these were quickly broken up by the government, the ringleaders already known and watched by the authorities. Although there were those among the intelligentsia who would support the concept of the revolution, there were few who would welcome its reality.

The scheme that found the greatest favour was the boldest,

a direct invasion of England. Had the Directory government but known it, it was the ideal time. Prime Minister William Pitt was desperate for money to prosecute the war and the Royal Navy was suffering strategic setbacks in the Mediterranean; the British had maintained the blockade of Toulon from ports in Naples and Corsica, but towards the end of 1796 the inevitable had happened: France's peace treaty with Spain led the Spanish to declare war on Britain, and delivered into French hands the mighty ships of the Spanish fleet. The relatively small British Mediterranean contingent of fifteen ships of the line now faced an enemy of thirty-five. Compounding the emergency, the Kingdom of Naples, once a British ally, had been forced to sign a peace treaty with France in 1797, which prevented access to her ports by the British. The Mediterranean Fleet of the Royal Navy was left with only the safe harbour of Calvi on Corsica, but was otherwise surrounded. Fearing imminent invasion at home, Admiral Sir John Jervis ordered a general withdrawal. The Mediterranean Sea became, in muttered jocularity, the 'French Lake'.

With this surge in French naval power, the Directory hoped to meet the British threat in the Atlantic and gain mastery of the Channel, at least long enough to support an invasion of Britain. On 14 February 1797, the Directory had their chance: twenty-seven Spanish ships of the line, making for Cadiz to unite at last with the French, were intercepted off Cape St Vincent by Sir John Jervis's fifteen battleships. Although several of the Spanish had more than 100 guns apiece ranged over four decks, their fleet was cut in two and so badly savaged by the British, and by Nelson in particular,[7] that the battered remnants retreated to port in Spain, reluctant to emerge ever again. The Directory's dream of an indomitable fleet for the invasion of England had been shattered.

The Directory's other hope, a British revolution, came closer to realization than they had ever imagined, though it was restricted to the Royal Navy. Only months after the victory at Cape St Vincent, British seamen at anchor in Spithead and on the Nore mutinied, commandeering their ships, several sailing up the Thames to threaten London with cannon fire if their demands were not met. But the Directory in Paris could take no advantage of the situation – they knew nothing of it. Although it was soon quashed by the Royal Marines and the ringleaders seized, some improvements to conditions were made and the disruption did not appear to affect tactical efficiency. Another French attempt to use an allied fleet against Britain was crushed several months later, when Admiral Duncan destroyed the Dutch fleet at the Battle of Camperdown in the North Sea in October that same year. The Directory had been frustrated at every turn, the victories of Cape St Vincent and Camperdown betraying none of the Royal Navy's internal unrest.

Despite these decisive naval blows to French strategic hopes, the Directory continued to draw up plans for the invasion of England. The man they wanted to lead the assault was Bonaparte, the saviour of the revolution and conqueror of Italy. In the footsteps of Caesar, Claudius and William of Normandy, the Armée d'Angleterre mustered on the coast in preparation. This was to be reinforced by the Toulon squadron, which could now sail freely from the Mediterranean unhampered by the British since their withdrawal – at least until they reached the Atlantic. Bonaparte inspected the coastal operations in February 1798 and found there were insufficient ships, funds and crews to win even temporary control of the Channel for a crossing – for much the same reason, the Toulon squadron was also bogged down and could not sail to reinforce the flotilla awaiting their arrival on the Channel coast. In such conditions, any invasion of England, as Bonaparte saw it, would rely upon the unlikely absence of the British navy. With so many unpredictable elements, Bonaparte refused to carry out the invasion plans. The Napoleon myth had already taken hold, and he was not prepared to destroy it with a foolhardy raid that would probably end in failure. Politically, and personally, the hitherto invincible Bonaparte could not afford to participate in a 'forlorn hope',[8] and he had no intention of doing so – especially considering the much more attractive alternative.

Talleyrand, appointed as Foreign Minister in July 1797, pressed the Directory for an expedition to Egypt. He was a firm believer in French trade and strategic interests in the eastern Mediterranean and began communicating with Bonaparte on the possibilities of expansion into the Levant. His timing could not have been better. Talleyrand calculated that the vast yet unwieldy Ottoman Empire was on the verge of collapse, but rather than waiting to let the giant fall and sift through the consequent rubble with other equally hungry European states, it was more in French interests to nudge it further into destruction. Even better, he reasoned, to be the first on hand to feast on the spoils. What better way to accomplish both tasks than to make a bid for the jewel in the sultan's silken crown – Egypt.

This grand design was not Talleyrand's alone. In late 1797 he had heard direct from Magallon, the French Consul in Cairo who had recently returned to Paris, that Egypt was fast descending into near anarchy. French merchants in Egypt were suffering at the hands of the warring Mameluke leadership, being stripped of profits, and even their goods, through extortionate taxes run more like protection rackets. It was a rich nation, he argued, yet its wealth was being taken from the thriving business community by the Mameluke households in their struggles for power. Intervention, in Magallon's view, was justified entirely by the Mameluke treatment of French merchants; he had been pressing for the conquest of Egypt for some time to safeguard French commerce in the region.

In early February 1798, Magallon detailed his plans to Talleyrand and then to the government. Talleyrand repeated Magallon's arguments to the Directory a week later, suggesting that Egypt would supply France with commodities such as sugar, coffee and cotton. There was also one further strategic and economic advantage for the occupation of the country: it would provide unhindered access to the Red Sea, and thence to the Indian Ocean. After their thwarted attempts to gather a fleet to attack Britain, here was the opportunity to cut off Britain's source of wealth in India.

The Directory had longed to ally itself with anti-British factions in India: Egypt would provide the means at last to do so. The closest ties they had enjoyed had been with the Tippoo Sultan – later referred to as 'Citoyen Tipou' by colonial French Jacobins. By supporting Tippoo, they could oust the British from the subcontinent and begin a new era of unmolested trade with India. Contact with Tippoo had been broken after the British took the French colony of Pondicherry in southern India in 1793; further, when Britain seized the strategic Cape of Good Hope on the southern tip of Africa from the Dutch in 1795, France lost direct access to the Indian Ocean. For two years the Directory's India strategy had gathered dust, but, in 1797, a French privateer sailed into one of the Tippoo Sultan's ports; negotiations opened once more, and the governor of the isolated French colony of Mauritius pressed Paris for French troops to support Tippoo's rebellion. Any doubts the Directory may have had about the Egypt plan were soon pushed to one side: India hung within the Directory's grasp.

Bonaparte knew well enough the debt owed him by the Directory and he enjoyed the patronage of Barras, the commander in the Paris streets of 1795 which Bonaparte had cleared with, as Carlyle later put it, a 'whiff of grapeshot' – Barras was now chief among the Directors and Bonaparte was so popular a figure that the government would not have dared defy his wishes too openly. Having listened to Talleyrand's arguments, twenty-eight-year-old General Bonaparte proposed in late February that the invasion of Britain be postponed in favour of his true ambitions, Magallon's plan to conquer Egypt. Magallon had insisted it could be done with roughly 30,000–40,000 men, and had proposed a schedule of key sites to be taken; as an agent-in-place he had done much of the reconnaissance work already.

To Bonaparte it was more than tempting. The Mediterranean was free of British ships; much of Italy was occupied by his own army; Naples was under treaty and Spain could keep watch over Gibraltar – the Ottoman Empire, the 'Sick Man of Europe', was ready to crumble and had let a precious province fall into the hands of barbarous hooligans: the time was ripe. Above all, for Bonaparte it would afford exotic glory everlasting. This would be a heroic rescue mission in the interests of patriotic merchants in distress, the extension of revolutionary liberty to the benighted and suffering people of the Nile and, further, lead to the liberation of oppressed and very wealthy allies in the Shangri-la of oriental trade on the subcontinent of India, utterly destroying Britain's source of commercial power.

The Directory concurred. It is also not inconceivable that they considered their precarious position, especially with the elections looming and the potential danger posed by Bonaparte's popularity and determination. They might be safer from Caesar's legions were he as far from the Rubicon as possible, and the distant deserts of Egypt were more than adequate. In March 1798, the expedition received the final stamp of approval. The Directors, having done this volte-face from England to Egypt, were about to make more of a mark on history than they could have imagined.

'Europe is a molehill!' Bonaparte reputedly exclaimed – it was a cramped, limited theatre where already, he believed, his glory was fading. The Low Countries and the Rhineland had been annexed, Italy conquered and the Habsburgs defeated. Yet soon the fêted hero feared he would become merely another once-victorious general. In just under five years he had outgrown the Continent with the itching ambition of an Alexander, and looked eastward for inspiration. Nowhere, so he believed, was power and glory so lavishly enjoyed as in the Orient, and he dreamt of an exotic rule among the palms of the Nile. His Eastern Adventure was about to become reality.

The Directory issued an order on 12 April 1798: Egypt shall be occupied. More specifically, Malta and Egypt shall be seized, Suez penetrated, the English ejected from their positions in the East, the living conditions of the Egyptian people improved and, more difficult, good relations maintained with the Ottoman Empire. There was little time. Bonaparte had to take advantage of the British absence from the Mediterranean and the apparent apathy of the Ottomans. As well as this, he had to contend with nature, which had its own timetable: to conquer Egypt he must invade before the Nile flood in August. The wheels were set in rapid motion. It was to be the greatest overseas invasion France had undertaken, and one of its greatest diplomatic gambles: Bonaparte's conflicting aims were to seize Egypt for France, while sailing ostensibly as a liberator of the oppressed Egyptians and trusted ally of the Ottoman sultan.

The sultan, however, had already been watching French troop movements with suspicion; after the dramatic French victories in Italy, Bonaparte had taken the Ionian Greek islands of Corfu, Zante and Cephallonia in 1797 – he saw these as more important than any other of his Mediterranean territories. All three islands provided swift access to the central Mediterranean, but control of Corfu had been a well-accepted strategy for centuries;[9] positioned within a short distance of the heel of Italy, these maritime posts could close off the Adriatic Sea to the north, protecting and controlling all naval commerce in and out of eastern Italy, the Balkans and, more particularly, the newly acquired Venetian trading empire.

The Ionian Islands, however, were on the doorstep of the

Ottoman Empire. As part of the Egyptian strategy dreamt up by Talleyrand, Bonaparte's interest in them was more for their proximity to the Levant than their threat to Venice; just as the possession of Egypt would afford access to Syria, he wrote that, should the Ottoman Empire collapse, he would be well placed to offer succour to the sultan, or preferably, to seize the shattered remnants of the eastern giant. As a result, relations with Constantinople suffered. Having taken the Ionian Islands, for Bonaparte to take Egypt as well, even in the pretence of friendship, would strain diplomatic ties to breaking-point. They would snap long before a single French soldier set foot on the banks of the Nile.

Although the orders came through officially on 12 April, Bonaparte acted in March. The first task was to equip the fleet at Toulon – ostensibly it was the sorry condition of these ships that had prevented the invasion of Britain. Neither would there be any naval support from Spain, the remains of their fleet blockaded after the Battle of Cape St Vincent. Yet within ten weeks, a squadron of French battleships, transports and merchantmen had been assembled at Toulon – history has graced Bonaparte himself with this extraordinary achievement, though the credit lies more with one Monsieur Najac, *commissaire ordonnateur*, the vigorous, newly appointed successor to a shambolic dockyard administration that was deeply in debt and owed arrears to its makeshift workforce. That the fleet was assembled at all is a wonder of logistics.

The army was comparatively easy to organize. Despite being scattered across much of southern Europe, most of the forces bound for Egypt were Bonaparte's men from the Army of Italy – he had chosen his own legions, battle-hardened veterans of previous campaigns. Some were in Corsica, and some in Rome to enforce the creation of the new French protectorate-republic; still others had recently seen action in Switzerland, having captured Berne. This region became the new Helvetian Republic, its millions in gold forming the source of the Egyptian expedition's campaign budget. Other units were brought down from the north of France, from the ranks of the now unemployed Armée de l'Angleterre. These reassembled divisions became the new Armée de l'Orient.

Including the roll of sailors, marines, support units and civilians, the expedition counted in excess of 50,000.[10] This army was so vast it would board its troopships from five separate embarkation points, Toulon, Marseilles, Genoa, Civita Vecchia and Ajaccio. Of this 50,000, not one knew for certain where they were bound.

There was one unit of the French forces which was to have more of a lasting effect on Egypt and, consequently, on history, than any other. It was not military, but civil, yet was a contingent assembled with the same vigour and efficiency as the army. Known generally as the *savants*, this was the Commission of the Sciences and Arts, consisting of 167 scientists, naturalists, botanists, engineers, technicians, physicists, chemists, artists, surgeons, scholars, surveyors, musicians and poets.

It is unclear which came first, the idea for the Commission or the government order to create it, for many commentators place its origins with Bonaparte, the scientist manqué. However, the concept of a scientific commission was by no means new to the republic. The eighteenth-century appetite for discovery had spawned similar commissions before: with the conquest of the Low Countries and the Rhineland, the republic had sent a commission of painters and art scholars to catalogue the native species of flora and fauna, and collect artworks for France's growing museums. The same was done in Italy in 1796 under the Governmental Commission for the Research of Scientific and Artistic Objects in Conquered Countries – a sponsored Grand Tour, marching behind Bonaparte's army, with orders to record and collect Italian sculpture and artwork, just as visiting antiquaries from all over Europe had been doing for decades.

In the same fashion as the British Museum would later expand thanks to Henry Salt and others, so the Louvre swelled with fine Italian treasures.

Two men involved in these previous commissions were Gaspard Monge (1746–1818) and Claude Louis Berthollet (1748–1822). Monge was an enthusiastic revolutionary and scientific polymath who had exhibited extraordinary talents from the age of just sixteen. He had worked in pure mathematics and had devised the discipline of descriptive geometry, and was credited with the discovery that water was composed of hydrogen and oxygen. He worked with the Committee of Weights and Measures, which pioneered the metric system, and he eventually rose to political prominence as deputy of both parliamentary houses. He was given various government commissions regarding steel manufacture and ironworks, and was one of the founders of the École Polytechnique.

Berthollet had been a physician before he developed a reputation in applied chemistry, in particular with his work in bleaches and dyes and later in gunpowder and explosives. He held the chair in chemistry at the École Normale in Paris, and made several key discoveries, establishing the basis of the modern system of classification of chemical compounds. Both members of the highest academic body in the land, the Institute of France, Monge and Berthollet became colleagues and close friends. When Bonaparte was made a member of the Institute, First Class, in Mathematics,[11] they became companions and confidants of the young general, their fortunes soon to rise with his.

Although Monge initially avoided enlisting on the expedition, he and Berthollet became the firm foundation of the new Commission. It has been suggested that Bonaparte expressed his yearnings for the East to the two academics and broke silence regarding the true destination, possibly not yet even an open secret at the time. In his early fifties, Monge was old enough to be Bonaparte's father, and it seems Bonaparte confided in him when they met again in Milan in the summer of 1797, just one year prior to the expedition.

The peg-legged Brigadier Caffarelli du Falga of the Army Engineers[12] was one of the general staff closest to Bonaparte and chosen to command the new Commission. He prepared a speculative list of names for Bonaparte's consideration, and together with Monge and Berthollet rounded up potential academic recruits. By the end of March 1798, a recruitment drive was under way, and a circular had been prepared by the Ministry of the Interior. Potential members were assured that their academic or professional posts would be kept open and that their regular salaries would be paid direct to their families while each member would also receive an additional fee for embarking on the adventure. The precise nature of the adventure, however, remained unspecified; although some might have suspected their destination, with few exceptions none of the men who signed on knew for certain that they were bound for the sands of Egypt – the thrill of the secret Commission was sufficient incentive for most.

The call went out to the major institutions in Paris: the École Polytechnique, the École Normale, the École des Mines, the École des Ponts et Chaussées, the Conservatoire Nationale des Arts et Métiers, the Musée d'Histoire Naturelle, and the Observatoire, all were asked to put forward a list of candidates. Jean Baptiste Joseph Fourier (1768–1830), a mathematician and professor at the École Polytechnique, was so enthused he succeeded in drafting five colleagues and some forty students and graduates. One of Fourier's ex-pupils was Captain Étienne Louis Malus of the Engineers, a brilliant mathematician of twenty-three, who would go on to cure himself of the plague in Syria, discover the principles of light polarization and be awarded the Rumford Medal by Britain's Royal Society in 1811. Further names were added: Aimé Dubois-Aymé, Édouard de Villiers du Terrage, the twenty-six-year-old professor of zoology,

Étienne Geoffroy Saint-Hilaire – whose theories are said to have anticipated Darwin's – Nicolas-Jacques Conté, an aeronaut who formed the very first airborne unit employing the reconnaissance balloon *L'Entreprenant* in the Battle of Fleurus in 1794, and who drew up a plan for the airborne invasion of Britain. He also invented the modern graphite pencil, a particular brand of which bears his name today. A mechanical genius likened to a latter-day Merlin, one of the most indispensable men of the expedition, he would later be able to machine tools that could in turn tool machines.

It would be understandable to suppose that the mere mention of Bonaparte's name was sufficient to attract candidates – but although it undoubtedly was for some, this was not the case for all. Georges Cuvier,[13] one of the finest naturalists in Europe, declined. One who gladly assented to the grand adventure was Antoine-Vincent Arnault (1766–1834), author and playwright, once exiled to England and later arrested in France for royalist sympathies, but who later rose to high office. He met Bonaparte in 1797 and was given the task of organizing the government of the Ionian Islands. That Bonaparte would have entrusted such a strategic territory to Arnault suggests he was far more than a playwright and librettist. Although the poet Jean François Ducis refused, poet and translator François Auguste Parseval-Grandmaison (1759–1834), later Member of the Academy, begged Arnault to let him accompany him on the journey, declaring, 'You are going to Egypt! The whole world knows that!' Bonaparte also hoped to include performers in his train, though this did not materialize so easily – the composer Étienne Nicolas Méhul and singer François Lays both refused Bonaparte's invitation; however, the famous pianist Henri Jean Rigel and singer and musicologist Guillaume André Villoteau accepted what was clearly going to be the most exotic booking of the season, and joined the roll of specialists.

Artists Jean Gabriel Caquet, André Dutertre, Jules Jean

Baptiste Joly, Michel Rigo and the sculptor Jean-Jacques Castex joined the expedition. Linguists and orientalists from the École des Langues Orientales were drafted into the ranks to act as interpreters and translators, one of whom was Jean-Michel de Venture de Paradis, who later died of dysentery on the expedition. Another, Louis Matthieu Langlès, curator of oriental manuscripts at the Bibliothèque Nationale and an Indian and oriental specialist, heatedly refused to join Bonaparte in his desert bivouacs despite the general's demands. Monge was detailed to find a replacement and enlisted Jean-Joseph Marcel, who later played a key role in the research of the Rosetta Stone. It would not be difficult to imagine Langlès's professional curiosity or possible regret on hearing the revelations from Egypt.

At the age of fifty, one of the oldest men to sign up was the well-known artist, diplomat, raconteur and gentleman arts scholar Dominique Vivant Denon (1747–1825). Initially overlooked by Bonaparte for the expedition, Denon had to wage a lobbying campaign to secure himself a place, eventually succeeding after the efforts of friends Vincent Arnault and Josephine Bonaparte. History should be grateful, for Denon's relatively short stay from 1798 to 1799 resulted in *Travels in Upper and Lower Egypt*, the most popularly read French account of the occupation of Egypt and one of the few sources of the period translated into English at an early date. His talents ranged from quick life-sketches of native Egyptians and archaeological sites to exquisite paintings of wildlife produced for the naturalists of the expedition. He was also one of the first members of the Commission to travel through Upper Egypt and record its monuments and hieroglyphs.

The geologist and mineralogist Déodat de Dolomieu (1750–1801)[14] – after whom the rock dolomite was named – reportedly accepted only on the assurance that there were rocks and mountains for him to examine upon arrival. Henri-Joseph

Redouté, Marie-Jules César Savigny,[15] the botanist Hippolyte Nectoux; the astronomer François Marie Quesnot and the student Jerome Méchain and Nicolas Auguste Nouet – some of these were the most illustrious names in France and the finest minds in Europe. As the ranks of savants steadily swelled, an expedition library was amassed in preparation and packed into specially built cases which would later be quickly converted to shelves. Brigadier Caffarelli, it is estimated, spent some 215,000 *livres* on the necessary equipment for the numerous branches of the Commission.

One of the peculiarities of Napoleonic conquest was the establishment of propaganda newspapers in vassal states – these were partly to inform and possibly sway a vanquished populace in favour of their conquerors, but also to maintain army morale, reminding troops of their homeland and the revolutionary cause. Egypt was to be no exception. But Dubois-Laverne, the Director of the Presses of the Republic, refused to relinquish his valuable typefaces to the expedition until the Ministry of the Interior intervened – however, the expedition press needed Arabic fonts, not to be found in Paris. Events in Italy provided Bonaparte with a solution: Monge had been sent to Rome to investigate the murder of General Duphot, allegedly killed by rioting papal soldiers. In response the Directory in Paris had ordered the deposition and arrest of Pope Pius VI[16] and the formation of a Roman Republic under French occupancy. Taking full advantage of the situation, Bonaparte asked Monge to procure the necessary printing materials from the well-stocked works of the Vatican propaganda information offices.

Monge not only obtained the fonts but procured further surveying equipment, interpreters and Levantine students for the expedition, and generally satisfied Bonaparte's desires for everything – from the requisitioning of carriages to bottles of wine in their thousands. He had done all this, however, while still reluctant to accompany the expedition. Bonaparte was determined to take him on the journey, but Monge prevaricated, despite Bonaparte's threat to sail up the Tiber to Rome to get him if need be. Eventually Bonaparte discovered that the higher authority holding such sway over Monge was actually Madame Monge. Bonaparte paid her a personal visit, and although mistaken at first for a student of the great professor, prevailed in his arguments.[17] Monge, at last, was officially enlisted.

On 2 April 1798 those members of the Commission in France were ordered by the Ministry of the Interior to prepare to head south. Just over two weeks later, they received Caffarelli's instructions to proceed to Lyons, and travel down the Rhône to the Mediterranean port of Toulon, which they reached on or about 30 April. Toulon harbour bristled with mastheads, Najac's achievement made manifest by thirteen ships of the line, seventeen frigates, brigantines, corvettes and numerous merchantmen and barges, enough to hold the tons of equipment, instruments and provisions, including the millions of francs in gold taken from Berne. This sight was later to be exceeded in spectacle by the arrival of the Marseilles convoy on the 11th, bringing the total number of warships in Toulon to fifty-five, and the list of transport vessels to nearly 150.[18]

Rumours abounded among the troops and seamen as to their true destination – the arrival of the cream of French academe would have done little to quieten such speculation. The Directory had taken great pains to maintain secrecy, employing a deception campaign to foster the illusion of an invasion of England.[19] Keeping the troops ignorant worked very well: the men had not even been issued with water-bottles or lightweight tropical uniforms, though it is more likely that haste and not military secrecy was the cause of this oversight.[20] Some predicted they were to take Malta and Sicily, or Sardinia, or raise the blockade at Cadiz, others that they were to invade England. Still others believed it was to be Egypt and from there to India. Army Captain Joseph-Marie Moiret bore witness to all this from his troopship in Toulon harbour: 'The clever young men, known to us as the Scholars, as well as the artists, were almost all of the latter view.'[21] Within a few weeks, their curiosity would be satisfied.

3

Triumph and Disaster

Napoleon and Josephine Bonaparte arrived in Toulon on 9 May. The general addressed the troops, urging them to rise to their next challenge as did the Roman legions in the age of Caesar and Augustus, causing them to break into patriotic song. They had been promised much, in particular six acres of land each upon their return.[1] Bonaparte needed to maintain their devotion: it was all they would soon be left with in the infernal desert. At six in the morning on 19 May 1798, Captain Casabianca of Bonaparte's flagship *L'Orient* sent a fleet signal to weigh anchor and set sail. The combined Toulon and Marseilles convoys filed past the towering three-decked battle-ship under Bonaparte's gaze for nearly eight hours.

The journey from Toulon bewildered the troops even as they sailed, their destination still unclear from the circuitous route. The fleet made a successful rendezvous with two other convoys, first from Genoa and later Ajaccio off the coast of Corsica, but did not meet the ships from Civita Vecchia until the coast of Malta. In entirety, the fleet comprised nearly 400 ships, covering four square miles of the Mediterranean. It is remarkable to note that part of Bonaparte's argument against the invasion of England had been that the Toulon squadron was unfit for action and that there were insufficient funds for repairs and recruitment of the Boulogne fleet. Najac's success in Toulon had proven this to be groundless. The heart of the matter was that Napoleon Bonaparte had wanted to invade Egypt more than he had wanted to invade England.

England, meanwhile, was in the grip of an invasion fever, the population convinced Bonaparte could land at any moment. Aware of the extraordinary naval activity at Toulon, Earl Spencer[2] wrote a letter to Admiral Jervis, now Lord St Vincent, requesting that Nelson be sent with a squadron through hostile Mediterranean waters to establish the nature of the French preparations. In this message he emphasized the gravity of the situation as interpreted by the Admiralty, with a tone of chilling determination,

> when you are apprised that the appearance of a British squadron
> in the Mediterranean is a condition on which the fate of Europe
> may at this moment be stated to depend, you will not be surprised
> that we are disposed to strain every nerve, and incur consider-
> able hazard in effecting it.[3]

Jervis had already ordered Nelson to Toulon, but could spare him only six warships for the task. Admiral Brueys's[4] Toulon fleet alone had thirty. Nelson was plagued by difficulties; half his squadron was damaged in heavy weather and had to put in for repair, and he was not reinforced by a further eleven ships of the line until a week later. When finally he took up station outside Toulon on 27 May, his quarry had vanished – its objective possibly Britain.

The island fortress of Malta, last bastion of the noble order of the Knights Hospitallers, or Knights of St John, who had with-stood the atrocities of the Great Siege by Suleiman the Magnificent in the mid-sixteenth century and accounted for the loss of nearly 50,000 Turks, collapsed before Bonaparte like a house of cards. Over the centuries the knights had become a crusader force without a crusade. Since their island home was in the ideal position to drain the Ottoman and Barbary states of rich trade and booty, they had become prosperous, undirected and idle, their knightly efforts at times tantamount to piracy, justified by an outdated religious war against Islam. Moreover, of some 350 knights in total, 200 were French, and of that number, some had republican leanings sufficient to spread discontent and confusion among their fellows.

The arrival of the French Civita Vecchia convoy on the horizon on 6 June caused panic. When it was joined by the rest of the Egypt expeditionary fleet on the 9th, the result was pandemonium. The sea black with French warships, resistance by 350 men and their retinue seemed more foolish than merely futile; the next day, the 10th, the Treasurer of the Order, Bosredon de Ransijat, flatly refused to fight his countrymen, throwing the council of knights into further disorder. The indecisive leadership of the Grand Master, Ferdinand von Hompesch zu Bolheim, who had left Malta poorly defended over the previous months, caused chaos in the Maltese militia and in the streets of Valetta. Faced with so little resistance, the one-legged Brigadier Caffarelli, being rowed into the harbour to parley, remarked that he was pleased there was at least someone in town to open the gates for them.

After an assault on the neighbouring island of Gozo with the loss of only three men, Bonaparte landed a force of 10,000 on Malta to encircle Valetta from the landward side. No longer devoted to the knights' cause, the Maltese militia fell back as French troops scaled the fortress walls, singing the *Marseillaise*. Von Hompesch sued for peace. Thus, after two days, the island was handed to Bonaparte on a Hospitaller silver salver – as were some six to seven million francs of gold and treasure, stripped from the gilded and ornamented interiors of the knights' church of St John and the rest of their island stronghold. Once the treaty was signed, and the pensions (or bribes as some have called them) agreed for the leaders of the once proud order, Bonaparte roughly ejected the knights, permitting them to take only a handful of francs with them. On 17 June, Grand Master von Hompesch was led ignominiously from the island fortress he could have defended.

Bonaparte immediately embarked on a number of measures to recast the state of Malta in an entirely new form. In the space of a week he converted the island from an anachronistic fortress of medievalism to a colony of republican France. He rewrote the constitution, reorganized the hospitals, reduced the political power of the Church, set teachers' salaries, arranged for the Parisian education of the children of Maltese nobles and, applying the tenets of the revolution, abolished slavery.[5] He released nearly 2,000 Turkish and Arab prisoners from the fortress cells and composed statutes forbidding slavery by law, far in advance of Britain's William Wilberforce. These were not the actions of a general, but a statesman; and with the acuity of a statesman he made certain the beys of Tunis and Algiers were informed of his pro-Muslim humanitarian deeds, in the hope the news would precede him and allay any Ottoman doubts of his motives.

From Malta, the Egypt expedition could be reinforced and supported, the island used as a halfway house for troops from France or Italy, as well as a useful source of income for the desert campaign. Bonaparte garrisoned 3,000 men on Malta to hold the island against the British, who would inevitably make an attempt to recapture it. The conquest of Malta, while admittedly effecting positive change and of unquestionable strategic importance to the future of the Egypt campaign, had dramatic diplomatic repercussions. The mentally unstable Tsar Paul I, outraged at Bonaparte's conduct against the sanctity of the Christian warrior-monks, changed allegiance, allying Russia with Britain and his old enemy, the Ottoman sultan. This change in the balance in power isolated France in the Levant. When Bonaparte set sail from Valetta on 18 June at the head of his armada bound for Egypt, he was unaware how far his latest success would unravel French diplomacy with the Ottoman Empire.

The day before the French fleet left Valetta, Nelson reached the Bay of Naples and learned from Sir William Hamilton, the British Consul, that the French were possibly somewhere off Malta, their destination still unknown. Nelson was convinced they were headed for Egypt to pursue plans for India. Nelson's squadron of fourteen ships of the line streaked across the Mediterranean — so fast that they overtook the French fleet and passed within just a few miles of it on the night of 22 June, reaching Egypt a week before Bonaparte. Captain Hardy approached Alexandria to make a reconnaissance, but he saw only a few old Turkish ships; the French were nowhere in sight.

The Egyptian chronicler Sheikh Al-Jabarti described the encounter between the British and the port authorities, as the Royal Navy warned the Egyptians of the approaching French fleet and the possibility of invasion:

> However, Al-Sayyid Muhammad Kurayyim did not believe their words and thought them to be trickery. The English thereupon requested: 'Sell us water and provisions according to their value and we shall stay in our ships lying in wait for them. When they come we shall take care of the matter and save you the trouble.'
>
> The above-mentioned Muhammad Kurayyim declined their offer and said: 'We do not accept what you say nor will we give you anything.'
>
> Then he expelled them that God's will might be fulfilled.[6]

And so it was. Nelson headed to Sicily, then back to Greece. For the next few weeks, he drove himself to near nervous exhaustion, chasing an unperturbed enemy who was, for at

least some of the time, sailing sedately in his wake, utterly unconscious of his presence.

We can hardly begin to imagine the reactions of the Levantine
traders who would normally have plodded their mercantile
course up and down the Nile, or the *fellahin* peasants who came
to market, when they raised their heads from their morning
labour to see the first of 400 French ships bearing down on the
twin harbours of Alexandria. The spectacle of the fleet must
have seemed like the end of the world. As Nicholas the Turk
wrote, one could not see its beginning, nor its end. Ottoman
ships were large, but the giant *L'Orient*, carrying 118 guns over
three decks, would have been the size of a small Nile castle, –
it dwarfed even some British ships of the line. Caravels, sloops,
barges, *djerms* and low-slung *feluccas* in Alexandria's waterways
must have lurched and dipped in the sudden swell as Napoleon
Bonaparte heaved-to. At last he had arrived in the East.

The six-week journey from Malta had been miserable.
Although there had been diversions such as concerts, gambling,
exercise, and perhaps the pleasing conversation of Commission
members, the conditions were barely tolerable. Officers wrote
letters home of rough seas, widespread seasickness, of the troops
crammed in their holds, unable to change or launder their
clothes, their food foul and rotting and their water revolting.
Bonaparte himself expected to be laid up in bed with *mal de
mer* for most of the time, and had castors fitted to his bed in
the hope that this would obviate the worst effects of the lurching
movement of the ship. The image of Bourrienne, his personal
secretary,[7] reading to the general as he rolled about his state-
room borders on the comic, but is possibly close to the mark.

When the ships sighted Pompey's Pillar at Alexandria on 1 July,
the troops gazed out upon dull, barren scrubland and the derelict
remains of Alexander's once-proud capital. Many uprooted from
the rococo ornament of Italy, possibly replenished with glowing

memories of Malta, their wary hopes had not been high – but neither had they expected such a drab landfall, especially not in the footsteps of the mighty. This disillusionment was to be a characteristic of their first weeks in Egypt. Their trials were just about to begin.

Bonaparte had learned from Magallon, now in Alexandria, that Nelson had departed only two days previously; he also discovered that to land an army of nearly 40,000 troops in Alexandria's two harbours was impossible – the inhabitants had already made a desperate scramble for arms, rallying a makeshift militia ready to take pot-shots from rooftops and windows, and sending for help to the Bedouin nomads and the Kashiff of Al-Buhayra.[8]

In lieu of Alexandria, Admiral Brueys insisted Aboukir Bay was the most sensible landing-site, some fifteen miles round a headland to the east, but Bonaparte believed he had only two or three days before Nelson's inevitable return; Aboukir would take time to reach and was so perfect to land troops he knew Nelson would head straight for it. Bonaparte overruled Brueys and moved the fleet to the open shores of Marabout, only eight miles west of Alexandria, but by far a more treacherous landing-site for the men. By evening the weather had worsened and a storm brewed. As darkness fell, many of the wretched soldiers were lowered by ropes into heaving boats and expected to row across three miles of sea, past rocks and reefs, through a heavy swell to reach the shore. Tired, seasick and starving, the Armée de l'Orient struggled for eight hours to reach the beaches in their heavy, sodden uniforms. Had there been an enemy force ready to meet the invaders it is doubtful that Bonaparte's men would have stood much of a chance. Bonaparte shared the misery with his men, and headed for shore himself with Admiral Brueys and a number of his senior officers.

By dawn the next morning, he had landed roughly 5,000 men – and several women camp followers of the army train as well, who had accompanied their menfolk in the hazardous crossing. Bonaparte marching at their head, the advance guard of the Armée de l'Orient, armed only with musket, pistol and sword, set out across the desert, intent on taking the walled capital of Alexandria. No horse or cannon had yet been brought ashore – the 5,000 storm troops were utterly without support. This punishing journey was still a blessed relief to some who were grateful to be on dry land. But it proved to be too dry – no water, no wells en route, they had nothing, not even a crumb of bread.

With the armada standing off the coast, Egypt was now in the grip of a frenzied terror. Al-Sayyid Muhammad Kurayyim,[9] who had dismissed Hardy's warnings, now sent a stream of messages to Murad Bey in Cairo, as the French advanced 'like a swarm of locusts'. There was an encounter with mounted Bedouins who rode off with several stragglers from the French columns, including some of the unfortunate women. In Cairo, at the emergency divan called by the Ottoman pasha, Abu Bakr, the recriminations and protestations of the beys eventually died down, records Al-Jabarti, scornful of the Mamelukes' excuses for leaving Alexandria virtually undefended. The fearsome Murad Bey lost little time in amassing a sizeable force and rode north with an army of 20,000.

Bonaparte reached Alexandria on the morning of 2 July and took the fortified city by noon, despite a spirited resistance by the inhabitants. Though forewarned by the arrival of the fleet they were unprepared, and had insufficient ammunition, quickly reduced to pelting the French with stones. Once inside the walls the French took the city house by house, until a surrender was brokered by a Turkish sea captain, and Bonaparte's proclamation of friendship – already printed in Arabic at sea by the new printing press – was distributed, declaring his intentions to liberate the defenders from their oppressive Mameluke warlords and tax officials, which cheered the traders greatly.

Alexandria was a disappointment to the troops who had been expecting oriental, or at least classical splendour: as Captain Moiret stated in his memoirs, the houses were of a 'matchless squalor'. However, the men were impressed by the grandeur of the Alexandrians instead, and their majestic dress of turban and gown. Bonaparte endeavoured to minimize the burden of his conquest by winning the favour of the populace and at first was successful. On the whole the mercantile population was pleased at the prospect of waving goodbye to the Mamelukes, and Muhammad Kurayyim wisely stayed very close to Bonaparte in that first week, cleverly assessing French intentions and strength.

The commander-in-chief remained in the ramshackle and derelict capital organizing his army, but within only a few days of taking the city he sent four divisions south from Alexandria. These men would meet up with other divisions under General Claude François Dugua, sent out later to take Rosetta and travel southwards along the Nile to rendezvous at Damanhur. Two of the divisions on foot, under Generals Louis-Charles Desaix and Jean Louis Reynier, crossed what appeared to be a scrub plain but which became a hellish inferno, pocked with dried-up wells: the Nile flood had failed to reach the plains the previous year – the wells were mostly empty. With this unforeseen misfortune came a drying wind, the *Ghibli*, blowing the dust into a red haze, burning the eyes and throats of the troops who had first been half-drowned in the surf upon landing, driven by thirst to take Alexandria and next scorched in the desert. It was from here that Europe would learn of that nightmarish and maddening phenomenon, the *mirage*.[10]

Most without canteens, fed at sea on salt meat and dry biscuit, in heavy tunics and almost entirely without horses or drawn transport, the divisions stumbled through soft sand, harassed by Bedouins, only to reach cisterns moistened by the dregs of foul brown water – men trampled their comrades in their haste to get to it. Some shot themselves in their anguish. Unable to offer relief, Desaix and the other generals left trails of parched corpses in their wakes. When Reynier's division found a well filled to the brim, they fell upon it with joyful abandon, drinking themselves into a stupor, the damned reaching paradise. That these ill-prepared men were then able to continue their march to Cairo is a testament not to Bonaparte, who was content to accept their tormented and agonized deaths as an acceptable casualty rate, but to their devotion and determination. Eventually this, along with their very lifeblood, would be wasted, drained into the indifferent sands.

The morale of the troops had plummeted, and they did not conceal their dissatisfaction. There is a tale of Bonaparte listening stonily to the complaints of his senior officers and generals in a barn at Damanhur before stalking out, saying nothing. He later wrote of his disgust for the army in those first weeks, mitigating the generals' complaints with the understanding that they were the Army of Italy, gentlemen of leisure, used to the comforts of the palazzo, not the desert.

After their brief period of rest among the watermelon field and market-places of Damanhur, where the soldiers had haggled with traders using uniform buttons as currency, Bonaparte had marched them to Al-Ramanieh. Moiret recounts a review of the troops which gave rise to hopes in the ranks for a swift return to France or a comparatively comfortable invasion of England. Instead, Bonaparte had better news for them; he had received word of Murad's Mameluke forces massing further south, and that battle was imminent. The effect was electric – in moments, recalled Moiret, their commandant had swept away the grumbling complaints and promised them the task for which they were most suited. They marched southwards to face Murad Bey.

The Battle of the Pyramids is often cited as the first decisive meeting between the Orient and the Occident, but the armies clashed first at Shubra Khit, also known as Chebreiss, on 13 July, a week earlier. It was here the Mamelukes first confronted the disciplined army of France en masse. It was to be an unhappy encounter for them. By dawn of that day, the French were reinforced by a flotilla of gunboats on the Nile, and Bonaparte had set the men into their divisional square formations, cavalry and baggage train in the centre, a daunting hedgerow of spike bayonets ranked six deep on the outside, each corner defended by cannon.[11] Not only was it nigh impossible for enemy cavalry to penetrate with any success, the square also became a mobile fortress: as Moiret recounted, the commanders gave the word to advance in echelon.[12]

This was also the closest the French had been to the Mamelukes. These were the elite cavalry troops of Murad Bey, a great warrior in the eyes of his followers, who could decapitate a horse with a single blow of his scimitar.[13] Al-Jabarti wrote that once Murad arrived at his destination, so it was believed, 'victory would be theirs'. The mounted Mamelukes presented an impressive sight, arrayed on their Arabian horses, dressed in sumptuous silks and jewel-encrusted robes, some armed with swords, pistols, maces or axes, each as skilled as the Mongol horsemen and Cossacks of the steppe. Shubra Khit gave the Mamelukes a chance to stop the south-ward march of the French and test their mettle, but they were outnumbered and utterly unable to penetrate the squares, their cavalry charges dodging through volleys of musketry fired at point-blank range. However, Murad had also come supported by gunboats on the Nile, and eventually the fighting grew worse on the river than on land – Monge and others had been placed aboard the French ships for their safety but soon found themselves in the midst of battle. Failing after some hours to break the French squares, Murad Bey and his warriors retreated, the Nile blazing with the remains of his river fleet.

Murad's defeat came as a great shock, and plans for the defence of Cairo were immediately put into effect by the sheikhs and beys, who ordered the construction of earthworks and gun emplacements. Ibrahim Bey, the joint Mameluke ruler with Murad, raised a militia from the city, wrote Al-Jabarti: 'The people were summoned to the entrenchments. This call [to arms] was repeated time and time again. People closed their shops and markets, and everyone was in an uproar.'[14]

What had particularly alarmed the sheikhs was Bonaparte's proclamation. Intended to reassure Egyptians that the French were enemies only of the Mamelukes and respected Egypt's sacred beliefs, it expressed a reverence for the indivisible God, 'with no Son', as an appeal to their Islamic faith. It reported Bonaparte's success in Rome in 'destroying the papal see', as if to demonstrate how the republic would seek out all evil, no matter how lofty, but this backfired. As Al-Jabarti recorded with some disgust, this indicated that the evidently non-Muslim French were also not Christian either: instead, much worse, they were godless materialists. It also appeared as if the French claim to friendship with the Ottoman Empire had backfired as well: on the whole, the average Egyptian had little affection for the alien dominance of the imperial forces. Terrified of what might yet come, the panic-stricken citizens of Cairo roused themselves to meet the invader. The fight with the French was declared a *jihad*, a holy war.

In the eight days that followed Shubra Khit, Ibrahim, Murad and Abu Bakr Pasha made ready their defences. On the dusty horizon, the Pyramids would preside over the battle to come.

As the Egyptians must have gaped at the French fleet on its approach to Alexandria, so too must the French have stared, awe-struck, at the monstrous proportions of the Pyramids. It is a shame for the world of art and drama that the Battle of the Pyramids was not fought at the base of Khufu's monument or under the chin of the Sphinx as it was later depicted – it was fought some nine miles from the temple plain of Gizeh, but still the Great Pyramid stood visible, to the rear of Murad Bey's Mamelukes. Although Moiret does not record the announcement, and the fact that the army was spread over some miles of wild terrain casts further doubt upon the story, Bonaparte claimed later he had declared historically, 'Soldiers, forty centuries look down upon you.' He had little time for such pronouncements, but he would not have been far wrong: the valley that had once reverberated to the sound of the pharaohs' massed chariot wheels would echo now to the thunder of French cannon.

'The heat was suffocating and we found it almost impossible to breathe,' wrote Moiret.[15] They did not go far before encountering the forward outposts of Murad's forces, and pushed them back, village by village, to the bulk of the Mameluke army, which they met at roughly two o'clock on 21 July. Entrenched in the village of Embabeh, on the banks of the Nile just opposite Cairo, were Murad's forces, over 21,000 men, 6,000 of whom were mounted carabinier Mameluke cavalry complete with artillery batteries. 'There they sat on their Arab horses, each armed with a London pistol and a shining carbine, making their superb damascene scimitars flash before our eyes.'[16] On the other side of the Nile, with Ibrahim Bey at Bulaq, there waited the levy of every able-bodied man from Cairo. There were over 100,000 of them.

Murad's Mameluke cavalry charged, but the French had been marching in their divisional squares since morning and were drawn up ready. Sitting behind their ranks of bayonets, soldiers reported the magnificent spectacle of the Mamelukes at full gallop, firing their pistols from bandoliers then drawing a scimitar in each hand, the reins held between their teeth, their gold and silver harness dazzling in the sun. Bonaparte's artillery held its fire until the last moment and broke the charge against Desaix and Reynier's squares, blasting the riders to pieces. Moiret recalled how his division was prepared to give the Mamelukes a 'hearty welcome', and were waiting when the second charge came at their rear – it dissolved in a cloud of musket-fire. Some Mamelukes leapt the rows of bayonets into the centres of the squares, their sabres slicing through ranks of raised musket-barrels in a single stroke before they were over-whelmed. The reckless courage and suicidal cavalry charges cost the Mamelukes dear as the French squares cut them to ribbons. The French outflanked the entrenched positions on the riverbank and attacked their rear: Al-Jabarti recalled how the muskets of the French were like a 'boiling pot on a fierce fire'. General Dugua cut off the Mameluke's route to the city and, with Desaix in pursuit, Murad once again took to flight across the desert, followed by those Mamelukes not trapped by the French counter-attack, and fled the field. Others, trying to escape by swimming the Nile to regroup on the far shore with Ibrahim Bey, were drowned in the stampede of the terrified levy troops stranded on the riverbank.

Once the French took the batteries on the western bank, they redirected the captured artillery at Ibrahim and the defenders on the eastern shore. Ibrahim and the Ottoman Pasha Abu Bakr took to their horses. Seeing their leaders flee at the gallop, the civilian militia, now being pounded by constant barrage, fell back towards the city and villages in panic. 'In their great alarm they took to their heels and ran like the waves of the sea'.[17] The battle lasted for the next two hours, until nightfall, the Nile Valley littered with the dead, each bejewelled Mameluke corpse looted for booty by the victors, the river filled with the dead gently floating downstream. The great levy surged back to Cairo, a desperate mob trying to escape. Looting began, and the grand homes of Ibrahim and Murad were set alight.

Moiret recorded General Berthier's terse conclusion, adopted by military historians since that day: 'No battle has ever shown more clearly the superiority of European tactics over the undisciplined courage of the Orient.'[18] French casualties are commonly listed as 'few' or 'several', but amounted to some 300, whereas the Mamelukes and Egyptians lost men by the thousands.

On the night of 22 July, the band playing, the French marched into a deserted capital, the inhabitants having fearfully locked themselves away in their homes. On the 24th, escorted by only a few of his men, Bonaparte quietly entered Cairo and took up residence in the palace of Muhammed Bey Al-Alfi.[19] In the passing of just over three weeks he had landed an army, destroyed the enemy, occupied his key ports and seized the capital city. He could now stand equal to the glory of Ashurbanipal, Cambyses, Alexander, Caesar and Selim of the Ottomans, and adopt the most illustrious title of the ancient world, 'Conqueror of Egypt'.

As with all conquests of Egypt, however, this triumph would pass. A week later, the laurels from this extraordinary feat of survival, determination and discipline would hang in tatters: Nelson was about to maroon Bonaparte like a castaway on a desert isle.

After the Battle of the Pyramids, one of the most famous land battles in history, there followed one of the most famous naval conflicts in the annals of the Royal Navy. Known also as the Battle of Aboukir Bay, it would turn the tide of fortune against the Egypt expedition.

The vast majority of the French armada long since returned to France, Admiral Brueys moved the invasion fleet's thirteen remaining great battleships, four frigates and several smaller craft, to Aboukir Bay, fifteen miles east of Alexandria – the spot he would have preferred to disembark the men of the Armée de l'Orient four weeks earlier. Naval historians and tacticians have often speculated why this invaluable battle squadron was left in such a loose line while at anchor in the bay. Prudent naval practice would have called for the ships to be cabled together closely enough for there to have been an uninterrupted line of cannon facing out to sea, providing a curtain of fire by some 500 guns. Instead, the ships were strung out with large gaps between. In Brueys's defence it has also been suggested that, in the three weeks he was in Aboukir Bay, he was too deeply involved with disembarking tons of equipment and materiel to engage in complex manoeuvres so close to the shore, and possibly felt safe enough with the shallows of the bay to one side – thinking that no British captain would dare risk trying to slip between the French ships and the shore; but this is precisely what they did.

After chasing across the eastern Mediterranean, Nelson returned on 1 August. Having reconnoitred in Alexandria, the British squadron had raced round the coast to Aboukir Bay, just as Bonaparte had anticipated a month earlier, and Nelson led his fourteen sail into the attack. When the British were spotted and the alarm was sounded at 2 p.m., Brueys's squadron was short of roughly a third of its crews – many were ashore and hundreds were miles away in Alexandria and Rosetta fetching new supplies.

Too late, Brueys ordered his ships be cabled and drawn in to close the gaps in the line, but in haste and undermanned, the task was not performed adequately. The British ships surged forward, each trying to outstrip the other, the crew of Captain Hood's *Zealous* roaring out three cheers as the *Goliath* under Captain Foley sped past to be first at the prey. They came into range of the French guns just after six o'clock, and *Goliath* sailed round the leading French battleship *Le Guerrier* taking Brueys utterly by surprise – making a quick assessment of the shoreline Foley sailed *Goliath* between the French ships and attacked on the landward side. As *Goliath* passed by, the ineffective shore batteries on Aboukir Island opened up. The Battle of the Nile had begun.

Culloden ran aground but four ships followed Foley's example and slipped between the French and the shore, dropping anchor opposite their chosen targets in such a way that they could fire on two French ships at once. Nelson in the *Vanguard* led the attack on the seaward side of the bay, the squadron trapping the leading French ships and those in the centre in a crossfire from which there was no escape. The first casualty was *La Sérieuse*, which opened fire on HMS *Goliath* but was hit in the rudder and sunk by a broadside from HMS *Orion*. The rear of the French line, under Admiral Villeneuve,[20] was not yet involved in the battle but could not advance to assist owing to contrary winds; he watched impotently as Nelson tore into his squadron.

The cannons often fired at point-blank range, and the British crews sent aloft blood-curdling cheers when they struck their target. As the battle raged through the next four hours, the most remarkable action was the attack on *L'Orient*. The 74-gun third-rate HMS *Bellerophon*, known affectionately as the 'Billy Ruffian', charged valiantly at Bonaparte's magnificent 118-gun flagship, only to be pounded by her huge battery of guns until dismasted and near-crippled, and forced to withdraw as other British ships joined in the attack. At seven-thirty, Admiral Brueys met his end aboard *L'Orient* – though severely wounded, he had insisted on remaining at his post until finally a cannon-ball snatched away his left leg, and he expired on the quarterdeck.

Around 9 p.m. *L'Orient* caught fire and five British ships moved in for the kill, *Swiftsure*, *Alexander*, *Defence*, *Goliath* and *Leander*, each trying to inflict the final blow. Still withstanding the barrage, the order to abandon ship was given only when the fire raged out of control. Just after ten o'clock, hundreds dived into the waters of Aboukir Bay as the flagship burned fiercely. Within fifteen minutes, *L'Orient* exploded. The blast was heard twenty-five miles away.[21]

As the burning remains of *L'Orient* rained down, the opposing squadrons' guns fell silent. For ten minutes, claim witnesses, the scene was still, the bright moon almost snuffed out, the bay wreathed in a heavy fog of gunsmoke. Firing then recommenced and continued throughout the night, breaking only for some few hours in the early morning. Eventually, *L'Artemise* was scuttled and exploded, with the same force as *L'Orient*, and the battered French ships struck their colours and surrendered independently.

Admiral Villeneuve, still at the rear, unable to participate in the battle, took advantage of a new wind and pulled his flagship, *Le Guillaume Tell*, another battleship and two frigates from the carnage, his sad duty to rescue the remnants of French naval power in the Levant. Two days later, on 3 August, the Royal Navy took possession of Brueys's proud squadron and over 3,000 prisoners.

Nelson had received a head wound and later recuperated in liberated Naples, enjoying the hospitality of Sir William Hamilton – it is popularly believed this is when he began his affair with Hamilton's wife, Emma. Nelson was made viscount, his coronet crest later incorporating ships under sail, his newly sanctioned heraldic arms bearing a palm-tree to represent Egypt. For the moment, it seemed Britain had dealt a decisive blow to the French – of seventeen French ships, only four escaped destruction or capture – rendering, so it was believed, an end to French naval plans for invasion.

What was achieved in Egypt was no less than the isolation of an entire army, along with the invincible Bonaparte, unable now to execute his plans to reinforce Tippoo Sultan in India, unable to threaten Europe and certainly unable to lead an invasion of England. Bonaparte and the Egypt expedition were now imprisoned in their new colony on the Nile.

4

The New Colony

Upon landing in Alexandria, the savants were not received with quite the ceremony one might expect for ambassadors of European culture and learning; instead they were largely ignored and left to fend for themselves by Bonaparte and the army, who were engaged in military operations. The Commission members had been shaken by the conditions of the voyage and, like the troops, were further dismayed by the state of Alexandria. Monge and Berthollet, the most senior among the Commission, had gone with Bonaparte on 7 July to Cairo,[1] but the remainder were to stay temporarily in the Delta, most in Alexandria, with a group of some twenty moving to Rosetta with General Dugua, who took the town with ease on the 8th.[2]

In the opening phase of the conquest, there were few specific scientific tasks for most of the savants to undertake, and they had no facilities with which to conduct detailed work. Those not employed as engineers by the army found themselves being used in administrative clerical duties, like civil servants rather than the cream of the French academic community. In the opening phase of the expedition Monge and Berthollet in particular were employed in uncovering Mameluke treasure and devising new taxes and fines to impose upon the Egyptian rich. In Alexandria the savants constructed barracks, conducted surveys, examined the Alexandrine canal, while Conté and the engineers built a furnace for creating 'hot shot' heated cannon-balls, and designed a river-borne fire-engine.

In Rosetta the savants had to make do with their commandeered billets, some living communally with cooking and cleaning rotas, suffering poor food, mosquitoes, vermin-infested houses filled with refuse and 'disgusting filth', reported Jollois, the engineer. Once supplies reached them and servants were found, life for most took on a sense of normality. They occupied themselves as best they could – mathematicians and poets became quartermasters and worked on 'supply commissions'; the composer Villoteau volunteered to become the secretary of the newly appointed Governor of Rosetta, the ageing General Jacques-François Menou.[3] They enjoyed cordial relations with Menou, who particularly appreciated their intelligent and cultured company and after-dinner conversation. The Rosetta district had its uses – it was a paradise of plant life and bird species for the botanists and zoologists. Jollois marched about the countryside, wearing sunglasses, armed with a shotgun shooting specimens for Geoffroy Saint-Hilaire, who consequently made great strides in his ornithological research; he also began to catalogue and record the marine life of the Nile.

Despite the occupation of Cairo, the countryside was far from subdued. In September Vivant Denon joined an excursion party into the Delta east of Rosetta, led by Menou and General Marmont,[4] with twelve 'artists and men of learning' from the Commission. After the destruction of the fleet at Aboukir, the Delta towns had become dangerous, even for the fully armed garrisons left behind by the army on the southward march to Cairo. News of Nelson's victory had spread across Egypt and the Levant, carried over the desert by the Bedouin faster than French couriers, bolstering localized resistance. With the whiff of a French defeat on the breeze, the town of Al-Mansuriah rose up and slaughtered its entire contingent of French soldiers; a single survivor escaped the townsfolk by leaping into the Nile to drown himself, yet was rescued by the inhabitants of a nearby village. Denon and the twelve Rosetta savants were to come face to face with this unanticipated violence themselves.

After a few days' travel without sighting much in the way of ruins to sketch, most of the savants broke off to visit elsewhere, leaving the geologist Dolomieu, Denon, an anonymous surgeon, two guides, an unnamed young man of Rosetta and Joly, the painter – to whom Denon refers as an anonymous 'draughtsman' – all under the military care of Generals Menou and Marmont and a sizeable escort of 200 cavalry. Having previously enjoyed a good reception by the sheikhs of many Delta towns, who afforded them the alluring spectacle of the *almeh*, the seductively veiled dancing-women, the excursion party rode some two miles ahead of its escort on the approaches of the fortified town of Kafr-Shahabas. The cry went up from the guides that the inhabitants had 'come upon them', armed with muskets, and rather than parley, as Denon related with some alarm, fired several badly aimed volleys. Denon assisted Dolomieu with his startled mount and the pair turned to ride out with the others – but the artist, Joly, panicked and fell or jumped from his saddle, trying to escape on foot. Menou wrote to Bonaparte how they called to him several times to remount or at least climb up behind another rider, but Joly 'lost his head' as a second group of attackers outflanked them, nearly cutting off their only retreat. Still mounted, Menou, Marmont and the others were obliged to gallop out of trouble, bullets whistling overhead. According to Menou, Joly was regrettably left behind, captured and killed. Marmont wrote that after their counter-attack to take the town they found his headless body.

Although Bonaparte claimed total victory and dominion over his new colony, in reality the fighting was not over. He might well have reflected it took William arduous years of war after Hastings before the barons called him 'Conqueror'. Joly's death, an example of the ever-present danger of their unstable environment and equally volatile hosts, must have shaken the Commission members. On their return to Rosetta after a fruitless journey for antiquities and ruins, more of Menou's savants were called to Cairo, including Denon. It is unlikely that many were unwilling to attend the facilities which had already been prepared in the perceived safety of Bonaparte's new capital.

Captain Moiret recorded his first glimpses of Cairo, remarking on miserable hovels, crumbling buildings of piled stone and brick which, falling in ruins, were left abandoned, and hastily built structures erected elsewhere to rehouse the homeless occupants. The genius of the Pyramids stood in stark contrast to the collapsing accommodation within the capital.

There was soon an area of Cairo which came to be known as Little Paris, where the troops drank and smoked – not all Egyptians abstained rigorously from alcohol and many could be seen fraternizing with the new visitors. Moiret and his men enjoyed the donkeys, which they used to ride at great speeds through the winding unpaved city streets. The early days were almost festive, though the troops were at first frustrated in a search for companionship – to touch the womenfolk of the rich, Moiret found, was most imprudent, and also very difficult, as they were usually kept locked away at the behest of 'jealous tyrants' in grand palaces, which were staffed in some cases by hundreds of slaves and concubines. At the other end of the spectrum, the squalid brothels and their hostesses were apparently too unappealing. There were many later couplings between Egyptian women and the occupying soldiers, but after hearing his officers' complaints one of the items on Bonaparte's early supply requisitions sent to the Directory in Paris was for a quantity of wives.

The new liberators enjoyed good relations with the bemused natives for some while, though the Egyptians were appalled by

European manners. Al-Jabarti found their habit of walking across carpets indoors in their boots, and apparently blowing their noses on furnishings, particularly abhorrent. He also discovered that the French did not shave their heads or pubic hair. The meeting of cultures was difficult but not an impossible chasm to bridge. It is ironic that the 'civilized' Europeans looked down upon the Egyptian people who, likewise, held their alien visitors to be barbarians.

Bonaparte had serious intentions towards Islam and did his utmost to convince the beys and pashas in Tripoli, Mecca and Constantinople that his army had come in friendship. This was by no means rhetoric for diplomatic consumption. Having dispensed with Christianity, Bonaparte envisaged a new empire in the East, its hub the French colony of Egypt, himself at its head, a 'new Koran in hand'. Except for the Bey of Mecca, who would depend on the French for the protection of pilgrims, no Muslim potentate responded to these protestations of brotherhood – instead, the famously savage Ahmed Pasha, ruler of Acre, also known as 'Al-Jezzar' ('the Butcher'), threatened the French emissary Beauvoisin, that if Bonaparte the infidel would not leave Egypt, he would 'throw him into the fire' with his bare hands.

As Alexander had become overtaken by Persian culture after his successful conquest of the Asiatic empire, so perhaps did Bonaparte in Egypt. There is a tale of the commander-in-chief attending dinner one night in Cairo in full Egyptian dress and turban. His officers burst out laughing, thinking it was a joke. Mortified, he never repeated the spectacle, but must have been disappointed. He had finished with the European 'molehill', which offered nothing for the man of vision. Egypt, by comparison, was ripe with opportunity for a new leader, laid low in the dust with the vilest poverty and thus filled with the most rewarding promise.

In those first few weeks of August 1798, it seemed the entire Levant and the whole of Syria knew of Nelson's victory and its effects before Bonaparte. Even Murad Bey in self-imposed exile in Upper Egypt knew of it – so that when Bonaparte sent Carlo Rosetti, the Austrian Consul in Cairo, to offer the Mameluke leader peace terms, Murad's confident response was to offer the French terms for their withdrawal, and sums of gold to cover their expenses. This insulting note, claimed Nicolas the Turk, spurred Bonaparte to send General Desaix southwards after Murad while Bonaparte himself went north-east to find the other Mameluke leader, Ibrahim Bey; but his sortie was unsuccessful. Returning two weeks later from the Sinai border-lands, Bonaparte was informed of the catastrophe at Aboukir.

Eyewitnesses say Bonaparte absorbed the shock of the Battle of the Nile without a flicker of emotion. Perhaps, to the commander-in-chief, the greater blow was to his reputation: he had suffered a defeat at the hands of an enemy. Though he paid tribute to Brueys and Villeneuve in his reports to the Directory, he would later blame these two admirals for the disaster, and not without reason. But the damage had been done, and Bonaparte was no longer perceived as the invincible god-general. Yet, in this sudden crisis, Bonaparte's determination motivated his troops; they were now obliged, he wrote in his memoirs, to accomplish great things. He compared their struggle to that of the heroes of ancient history. He spoke not of an eventual safe return to France, but of taking Africa, and Asia, as if what remained of his 40,000 men could conquer indefinitely. His plans for India would now involve the overland dominion of all that lay between the subcontinent and the Nile. For the sake of his plans, he refused to acknowledge any defeat whatsoever.

It was this determination of Bonaparte to carry on and establish his colony that enabled the scientific and archaeological works of the savants. The Egypt expedition was to continue – especially as their boats had most certainly been burnt.

When they reached Cairo, the savants were conveyed to the suburb of Nasriyah, to the abandoned palace complex of the Mameluke lords Hassan and Qassim Bey, both of whom had fled to the side of Murad in Upper Egypt. The palaces were surrounded by gardens and high walls, providing a luxurious headquarters for what would become the first academic association of its kind outside Europe, the Institut d'Égypte.

Not all of the 167 savants became members of the Institute, and not all members of the Institute had been drawn from the ranks of the savants. Membership had been limited to some fifty of the most senior or most exceptional specialists,[5] but included army officers and military engineers such as Malus, Sulkowski, Desgenettes and Caffarelli, who would have a genuine contribution to make to discussions. This anchored the Institute firmly within Bonaparte's military operations, binding the two inextricably, and the Institute's aims became those of the military expedition as a whole.

Modelled on the Institut de France,[6] the organization of the Institute of Egypt was devised on 21 August by a committee consisting of Bonaparte and two of his generals, Andréossy and Caffarelli, and senior members of the Scientific and Artistic Commission: the inseparable Monge and Berthollet, the zoologist Geoffroy Saint-Hilaire, the mathematician engineer Louis Costaz and the army chief medical officer, General Desgenettes. The Institute was subdivided into four departments, or sections: Mathematics, Physical Sciences, Political Economy, and Literature and the Arts. Each section had twelve allocated seats for a total of just forty-eight men. With some of its members still in Rosetta and Alexandria, the Institut d'Égypte met for the first time in the exotic surroundings of the harem of Hassan Kashiff Bey, on the morning of 23 August 1798. At this first meeting, Bonaparte allowed the multi-faceted Monge to be elected president and himself vice-president – Fourier, the mathematician, was appointed secretary.

Despite his military successes, Bonaparte did not view the army as his true vocation: he often stated that had he not pursued a military career, he would have chosen a life in the sciences, mathematics in particular, and was duly proud of the honour accorded him by the Institute in Paris when he was made a member of the Mathematics Section after his conquest of Italy in 1797. In Egypt, even after all he had achieved in Germany and the Low Countries, Italy and Malta, he styled himself 'Member of the Institute' first and 'general' second. With such genuine interest in its foundation and proceedings, Napoleon Bonaparte took his place among the savants at the high table of the Institute.

Although not the president, when Bonaparte spoke the members deferred to him. However, some, such as Desgenettes, were not afraid to contend with him in discussion. Detractors of Bonaparte might point to his mundane demands on these gathered *illuminati* as evidence of his inability to consort with them as an equal, but this would not be accurate. Though he was by no means a Berthollet or Conté, he was more than a competent mathematician, and more than willing to learn, asking Berthollet at one point to give him chemistry lessons amid the daily tribulations of redeveloping a nation. His first questions posed to the Institute were certainly very practical and have been interpreted as somewhat beneath the great minds of the savants – they ranged from purifying Nile water for drinking and brewing beer for the troops to improving Egyptian civil and criminal law.

The Institute began work on many long-term investigations: studies in agricultural improvements and irrigation; the feasibility of introducing or breeding new crop species; the control of contagious diseases involving Desgenettes's use of statistical analysis of public deaths; and, most famous, the potential of reopening the ancient Suez Canal.[7] The geography and geology of Egypt was surveyed and analysed more fully than ever before. Cairo was mapped, engineers moving from street corner to street corner with theodolites, before the eyes of baffled onlookers.

The palatial Institute headquarters in the Cairo suburbs, with its gardens, fountains and cooling colonnades, has since been compared to Plato's Academy. The thousands of volumes brought by Bonaparte across the sea became the Institute reference library; a museum was created for the antiquities being collected in and around the capital; halls and chambers were converted into chemistry laboratories and workshops and cellars slowly filled with botanical and zoological specimens, while the fertile gardens sprouted working horticultural experiments. The aeronautical inventor, Conté, oversaw a metal foundry, and among his first tasks was the fashioning of scientific instruments lost in the Battle of the Nile. The Institute buildings eventually housed the new state printing press, producing the *Courier de l'Égypte*,[8] a short, general newspaper, first published on 29 August 1798.[9] Later would emerge *La Décade Égyptienne*,[10] the formal journal of the Institute where the savants would publish their progress and findings.

The only other two known printing presses in the eastern Mediterranean were at Constantinople and Lebanon. Consequently, the first book ever printed in Egypt was produced in Cairo by the new state press, *Exercises in Literary Arabic, Extracted from the Koran For the Use of Those Who are Studying the Language*, in both French and Arabic. With its alien machines, laboratory experiments and public demonstrations, the Institute became a working embassy of eighteenth-century European technological and scientific achievement.

After the September uprisings in the Delta and the resistance encouraged by rumours of a French withdrawal, the country around Cairo was still potentially dangerous. It was therefore some time before the savants of the Institute were able to organize a visit to the greatest monuments in the world, some ten miles downriver. Denon, on his southward passage up the Nile from Rosetta, described passing the towering pinnacles of Gizeh, the Pyramids' appearance rendered almost diaphanous 'by the sheer volume of air they occupy'. Upon his arrival in Cairo on the celebration of the republican New Year,[11] he discovered that a party of 'curious persons' had gone with an escort of some 200 troops to see the site; in his meeting with Bonaparte he was advised to join the excursion – the commander-in-chief suggested that the opportunity of such an armed escort might not necessarily arise again. Denon hurried after them.

The Pyramids were measured and surveyed, Denon remarking that at first he felt their majesty lessen as he drew nearer, only to find it reaffirmed when he saw his colleagues moving before them as mere dots against their colossal size. Monge and Berthollet were among the party, as was Bonaparte, who encouraged the group to climb to the summit – which the ageing Monge did without qualm. Some entered the Great Pyramid, Denon recounting the event as a hellish ordeal of stifling, airless darkness and precipitous ledges, their only guide the flames of flickering torches ahead. There is an apocryphal tale of Bonaparte going inside the monument, and contemplating alone in the empty King's Chamber, as he believed Alexander had done before him. He is said then to have reappeared, visibly shaking with fright at some unspecified terror within, and refused ever to comment on the matter, even on his deathbed.[12]

The branches of the Commission destined to play a major role in the new science were largely the surveyors and draughtsmen, their minutely calculated records of the monuments of Egypt in many cases serving adequately ever since their execution. They were the first modern Europeans to measure the Pyramids and the head of the Great Sphinx – the only portion of the giant sculpture exposed above the sand at the time. Starkly visible even before its earliest excavations under Pharaoh Thutmosis IV in the fifteenth century BC,[13] the disembodied head of the Sphinx was a source of fear for many native Egyptians who called it the 'Father of all Terrors'. It yielded little more to the savants – with no historical narrative to rely upon other than classical sources, they were unable to interpret the Sphinx beyond its mathematical values, and set about measuring its every detail.[14]

Separate excursions of savants left for every region; a band travelling south with General Desaix were some of the first Europeans to explore Upper Egypt. Here was found the giant Memnonium of Thebes,[15] the Necropolis, the ruins of Karnak and Luxor, their temples and palaces recorded by the artists and surveyors. Such men included André Dutertre, the artist, engraver and lithographer who produced portraits of many expedition members and illustrations of ruins; Charles Louis Balzac, artist and architect, who made a number of drawings of Philae and the temple of Karnak; Prosper Jollois, a civil engineer and hydraulics specialist, who worked at Philae, Thebes and Dendera with the eighteen-year-old technician and artist Édouard de Villiers du Terrage,[16] both of whom made highly accurate drawings and descriptions of the Dendera zodiac, making their observations unsupervised, at night, and at great personal risk. In 1799 these same two would discover the tomb of Amenhotep III in the Valley of the Kings. Edme François Jomard, the surveyor, roamed all over Upper Egypt, recording remains at Philae, the temple of Karnak, and the Valley of the Kings – he was so touched by the ancient civilization around him he would study it for the rest of his days.

Of all these, however, the most famous is doubtless Vivant Denon, who provided breathtaking illustrations of the landscape and the people of Egypt as well as the great monuments. In November 1798 he convinced Bonaparte to let him leave Cairo and travel south to join General Desaix in his pursuit of Murad Bey, and while on the march with Desaix's troops, was able to sketch the great sites of the south such as the Temple Gate of Dendera and the ruins at Edfu. He recorded hieroglyphic inscriptions and carved reliefs meticulously, compiling a valuable record for his colleagues at the Institute. On this perilous adventure he sought no favours, and at the age of fifty-one carried his own kit and looked to his own resources, the soldiers taking to him so much that they happily stood guard over him to provide shelter from the sun if he stopped to sketch.

The work of the Institute and Commission of the Sciences and Arts ultimately vindicated Bonaparte's mission to Egypt. It is, however, ironic that the greatest discovery made by the French on this mission, that of the Rosetta Stone, was not a result of specific archaeological endeavour – it was found instead as a direct consequence of the military instability of the new colony, and the increasing threat of a host of enemies.

Contrary to Bonaparte's expectations, Foreign Minister Talleyrand had made no attempt to soothe relations with Ottoman Turkey and explain the purpose of the French expedition to Egypt. Worse, Talleyrand and the Directory made little attempt to contact Bonaparte to tell him so, failing to inform him of the increasingly precarious political situation. Although the British had blockaded the Nile Delta, it would not have been difficult for a courier ship to penetrate the lines at night with vital communiqués, as did several independent merchantmen. Bonaparte and his army had been abandoned by the Directory in Paris.

Isolated as they were, they had no idea that diplomatic relations with Turkey had collapsed and that French emissaries had been imprisoned along with all French citizens in many Ottoman cities. The rumours of war emanated from Al-Jezzar in Acre, who sent out copies of the sultan's *firman*, a printed declaration, against the French, urging the populace to rise up against the invaders. By late October 1798, the powder-keg of Cairo was set to blow.

Early in the morning of the 21st, the call echoed throughout Cairo for all men who believed in the One God and His Prophet to rise up against the invaders. The streets were soon overflowing with the murmuring mob. Leaderless and without aim or objective, the crowd exploded into action at around six o'clock and ran amok, attacking the Christian and Jewish quarters, particularly targeting the houses occupied by the French. Caffarelli's house was ransacked and three engineers and four savants were torn to pieces by looters, their precious surveying instruments stolen or destroyed. General Dupuy was clubbed to death in the streets, and General Sulkowski with a number of elite cavalrymen was attacked and killed.

The city collapsed into anarchy, the centre of the disturbance the area around the Al-Azhar Mosque where the sultan's *firman* had been read to the people. Bonaparte did not hear of the uprising until ten o'clock, as he inspected fortifications on Rodah Island on the Nile just outside the city. When he returned it was to find the gates closed and uproar in the streets. He ordered the artillery to be readied at the citadel and the Moqattam hills east of the capital. The following day he issued an ultimatum to the Al-Azhar Mosque, by now completely barricaded and occupied by hundreds of armed rebels: surrender or be destroyed. With no answer forthcoming, the bombardment began the next day at noon, howitzer shells raining down upon the mosque, the surrounding houses, inns, shops and streets. It did not stop until sunset, when French cavalry and infantry crashed through the barricades and stormed the mosque, with orders to kill everyone inside. As the Al-Azhar was sacked and defiled by the drunken troops, horrified officers called in several savants to rescue as many of the ancient books and relics as they could before they were destroyed.

Once order was restored, Bonaparte's vengeance was swift. All rebels captured bearing arms were beheaded, their bodies thrown into the Nile, and those sheikhs considered to be ringleaders were rounded up, tried at the citadel and executed. Cut off from home, suspecting they were surrounded by enemies, the French expeditionary force now had to contend with a hostile native population.

Bonaparte refused to believe that the sultan's *firman* was genuine – Talleyrand, so he hoped, was engaged in negotiations in Constantinople. The first glimpse of the truth came when Turkish warships were sighted among the British blockade off Alexandria. After parleys with the British it became clear that Egypt was now under threat from the Ottoman Empire. Still Bonaparte would not believe the alliance – it was a ruse of the British. The final proof came in early 1799, when a French merchantman slipped into Alexandria harbour; the captain was rushed to Cairo and reported that the Ottomans had officially declared war on France, allied with Russia and Britain as Europe rearmed against the French Republic. This coincided with an intercepted message from Al-Jezzar and Ibrahim Bey to Murad and the Mamelukes still at large in Upper Egypt, planning a combined assault on the French.

In a great reversal of Esarhaddon's invasion of Egypt in 671 BC to safeguard conquests in Syria, Bonaparte, now Sultan Al-Kebir, the Great Sultan, would invade Syria to safeguard his conquest on the Nile – with a single blow he would destroy Al-Jezzar, Ibrahim Bey, take Gaza, Jaffa and Acre, deprive the Royal Navy of their Levantine bases and force the Ottoman Empire at the point of the bayonet to negotiate. This was to be the Syria campaign. Although the advancing Armée de l'Orient overcame great physical hardship on the long march through the Syrian desert and very nearly succeeded in threatening the heart of the Ottoman Empire, the residual impression of the campaign was atrocity and murder, rendering it the least glorious of Bonaparte's achievements in the Middle East.

Despite a large number of men having died or been stricken with bubonic plague in the annual Egyptian epidemic that came with the onset of winter, three divisions totalling some 13,000 men set off for Sinai in early February 1799. So many savants from the Institute joined the expedition that *La Décade Égyptienne* announced a brief suspension of Institute meetings until the members' return. Sheikhs, slaves, concubines, entourages – all were taken on what appeared as permanent a venture as the Egypt expedition itself.

They took the frontier fortress of El-Arish after eleven days of brutal fighting, and crossed the border into Syria. A month later, suffering foul weather along the Mediterranean coast or getting lost in the burning, waterless desert, the army laid siege to Jaffa, but at a terrible cost. The affair at Jaffa forever polluted the expedition with the taint of massacre: after days of fruitless losses at the city walls and bloody encounters with the obstinate defenders, the city governor unwisely beheaded the French officer sent in to negotiate a surrender – and displayed the result on a pike on the city walls. The enraged Armée de l'Orient poured through a breach in the walls and killed thousands of men, women and children. Worse was to come. When the savagery had run its course a day later, Bonaparte was presented with the unexpected problem of several thousand Ottoman prisoners. After hours of circular debate with his generals, he came to the decision that the prisoners should be executed. Unable to offer them the limited rations of his own army, and unwilling to turn them loose to fight another day and perhaps succeed, Bonaparte felt he was forced into this course of action by his officers. Segregated by nationality, Egyptians, Moroccans and Turks, some were herded to the seashore and shot in their hundreds – some bayoneted, others run down by cavalry. This mass murder lasted three days, in which time nearly 4,500 were killed.

By 18 March, Bonaparte's bloody caravan of destruction had reached the stronghold of Al-Jezzar at Acre. The French heavy artillery, still at sea aboard transport ships, was to rendezvous with the army. However, as it rounded a headland to meet Bonaparte, the ships were pounced upon by a small British squadron and seized in the relentless attack of HMS *Tigre*; on the first day of the siege of Acre, Bonaparte lost his artillery to the Royal Navy's celebrated hero, Sir William Sidney Smith.[17] In so doing Smith had doomed the French to a protracted and fruitless exercise.

Suffering from plague and dysentery, Bonaparte's forces mounted repeated assaults on the city but failed to take it in a three-month war of attrition. Despite their victory over a Turkish relief column at the Battle of Mount Tabor and the addition of new artillery to their arsenal, several further assaults on Acre were driven back. Having lost considerable numbers to disease,[18] Bonaparte pulled back on 21 May.

Although he had failed in his attempt to seize Acre and conquer the Middle East, he had rendered Al-Jezzar less of a threat to Egypt, delaying an overland Ottoman attack from the Sinai desert. Bands playing, captured banners flying, he returned to Cairo on 14 June amid a pre-arranged Caesarian triumph. His plans for a march of conquest across Syria and Persia to India lay in tatters: in May, the British army took the rebellious Indian fortress of Serangapatan and found the body of Tippoo Sultan buried beneath a heap of corpses. A French empire in the East was now out of reach.

The Ottoman Empire could send other armies without fear of exhaustion and enjoy undisputed mastery of the seas with their new British allies. Talleyrand's dreams of controlling commerce in the Levant were over: the valuable Ionian Islands had fallen into enemy hands and Malta had been blockaded. Rather than the formidable presence of French arms in the East, the Armée de l'Orient had become an exposed target. Justly feeling that he and his men had been deserted by the Directory, Bonaparte turned his attentions towards Paris. The only way to save Egypt would be from France.

The Stone – July, 1799

After the temporary success of Bonaparte's attack on Al-Jezzar's forces in the Holy Land, the swiftest means available for an Ottoman reprisal was by sea. An invasion could fall on any combination of three key targets in the Nile Delta: Damietta to the east, Alexandria to the west, or Rosetta between the two in the north-west. To hold the enemy, the French looked to their engineers to strengthen the Delta fortress defences: one such aged castle was Fort Julien, a fortified tower with a view of the whole of the river as it swept past the green and lush vistas of the vital port of Rosetta on the west branch of the Nile. With well-placed guns the old castle could theoretically command the river mouth and the seaward approaches to the town.

However, the fifteenth-century fort built by Sultan Qayt Bey needed immediate structural reinforcement. A unit of engineers under the command of Lieutenant Pierre Bouchard was assigned the task, his first job the renovation of the outer curtain wall. It was here that Bonaparte's expedition would make its most lasting impression on Egyptian history. During the demolition of this older structure, someone, labourer, engineer, or possibly Bouchard himself, saw a curious block of dark rock lying in the foundations: this block was the Rosetta Stone. There are no detailed accounts of how precisely the works proceeded, neither on which day, nor who had the first sighting of the arte- fact.[1] Over a month later, on 19 August 1799, as reported in the popular Cairo newspaper *Le Courier de l'Égypte*,[2] the first public notice of the discovery of the Rosetta Stone was published:

Le Courier de l'Égypte, n.37:

Rosetta. 2 Fructidor, Year VII (19 August 1799)

During the fortification works which Citizen Dhautpoul,[3] commander of the battalion of engineers, arranged to be done at the ancient fort of Rashid, today called Fort Julien,[4] situated on the left bank of the Nile, three thousand fathoms from Boghaz on the Rosetta branch, there was found in the excavations a stone of very beautiful black granite, of a very fine grain, very hard under the hammer. . . . Only one face, well polished, offers three distinct inscriptions separated in three parallel strips.

Pierre François Xavier Bouchard (1771–1822)[5] is regularly described as lieutenant, captain or merely 'an officer of engin- eers' in many accounts. At the time of the discovery he was a lieutenant on his first posting. In France Bouchard had been recruited into the Grenadiers after his initial studies and joined Nicolas-Jacques Conté in the new aeronautic squadron, seeing action in the extraordinary victory of Fleurus. Having completed his army service he enrolled in the newly established École Poly- technique, later accompanying the grand expedition to Egypt as a member of the Commission: he was no ordinary soldier, but a junior savant, and one of the rare group of engineering students to sit their final examinations in the Institut d'Égypte in Cairo under the invigilation of Gaspard Monge himself. He passed his exams and was commissioned into the engineers as a lieutenant. His first posting was to Rosetta. Of all the army officers in Egypt, he was probably the most appropriate to discover the stone in the rubble of Fort Julien.

Commentators differ as to the actual date of the find during the works at Fort Julien; however, this is linked directly to that of Bonaparte's victory at the Second Battle of Aboukir Bay.[6] On 15 July, possibly just as *chef de brigade* Dhautpoul was assigning work for Bouchard and the other engineers in the Delta, Bonaparte received an alarming message from General Marmont in Alexandria: a Turkish fleet had been sighted.

It was undeniably the seaborne invasion the French had anticipated: five towering Turkish battleships, three frigates and between fifty and sixty troop transports with an estimated 15,000 men aboard, dropped anchor in Aboukir Bay and began landing troops. Bonaparte acted at once. Within nine days he gathered his divisions, recalling General Murat from a renewed campaign of pursuit of Murad Bey and issued his orders to Generals Lannes, Kléber, Lanusse and Marmont. Having amassed some 10,000 men he arrived at Aboukir on 24 July, to find roughly 7,000–9,000 Turks[7] dug into positions on a well-defended beach-head, their backs to the sea.

Although the Turks were led by Mustafa Pasha, an experienced commander, they had trapped themselves on the spit of land which forms the northern horn of the bay, affording them possession of Fort Aboukir but nowhere to retreat or regroup. The next day Bonaparte's divisions outflanked and utterly destroyed the Turkish positions, driving them into the surf – those who did not perish by cannon and musket drowned in their attempts to escape. It was the most resounding victory since the Battle of the Pyramids – even the great Kléber, never a supporter of Bonaparte, was moved to embrace the commander-in-chief and proclaim his admiration.

This well-documented battle gives tempting clues to the date of the discovery of the Rosetta Stone, but still does not make it certain. Most believe that the stone was found approximately ten days before the battle, which took place on 25 July, and point to a report by Jean-Joseph Marcel, the savant orientalist and director of the press. In *La Décade Égyptienne*[8] he provided a summary of Institute sessions from 9 July 1799 to 8 September 1800:

> During the session of 1.er Thermidor [19 July, 1799] there was read out a letter in which the Citizen Lancret,[9] member of the Institute, related that the Citizen Bouchard, an officer of Engineers, had discovered in the town of Rosetta, some inscriptions the examination of which may offer much interest. The black stone which bears these inscriptions is divided into three horizontal strips: The lowest contains several lines of Greek characters which had been engraved under the reign of 'Ptolemy Philopator'; the second inscription is written in unknown characters; and the third contains hieroglyphs only.[10]

The date of the discovery, most presume from this report, must have been some time between 1 Thermidor (19 July) and the previous session of 21 Messidor (9 July). Many commentators arbitrarily choose the 14th or 15th or, more loosely, the first two weeks of July. Institute sessions, however, were numbered, and the session where Lancret's dramatic news was announced was Session 31. Unfortunately, Session 31 was incorrectly dated by Marcel in the report above.

It seems that *La Décade Égyptienne* had recorded the previous two Institute sessions, 29 and 30, both as 21 Messidor (9 July) – as if both had been held upon the same day.[11] Instead, Session 30 took place on the 19th and Session 31, therefore, ten days later on the 29th. This conclusion is supported by the fact that in the same session that featured Michel-Ange Lancret's exciting news of the discovery of the Rosetta Stone the gathered Institute members had to suffer an ode by the expedition's unappreciated poet, Parseval-Grandmaison, whose pen apparently knew no limits; this poem praised Bonaparte's great victory at Aboukir Bay – a victory which did not occur until the 25th. The unshakeable conclusion is that the discovery of the Rosetta Stone was announced on 29 July, and not the 19th as Marcel asserted in his report.

This then makes it more difficult to pinpoint the date of the stone's discovery – there is now no reason why it should have been found only a few days before the Institute session on the 19th. We can only speculate. Some look to a message sent to Bonaparte by General Menou from Rosetta, dated 18 July:

> I expect to be attacked at any time. I am vigilant and I hope the enemy will not take Fort Julien as easily as he took the fort at Aboukir.[12]

Even this is inconclusive; although Menou is concerned about the defensibility of Fort Julien, the message does not necessarily mean that the fort was reinforced, under renovation or lay still in semi-ruin. Indeed, the stone might even have been found after the great Battle of Aboukir Bay.

Considering the military situation, what is most likely is that works started on Fort Julien before the Turkish fleet was sighted on the 14th. The reading of Lancret's letter at the Institute session on the 29th can be interpreted in many ways: either that the stone was in fact found before the 19th but the announcement delayed owing to the dire circumstances of the Turkish landings; or that it was found *afterwards*, the news thus not being reported at the meeting, with the added possibility that the stone could have been found after Bonaparte's victory on the 25th. Unfortunately, there is no way to determine with any reasonable certainty at which point the stone was found; but there is no particular reason to believe it was in the first two weeks of July.[13]

When the cloud of dust hanging over the demolished wall of Fort Julien parted on the Nile breeze and the engineers spotted the stone lying in the rubble, Bouchard apparently recognized its importance immediately. Smaller pieces of inscribed stelai had been found before, similarly built into walls, but the Rosetta Stone was special – its size, state of preservation and legibility of the three evidently different scripts, all suggested an unusual value. Although it was not a decorative relic rich with images of gods or suns, the densely packed inscriptions of the Rosetta Stone were clearly trying to convey a message.

In the likely absence of his *chef de brigade* Dhautpoul, Bouchard went straight to General Menou with the news. Menou, all are agreed, was a man of learning, and he doubtless recognized the Greek characters at once and could probably tell that here might be an opportunity of comparing ancient Egyptian with a known language. He ordered the stone to be cleaned and taken to his tent.[14]

The Rosetta Stone is no mere fragment, but a tall, thick and massive piece of masonry weighing three-quarters of a ton – anything of such a size would have caused a stir, as would the inscription: three bands of script, including two recognizable languages, hieroglyphics at the top and Greek at the bottom. The middle band remained something of a mystery, but looked similar to those found earlier that year and, according to the *Courier* report, was declared to be 'Syriac', a form of Arabic.

General Menou ordered those savants in Rosetta to translate the Greek. As they did so, they revealed the most dramatic aspect of the stone. Although the bottom right corner had been broken away, the fragmented final line of the inscription declared:

SHALL BE ENGRAVED ON A SOLID STONE IN SACRED, IN VERNACULAR, AND IN GREEK CHARACTERS . . .[15]

It was not until this point that the savants had confirmation of the stone's significance. With this final sentence in the Greek there was now no doubt what they had in their possession: a code-key expressing the same text in three scripts: hieroglyphs, ancient Egyptian, and Greek, a known language.

Lancret wrote his letter to the Institute in Cairo, which was read out at Session 31, on 29 July. Searches were made for other fragments among the rubble at Fort Julien, presumably after Bonaparte's victory and the immediate threat of invasion had passed – but none was found. Later it was said these would have been 'worth their weight in diamonds'.[16] It must have been with some regret that the renovations at Fort Julien continued, the site of the discovery covered over, buried under the sands. Some time in mid-August, Bouchard was ordered by General Menou to take the stone to the Institut d'Égypte in Cairo, and it was duly sailed up the Nile. According to the *Courier*, it arrived by 19 August.

Many commentators have interpreted this as an honour for Bouchard, awarded him by General Menou, which might well have been partly the case; Bouchard had been, after all, a student of the École Polytechnique, and was a member of the Scientific Commission – it would have been fitting for him to transport the piece to the grand halls of the Institute where not long before he had sat and passed his exams. But by the middle of August (the end of Thermidor) when he sailed upriver to Bulaq, Cairo's Nile port, he had also been transferred to his next posting at the fortress of El Arish; the trip to Cairo might have been in recognition of his first command ending in scientific triumph but also to fall in with his new unit. His journals give a meticulous account of the months to come,[17] but he makes no mention whatever of the discovery of the Rosetta Stone, as if his delivery of the artefact to the Institute finished his involvement and, oddly, his interest in the stone.[18]

There is some question whether Bonaparte ever saw the stone. It would not have been difficult for him to have made the journey from Alexandria, where he remained after the Battle of Aboukir, but whether the man who had declined to enter the Great Pyramid would have been sufficiently interested in such a philological tool beyond the report he would doubtless have received is another matter – especially given the negotiations being enacted at Alexandria immediately after the victory. He was certainly well aware of its discovery, its basic composition and significance: though some of the detail was incorrect, he was the first to announce the find to the Institute in Paris, citing it as one of a number of great achievements of the Egypt expedition:

A tablet was found in the foundations of Rosetta, on which were engraved or carved three columns, carrying three inscriptions, one in hieroglyphs, the other in Coptic and the third in Greek. The Coptic and Greek inscriptions each state that, under the Ptolemies all the canals of Egypt were cleaned, and that it cost a certain sum. There appears no doubt that the column which bears the hieroglyphs contains the same inscription as the other two. Thus, here is a means of acquiring certain information of this, until now, unintelligible language.[19]

He had the opportunity of giving this address to the Institute in Paris only a few months after the Battle of Aboukir – for just as Bouchard was making his journey upriver to Cairo with the Rosetta Stone, Bonaparte suddenly returned to France. Rumours had come from Europe of French reverses in Italy and on the Rhine, and these were confirmed after the victory at Aboukir Bay: envoys were sent out to parley for an exchange of prisoners with Commodore Sir Sidney Smith aboard his ship HMS *Tigre*, which had come in support of the Turkish landings. Smith was well aware that bad news from the Continent could possibly take the great tactician home, leaving the army under different leadership, probably more amenable to a negotiated withdrawal.

Smith gave the envoys newspapers for their return to shore. Bonaparte apparently read these in his tent with occasional outbursts of rage at the government; battered by the devastating campaign in Syria, his worst fears for his European conquests realized in the papers before him, he also had proof by letter from the Directory's own hand that the government had effectively abandoned him and the Armée de l'Orient: their belated communiqué to him sent months earlier had reached him at last, suggesting blithely that he should attack the Ottoman Empire. Other than this advice they offered him no other support in Egypt.

However, the Directory wanted Bonaparte to return to France and rectify the European situation[20] – how much of his army he brought with him was a matter for him to judge. Return he would. After the defeat of the Turks, now was as good a time as any to put an end to the mismanagement of the European empire he had created for France. The Directory would come to regret their request.

He returned to Cairo by 11 August and began making arrangements, compiling sealed orders for his generals. Though his imminent departure was kept secret, according to Captain Moiret[21] rumours were rife in the army; yet not even Kléber, who was to take over as commander-in-chief, had been informed.[22] A message came down from Alexandria that many of the British ships had departed, probably for revictualling on Cyprus: the blockade was at its weakest – this was Bonaparte's chance.

Bonaparte left Cairo on 17 August in the middle of the night, ostensibly for a week-long tour of Lower Egypt, with a select group including Monge and Berthollet: his sending a carriage to the Institute for his two mentor savants nearly gave the game away – its arrival was announced at 10 p.m., forcing the pair to make their embarrassed excuses and pack their bags amidst the curious questions of their astonished colleagues. Some were convinced they were both going on more than a tour of Lower Egypt, and pursued them to the carriage door. Parseval-Grand-maison was so terrified of being left behind he packed his bags to join them without being invited.

A week later, on the night of the 24th, Bonaparte paced the beach at Alexandria with Menou, Marmont and Admiral Ganteaume, waiting for the wind and a clear passage through the thin British lines. He handed Menou sealed orders containing a proclamation to be made after his departure. Later that night, Admiral Ganteaume provided the frigate as he had been commanded. Denon, Monge, Berthollet, a clasp of generals, one Mameluke bodyguard,[23] a cook and the future Emperor of France, the Sultan Al-Kebir himself, bade farewell to their orange-scented dreams of the Nile, possibly wondering what might have been.

Four days earlier, just after Bonaparte had left the capital, Bouchard arrived in Cairo with his precious cargo.

Bouchard's *djerm* riverboat docked at Bulaq, the capital's old Nile port, and the Rosetta Stone was taken ashore. When it was finally carried into the hall of the Institute, the cry went up immediately:

> At this news each ran to see the marvellous stone; each wanting to analyse it in all its minute features, asking him for an account in all its detail; the scientists who were then in Cairo spent days before it, entire weeks, and this attentive examination served only to confirm the high hopes which they had placed in it.[24]

The savants' first step was to consider how best to make faithful reproductions of the inscriptions to circulate to colleagues, both within the Institut d'Égypte and in France – scrupulous artistic rendering would have been potentially inaccurate, however painstaking its attention to detail. As Saintine, Marcel and Reybaud recorded,

The first and essential requirement of any examination was to produce exact copies of the monument; without this preliminary operation, any later investigation, any scientific study would have been difficult, dubious – one can even say impossible.[25]

Well aware of Senefelder's new chemical process devised in 1796, the ever-resourceful Conté and Marcel, saw the stone's potential as a ready-made printing block. As an experiment in lithography, the depth of the incised inscriptions became relevant; the inscriptions on the Rosetta Stone are not deeply carved, as are many examples of temple hieroglyphs – although the grey surface of the stone, if stood even on temple steps in the sun, would have displayed sufficient bas-relief for the characters' shadows to be seen clearly, they were still more shallow than the printer would have wished. Marcel's use of the stone as a printing block produced a mirror-image, with 'white' characters against a black, inked background. Conté produced the reverse, much as in copper-plate printing, whereby the characters were filled with material that retained ink while the specially coated surface of the stone repelled it, thus providing sharp black characters on a white background. Raffeneau-Delile also suggested taking a sulphur cast of the stone, which, according to Saintine, clarified some of the typographical imperfections made in the printing process.[26] The effect was not achieved immediately – Marcel's copies were made on 24 January 1800, and Conté's some time after, in February, some six months after the stone's arrival in Cairo. The results were later given to General Dugua, who was to make his way back to France – by the summer, images of the Rosetta Stone had reached Paris and were presented to the National Institute.

The impact of these copies on the academic world cannot be overestimated; work was begun on them straight away – first by Laporte-Dutheil and later by one Monsieur Ameillion of the

Institute. Almost more interested in the demotic middle inscription than the hieroglyphs, Citizen Ameillion said:

> This discovery has produced the greatest feeling among those fascinated by ancient languages; it gave hope that one could, by means of the Greek inscription, decipher the hieroglyphic inscription and, above all, that which was in the native language.[27]

Upon his heroic return to France, Bonaparte had stimulated the European appetite for Egypt, now made all the more mesmerizing by the sketches and drawings by Denon and his fellow artists, doubtless the talk of Paris. Bonaparte had not only presented the mystery of the lost world, but also the key to unravel it.

That the copies were sent to France is a testament to the scholarship of the savants in Egypt – they had readily shared this find with their countrymen in the search for the inscription's meaning, rather than withhold it in the pursuit of personal academic glory. As Fate would later determine, these copies became invaluable, for these, Delile's mould and a last-minute plaster-cast, would be the only remnants of the Rosetta Stone to be taken back to France.

Thanks to the initial decipherment of the Greek in Rosetta, the savants knew what they had before them: a direct translation of two ancient Egyptian scripts in a known language. Their first translation of the Greek section at the bottom of the stone was curiously flawed, incorrectly attributing the relic to Ptolemy IV Philopator, father of Ptolemy V Epiphanes, as reported in the remainder of the first *Courier* report which emerged a month after the discovery:

> General Menou had the Greek inscription partially translated. It reads in the main that 'Ptolemy Philopator' had all of the canals of Egypt reopened, and that this prince employed in

these immense works a very considerable number of workers,
of immense sums and eight years of his reign.

This error was later compounded by a mistaken correction,
dating it to the reign of Ptolemy VI Philo*metor*, the son of
Ptolemy V Epiphanes. This was announced in *La Décade
Égyptienne*. It has often been asked how the savants could have
misinterpreted the Greek, but an inspection of the inscription
demonstrates that reading the stone was by no means a simple
task; English scholars working from neatly printed copies later
took some months to perfect their efforts.[28] Some of the Greek
also had an Egyptian influence, such as the name 'Ftha',[29] a
Hellenized form of the Egyptian god Ptah, a point which
Marcel makes himself in the rest of his note for *La Décade
Égyptienne*:

> The hieroglyphic inscription comprises 14 lines, of which the
> figures of a dimension of six lines are arranged from left to
> right.
>
> The second inscription [the demotic] which had been
> announced as ancient Syriac at first, then as Coptic, is
> composed of 32 lines of characters which follow the same
> direction as the upper inscription and which are obviously
> cursive characters of the ancient Egyptian language. I have
> found identical forms on several rolls of papyrus and on several
> linen strips which are part of the wrappings of human
> mummies.
>
> The Greek inscription which comprises 54 lines is above all
> remarkable for containing several words, among others that of
> $\phi\theta\propto$ 'Ftha' (God), which are not at all Greek, but Egyptian,
> and indicate that the age in which, despite the efforts of the
> Ptolemies, the ancient language of the Egyptians began to mix
> with that of the Greek, their conquerors – a mixture growing
> successively – finishing in about the fourth century AD by forming

the ancient Coptic language of which one finds invaluable traces in modern Coptic.

This stone seems to have been engraved in about 157 BCE[30] in the beginning of the reign of Ptolemy Philometor, and not of Philopator, the name of this latter prince who reigned about 195 BCE is to be found among those of Philadelpho, Euergetes, and Epiphanes in the enumeration of gods or deified kings, predecessors of the prince of whom this inscription reports the coronation and inauguration. The details on this infinitely interesting stone and the ceremonies which are described on it will be the subject of a special paper. (Note of Citizen J.J. Marcel)

It was later established that the stone was erected not for Ptolemy Philometor or Philopator, but Ptolemy V Epiphanes and gives thanks for a victory at Lycopolis of 197 BC. One would like to believe that the *Courier* report of the first attempt at translation recorded only primary findings with understandable errors, for it was Jean-Joseph Marcel, the expedition's chief orientalist who recognized the 'Syriac' inscription of the middle band to be demotic – a Greek term for 'common' Egyptian, literally, 'of the people' – and a cursive form of hieroglyphs rather than Coptic. But Marcel's own summary above from *La Décade* does not support this theory and suggests simply that certain mistakes had been made at the time.

Identifying the demotic was a step forward, but the script did not yield to decipherment. The hieroglyphs themselves, though in such tantalizing proximity to the Greek characters, proved equally stubborn, the pictograms apparently not corresponding to any one word or letter of the Greek alphabet. At that time, despite Marcel's logical assertion in his note in *La Décade*, there would have been no indication that the hieroglyphs could be read either from right to left or from left to right, nor that the demotic was to be read, unlike the Greek, only from right to left, causing further comparative difficulty.

Marcel and the savant Louis Rémi Raige turned to the demotic inscription which, unlike the hieroglyphs, was at least complete. Eventually resorting to a mathematical approach, they subdivided the thirty-two lines of demotic and fifty-four lines of Greek script into relative proportions, presuming that one was the direct translation of the other. They noted the frequency and position of the name 'Ptolemy' in the Greek text – it appeared in eleven places. They next used a compass to determine the proportional position of the word in the relevant demotic sector, treating the characters like mathematical measurements. The technique was successful: for each of the eleven occurrences of the name 'Ptolemy' in the Greek, they found a corresponding series of characters repeated in the demotic.

Their next step was to analyse the demotic signs composing 'Ptolemy' to try to establish comparable values to the Greek letters – this was the first attempt to identify a demotic alphabet. The demotic symbols for 'P' and 'T' were identified not from 'Ptolemy' but from the positions of the Greek 'Pyrra' and 'Aetos' – but the Greek 'L', which they had hoped to find in a reference to Alexander or Alexandria, seemed to have no corresponding character in the demotic. With this obstacle, their work on the Rosetta Stone made little further progress at the Institute.[31] The frustrations involved led many of the savants to doubt whether the Egyptian was capable of decipherment.

When Vivant Denon returned to Cairo in the summer of 1799 and met Bonaparte just after the Battle of Aboukir Bay, the general had been so taken by Denon's drawings of the sites at Upper Egypt that he ordered two commissions be arranged to explore Denon's discoveries further. Prosper Jollois, Villiers du Terrage and others were led by Costaz to continue the work Denon had begun, leaving Marcel, Conté and colleagues labouring over the Rosetta Stone in Cairo. These commissions to record more of the works in Upper Egypt provided the opportunity to seek out further inscriptions which, it was hoped, would be of some use in deciphering the Rosetta Stone. Lancret himself, who had first revealed the news of the discovery to the Institute, compiled detailed descriptions of Philae and the Cataracts near Aswan, while Jomard catalogued Elephantine and Syene – as the savants' own history of the excursions relates: 'From Memphis to Philae, our savants . . . investigated the monuments stone by stone, copied hieroglyphic tablets sign by sign, figure by figure.'[32]

The savants made these remarkable efforts just as the Egypt expedition came under increasing threat of attack. Although Bonaparte had destroyed the first assault of the Turks at Aboukir Bay, the sultan continued to amass his land forces in Syria as the British began closing in. In the second half of 1799 the future of the virtually bankrupt French colony in Egypt looked ever more uncertain, its leadership a crown of thorns, as General Kléber was shortly to discover to his undying fury.

6

Assassins and the Pig-General

Kléber arrived at Rosetta the same night that Bonaparte sailed for France. All that he found at his rendezvous was a sealed packet of orders transferring command of the Armée de l'Orient to his hands. He was outraged. 'That *bugger* leaves us with his breeches full of *shit!*' he roared: 'We'll go back to Europe and rub them in his face!'[1] Compared to the small, pale and quiet Bonaparte, Kléber was every inch the warrior – tall, powerfully built, with a leonine mane of hair, a booming voice and a commanding presence – and one of the most popular generals in the army.

While Moiret's men rejoiced at the news, Kléber did not. As Bonaparte reached France and was carried to Toulon, hailed as the conquering hero returned safe from his adventures and victories abroad, Kléber began making plans for the extraction of French arms from Egypt, acting partly under the vague and confusing direction of the sealed orders left behind by the ex-commander-in-chief, but also out of a personal determination to save the army from a doomed enterprise. Kléber knew that the sultan's aged Grand Vizier in Constantinople was busily gathering forces en route to Egypt. The net was tightening and Kléber refused to sacrifice his men to the glory of Bonaparte.

In these months of instability the savants set off on their commissions into Upper Egypt in search of Denon's sites and to explore more fully the undiscovered regions south of Cairo. Yet the most relevant find in this first hunt for additional inscriptions was made a relatively short distance north of the capital, in the small settlement of Menouf, between the two branches of the Nile. As Lancret, Jomard Villiers du Terrage and others were recording Memphis, Dendera, Edfu, Karnak and Luxor, Jollois and Dubois-Aymé encountered another inscribed stele. Much like the mundane use which had been found for the Rosetta Stone, this relic had been converted into a bench-seat outside someone's home. Details vary, but it seems to have been much larger than the Rosetta Stone at 36 cm thick and roughly 1.2 metres in length. However, 'the bilingual stone of Menouf',[2] as it came to be known, bore only Greek and demotic Egyptian inscriptions, though it was believed to be part of a larger trilingual stele which would have borne hieroglyphs, long since broken away.[3] The savants recorded what they could, despite its poor condition, the demotic, however, identical to that of the Rosetta Stone. In the end this did not help Marcel or Raige back in Cairo, trying to reconstruct a demotic Egyptian alphabet, and the bilingual stele was passed over in the continuing search.

The expedition forces were in a state of great unrest; since landing in 1798 there had been a steady stream of personal requests to Bonaparte for premature passage home, from higher functionaries to senior officers. Bonaparte had tried to stamp this out with new regulations, but this served only to limit the number of supplicants. After his departure and the rumours of Kléber's determination to secure a negotiated withdrawal, the end seemed genuinely in sight, and a slow drain of petty officials and administrators continued to cross the Mediterranean. There was mutiny in several army units, the garrisons bewailing their fate as others returned to France, leaving the troops, so they believed, to rot in 'this faraway country', as Moiret put it.

The savants, many of whom were just as eager to return, would have been more than aware of the volatile political situation owing to their connection with the army through the Institute – the time left for their research seemed to be running out.

The peace overtures by Kléber created a certain disharmony in the French general staff, which could be roughly divided into two camps: a few who felt they should maintain and develop the colony, and the majority who felt honourable withdrawal the wisest course. However, Bonaparte, though he later countermanded the move, had opened the path to peace with the Sublime Porte himself. Swelled by the victory at Aboukir Bay, in his last days in Egypt he had written to the venerable Grand Vizier, Yussuf Pasha:

> What the Porte cannot attain by force of arms it can achieve by negotiation . . . France never intended to take [Egypt] away from you . . . Everything can be settled in a couple of hours' discussion.[4]

Kléber followed Bonaparte's lead, and used the redoubtable Mustafa Pasha, the captured commander of the Turkish forces at Aboukir, as an intermediary with the Grand Vizier to conclude peace terms. Negotiations to evacuate Egypt began in earnest.

At first, Kléber dealt only with the Ottomans, but Sidney Smith, still on station off the coast of Egypt aboard HMS *Tigre*, pointed out to the general that any treaty with Turkey must also be concluded with Great Britain under the terms of the Anglo-Ottoman alliance – a peace concluded with the Sublime Porte of Constantinople would not necessarily be acceptable to the palace of St James in London. Kléber duly appointed two men to conduct talks with Smith, Poussielgue, the comptroller-general of the expedition and an experienced negotiator,[5] and General Desaix, who hitherto had largely been pursuing Murad Bey from Cairo to the Cataracts and back.

The pair travelled north and were welcomed aboard the *Tigre*. It seemed that Smith's newspaper scheme had borne fruit: the intractable politician Bonaparte had gone, replaced by Kléber, the courteous and reasonable man of honour.

Captain Sir William Sidney Smith was no diplomat and held the rank of commodore only in a temporary capacity; it became clear to the French that he was keen to conclude peace terms as quickly as possible – possibly to his own credit. As talks proceeded it was Smith who had to be reminded that any terms he managed to conclude would equally have to be to the pleasure of the sultan.

Though Smith did all in his power, it was evident that he and the Porte were not speaking with one accord: while he and Poussielgue parleyed with Smith, General Desaix requested that the army of the Grand Vizier be halted and make no further advances towards Egyptian territory. Smith thought this more than reasonable and sent a letter to this effect, which was ignored. As the trio sat aboard HMS *Tigre* drafting terms, in December 1799 an extraordinary Ottoman force composed of bands of Syrians, Moroccans, Albanians and Turks thirsting for revenge, swarmed down from Gaza and encircled the border fortress of El Arish.

Although it has been suggested that at least half this number were camp followers, the Grand Vizier's army numbered some 80,000, while only 250 French defended El Arish – commanded by a Major Cazals and, among his officers, Lieutenant Pierre François Xavier Bouchard. Bouchard was sent out eventually to negotiate a surrender, but was promptly arrested. Discipline in the fort later broke down. The troops mutinied and sacked their own stores (including the liquor stores) and some unwisely flung ropes over the walls as a signal to the Turks that they could enter at will. The Turks scaled the walls and nearly slaughtered the French to a man; according to Édouard de Villiers du Terrage, a group of grenadiers scarified themselves, deliberately detonating the powder stores. Appalled at the massacre, a British colonel marching with the Grand Vizier managed to stop the bloodshed but only after half the complement of French had been butchered.[6]

Despite the slaughter of the garrison at El Arish, Kléber continued with the peace negotiations, which eventually resulted in the Convention of El Arish. It has been suggested that Kléber had no authority to agree such a withdrawal, though the previous commander-in-chief had apparently deserted his post and former news from France had spoken of near economic ruin with losses on all fronts – any prudent French general would have wanted to return the bulk of the Armée de l'Orient to Europe, where it could do more good than on the Nile. In the absence of any government orders, and in the absence of the previous commander-in-chief who had masterminded the mess in which Kléber found himself, it would be a harsh court indeed that would condemn him for his actions.

The agreement was generous in that not only were the French to be permitted to march out, under arms with full honours, baggage included, the Ottoman Empire would pay for their upkeep before evacuation and provide naval transports to take them home. The Turks had, however, not agreed to the unrealistic French demand to dissolve their new tripartite alliance with Britain and Russia. It was certainly Sidney Smith's belief that both Britain and Turkey wanted the French out as much as the French wanted to leave and would be prepared to go to any lengths to achieve it. It was a treaty entirely to the benefit of the French, leaving the original Ottoman keepers of Egypt to rectify the problems of their old province once the invaders had departed. Preparations for evacuation were put in place immediately, even while the army of the grand vizier continued to threaten Egypt.

The treaty was signed on 28 January 1800. It stipulated that Cairo be evacuated within a month, and all French troops withdrawn from the north-east and moved to Alexandria, Aboukir and Rosetta to await embarkation on Turkish transports. It should be noted that it was at this time that Marcel made his printed copies of the Rosetta Stone. As events unfolded, this proved very wise. The ratification of the peace treaty considered a mere formality, Kléber set up an administrative commission to oversee the evacuation of the capital and recalled the savants from Upper Egypt, taking steps to have their collections prepared for shipment in their absence.

On 4 February, several dozen savants embarked at the Cairo port of Bulaq, looking forward to a swift return to France, their collections and sculpture to follow, the Rosetta Stone included. However, this was to be the first in a series of trials unparalleled in their experience. Because several cases of plague had been declared in the Delta, the savants were intercepted before they reached Alexandria, and ordered to proceed instead to the Île de Warh,[7] a small island quarantine station in the Nile, opposite Rosetta. Here they stayed for several weeks, Édouard de Villiers du Terrage recording the dolorous duties in their grim surroundings: 'There was little to do to ease us, just having buried the victims of this malady in the island itself, at the extremity of our encampment.'[8] The ordeal was to continue as they heard the crushing news that was soon to follow.

With the arrival of *chef de brigade* Latour-Maubourg on a courier ship on 2 March, Kléber learned of '18 Brumaire' – the day in October when Bonaparte had staged his coup in Paris, ousted the Directory government, and made himself First Consul of France. This in itself was probably not a surprise to Kléber, who had despised Bonaparte's personal ambition, but among the newspapers, books and leaflets brought to him, there was not a single communiqué from the new Octavian in Paris, no instructions either to comply with the Convention of El Arish or to revoke it. Kléber once again had been abandoned with no clear signal to expect reinforcements.

In fact, in his original instructions to Kléber after the trickery of his false rendezvous at Rosetta in August seven months earlier, Bonaparte had promised reinforcement of a sort – they would not, however, be companies of grenadiers, cavalry or artillery, and neither would they include ordnance or ammunition – instead, Bonaparte had promised him a troupe of comedians. Since they were 'so important to the army', he had assured Kléber, he would insist on the actors' immediate despatch. Kléber must have thought Bonaparte mad. When finally Kléber did receive a definite instruction from General Berthier, Bonaparte's new Minister of War, it told him on no account to sign any treaty of capitulation. It had been dated 12 January – but received months too late: Kléber had already signed the Convention treaty.

Bonaparte's sudden rise to power changed the attitude of the general staff in Egypt. Among those who immediately disavowed Kléber was Menou, an arch-colonialist. He resented the El Arish treaty, much as Desaix had done from the start, holding it to be such a travesty of honour that it was tantamount to treason. He wrote to Bonaparte, Berthier and as many influential people in Paris as he could, telling them in a melodramatic and pompous manner that the treaty had 'plunged all those who love honour and fatherland into the deepest sorrow'.[9]

At the same time, Smith was stunned to receive news from Admiral Keith that the Cabinet in London found the treaty unacceptable as well, and that Smith, without intention, had overstepped his authority: any French troops discovered sailing on the high seas, declared Keith, would be captured and treated as prisoners of war. Smith, now accepted by Poussielgue as a man of his word, tried his utmost to end the matter favourably for all concerned, and conveyed this setback to Kléber, whose wisely diplomatic response was to renew negotiations. With the French drawn back from their north-eastern towns in the face of the advancing Turks, the Grand Vizier refused to compromise. Having ignored Smith's requests to halt during the peace negotiations with Poussielgue and Desaix, he continued on what he doubtless felt was the indomitable march of his invincible yet untested army. He demanded that Cairo should be evacuated as agreed in the treaty. Then Admiral Keith struck again.

With orders from Pitt and the Cabinet, Admiral Lord Keith took command of the fleet; bypassing Sidney Smith, he sent Kléber a letter predating the Convention of El Arish clarifying the position without Smith's diplomatic finesse. Shortly after he sent this note, news reached him that the Cabinet had changed its mind: they would uphold the terms of the Convention after all – but it was too late. Just after receiving the news of Bonaparte's coup and suffering the outrage of the new First Consul's lack of interest, Kléber received Keith's letter. Notable commentators have emphasized the 'insulting' tone and 'brutal' language of this note but, in defence of Keith, it was more blunt and matter-of-fact than insulting, a statement of continued aggression to an old enemy: the more than generous peace terms agreed with Smith were hereby utterly repudiated, declaring that nothing less than unconditional surrender would be acceptable to His Majesty's Government. It was a bitter blow after months of negotiation. Worse, by mid-March the rabble of the Grand Vizier's army had camped within reach of Cairo.

Offended by the suggestion his men would lay down their arms to an enemy without first being defeated, the leonine Kléber, according to Nicholas the Turk, let out a roar of anger.[10] He put an immediate halt to the evacuation, mustered 10,000 men within two days, and sent word to the Grand Vizier that the ceasefire was over. He ordered Marcel at the Institute to print Keith's message with his own curt orders beneath: 'Soldiers, one responds to such insolence with naught but victories! Prepare to fight!'[11] Charging out of the capital on 20 March 1800, near the ruins of Heliopolis on the outskirts of Cairo, Kléber's army of 10,000 smashed the Turkish host of over 40,000, chasing the Grand Vizier and his invincible troops across Egypt, back to El Arish on the border. He then set about recapturing all the northern towns from which his men had so recently with-drawn. In a matter of days, Kléber had effectively reconquered Egypt. It was a victory which matched, if not dwarfed, Bonaparte's triumph at Aboukir Bay.

The collapse of the Convention of El Arish frustrated the savants' efforts to return home. After their island quarantine, they continued to Alexandria in late March, having watched the departure of Generals Desaix and Dugua for France, wondering when their chance would come. It never did. When they boarded their ship *L'Oiseau*, ready for home, the news of Kléber's attack at Heliopolis cancelled all arrangements; there would now be no safe-passage through the British blockade. Stranded aboard their brig in port, they waited anxiously for permission to return to dry land, finally being released on 27 April. Still, no orders allowed them to return to Cairo, and they waited a further six weeks.

Some have suggested that the return of the savants to Cairo did not include the antiquities nor the Rosetta Stone, that they were left deposited in safety within the fortified city of Alexandria. This seems unlikely and later events imply this was not the case. The road to peace was no longer clear: had the savants left their invaluable cargo behind in the Delta, there would have been no guarantee that they would have seen it ever again. Instead, it would appear that the Rosetta Stone never went further than being loaded on to a barge at Bulaq[12] just before the collapse of the El Arish treaty, whereupon it was promptly returned to the Institute buildings.

The greatest tragedy of the moment – and Kléber saw it – was that the victory of Heliopolis, though satisfying, was hollow, serving only to prolong the uncertainty of the situation at the cost of more French lives. Menou, on the other hand, was filled with pride, not fully grasping the precarious position of the expeditionary forces. He wrote a patronizing letter to Kléber, at once congratulating him but also chiding him like a foolish child for agreeing to terms at El Arish, finishing with an admonition worthy of Bonaparte: 'Remember who you are and you will be the founder of a magnificent colony!'[13] Well aware of Menou's backstage efforts to blacken his name without suffering the difficult decisions of his position, Kléber replied with customary directness:

> Citizen General, my stupidity is so enormous that even today I do not believe that the Convention of El Arish was a political mistake or that there is any reason to lose one's head over the victory I have won with my army. Even today I am profoundly convinced that, by means of that treaty, I had succeeded in putting a reasonable end to an insane enterprise. Even today I remain convinced that we shall receive no help from France and that we shall never . . . found any colonies in Egypt . . . You General, have your face turned to the East, mine is turned to the West. We shall never understand each other.[14]

Kléber received little reward for his efforts. As the French pursued the Grand Vizier into Lower Egypt, a force of Turks led by the vizier's son and the exiled Mameluke beys entered Cairo, declaring the French defeated. The result once again was civic revolt: Cairo flew into a second anarchy, as it had in 1798, of looting, rapine and robbery. Murad Bey, pursued for over a year, did not enter the city, having been won over to French rule at the last minute; Fourier, the Institute Secretary, had taken a message to him to confirm this. It seemed that Murad was not happy to meet the Turks – he had not paid the sultan tribute for some years and was not keen to start. He preferred to side with the French, who had offered him the governorship of Upper Egypt. Almost certainly he was waiting until the French ejected the Turks before plotting afresh. The violence in the streets was not fully quelled until mid-April, a month later, after Kléber had starved and bombarded the city into submission. He imposed punitive fines on the Cairo sheikhs for allowing the uprising, and those who did not pay were imprisoned, and some-beaten. With the sudden influx of cash, by the end of May the army had received nearly a year's wages in arrears.

In June 1800, Kléber's command came to an abrupt end as he walked in the gardens of his headquarters in Cairo. He was accompanied by Protain, one of the savant architects, when he was approached by a young man he took for a beggar seeking alms. The man was in fact a student of the Al-Azhar Mosque named Solimann. He was a paid assassin. As Protain moved off in search of a sentry to chase away the interloper, Solimann drew a dagger without warning and stabbed Kléber violently several times in the chest. Protain rushed to the general's aid and beat at the murderer with his walking-stick until he fled. But it was too late – Kléber was dead. The Armée de l'Orient had lost its truest champion, and its only chance to return home intact with dignity and honour.

As the dread news went out across Egypt, the role of commander-in-chief fell to the most senior but least likely member of the general staff, Jacques-François Menou. Unlike the nobly intentioned Kléber, Menou had quite a different agenda altogether. Solimann was pointed out in the mêlée that followed Kléber's murder and seized almost immediately. Menou convened a court and put Solimann on trial – something which surprised the chronicler Al-Jabarti as there was clearly little case for the defence. Menou adopted Bonaparte's parting advice on maintaining order, to 'cut off six heads a day and keep smiling', and three accomplices from the Al-Azhar Mosque were executed. Something entirely more appalling awaited Solimann of Aleppo. He was condemned to death according to local custom: his right hand was to be burnt off, and he was then to be impaled. His sentence was carried out on the day of Kléber's funeral.

To understand the death-throes of the French expedition and how the British Museum began its collection of Egyptian colossi, it is necessary to appreciate *général en chef* Menou. Jacques-François Menou, Baron de Boussay, was born in 1750, a son of the nobility, his exalted father no less than the *'haute et puissant'* marquis René-François de Menou, Chevalier, Lord of Boussay, Genilly, Chambon and other lands, and Marshal of the Armies of His Majesty. Like many of his class, come the revolution, Jacques-François Menou was forced to become a fierce republican as a matter of survival; however, it is more than likely his ardour was genuine.

Although he reached the most senior staff position in Eqypt, he had very little military experience. His first duty was the suppression of the revolt of the Vendée peasants, in the course of which campaign he was heroically wounded. Though he continually solicited the post of an inspector-general or governor in a far-flung colony, his requests fell upon deaf ears, and his wounds led him to the impressive rank of General of the Interior in the crucial days of counter-revolution. When the royalists massed their attack on Paris, he blundered through the day with more enthusiasm than tactical efficiency and disaster was averted only by Bonaparte's artillery. Menou's incompetence had set the scene for Bonaparte's stardom. The two were to be bound in stranger circumstance still: summarily removed from his post as General of the Interior, Menou sank ignominiously from sight until Bonaparte offered him a place on the Egypt expedition.

There is doubt, however, that Bonaparte ever wanted Menou to command a division in battle and possibly wanted him more as a fervent republican administrator – as biographer Georges Rigault wrote of him, 'He was one of those men of 1789 who learned political science in governing France'[15] – it was from this group Bonaparte chose a large number of his administrators. What Menou lacked in military genius he made up for with raw courage, leading his troops from the front in the assault on Alexandria. Severely wounded in the process, possibly in yet another attempt to prove himself in the field, he gave Bonaparte the chance to sequester him in Rosetta as governor, giving his division to General Vial. Menou had his wish at last, power in as exotic a colony as he could have imagined.

He was not the most appealing of officers, and not one of Bonaparte's favourites; 'he had no military air – he was fat and balding, one would have taken him for a financier'.[16] Badly dressed and lacking any real grasp of personal grooming, with unkempt locks of straggling, unwashed hair, Menou was not the sort of man Bonaparte wanted decorating the scented palaces of Cairo. As General Marmont later wrote of him,

> His character, one of the oddest in the world, came very close to lunacy. He was an eccentric . . . amusing enough sometimes, but a curse to all that depended on him.[17]

However, Menou, above all others, seemed to take the political propaganda of their presence in Egypt at face value, and was devoted not only to the ideals of a French colony on the Nile but also to Bonaparte himself, who had saved his career and reputation. In a demonstrative act of this devotion, and one that endeared him to Bonaparte thereafter, Menou became famous throughout the expeditionary forces by converting to Islam, and becoming, quite suddenly, 'Abdallah Pasha'.[18]

This would have been a remarkable notion at the time. Although the French Republic had effectively dispensed with the Church, the rank and file disapproved. Not even Bonaparte followed his own suggestion of conversion, blandly remarking to the sheikhs in Cairo when questioned if he had become a Muslim, as he had promised, 'I *am* a Muslim,' and claimed he was probably a better one than the sheikh who had asked. The sheikhs, understandably, were somewhat confused by this. Menou, however, was now very clearly a Muslim, and attended the mosque on Fridays and reputedly saw to his five daily prayers. Both French and Egyptian opinion believed his conversion was merely a ploy, both to curry favour with the Egyptians, and to marry Zobeida, the daughter of a Rosetta bathkeeper.[19] The other generals found this most amusing. Marmont wrote to him several times enquiring about his new wife and whether Menou would be following Islamic tradition by taking three further wives. Menou responded ingenuously that no, although the Holy Prophet permitted four wives (concubines notwithstanding) he found Zobeida sufficient for his needs, endowed as she was, so he said, like all Egyptian women 'of vehement appetite'.

Bonaparte appointed Menou Governor of Cairo in late 1798. His new Islamic status could undoubtedly prove useful in such a politically sensitive centre, but Menou asked if he could accept this honour some time later as, owing to the British blockade of Alexandria, his presence might be needed in the Delta (it was not, and Marmont would have been unlikely to ask for it). Frustrated by this, Bonaparte gave the post to General Dugua. Menou's only other military task before his ascent to power after Kléber's death was to join Bonaparte's expedition to Syria in February 1799. Bonaparte had made the request with the intention of making him Governor of Palestine. Menou fumbled here as well: missing the rendezvous and told to catch up with the army when he could, by the time Menou got his great caravan ready and reached the border, he encountered Bonaparte coming in the opposite direction – on the march back from Syria. Menou had missed the entire campaign.

In 1800 he reached fifty years of age, but seemed older. According to his memoirs, at the time Bonaparte had thought Menou was sixty. His time under Kléber was marked by a number of pompous declarations and irritating letters as he informed his superior officer how best to run Egypt, giving great lectures on what a prosperous colony it would be under the direction of France. His letters tired Kléber: at one point, in defence of his republican spirit, Menou begged to be made a simple grenadier so he might join the ranks. Kléber's response was that he had thought Menou too busy writing letters and memoranda to take up any military duties. Relenting, Kléber offered him the command of Cairo as Bonaparte had done, which Menou at last accepted – he was taking up this post just as Solimann lunged with his knife.

Menou did not want to become commander-in-chief. He suggested General Reynier. Reynier was reluctant to take the post as well, and passed it back to Menou. After much deliberation, Menou accepted it, and no sooner had he done this than Reynier began to wish he had grasped the crown; the two men would be at loggerheads for the best part of a year. There was also discontent among the generals at the new change in command; Menou, the administrator, behaved more like a political commissar of the republic than a general. He purged the upper echelons of Kléber's supporters and all those who wished to evacuate Egypt. He sacked the admirable Comptroller-General Poussielgue and a number of senior officers, and sent them home to await court-martial, firmly believing that Kléber had had no right to concoct the Convention of El Arish. The effect on the army was disastrous. In his first proclamations to the troops he emphasized the notion that the government, and not the army, should dictate when and where the army should go, and signed off as 'Abdallah Menou'. As Moiret put it, how could they trust a man who had turned his back on all he had known in France to embrace this foreign culture? Having bound himself to a woman of this land would he not rather stay in his voluntary exile than return to his homeland with a family which would be despised by all?

To the troops looking forward to a quick return to France through Kléber's efforts it was devastating: far from relieving general despondency among the men, wrote Moiret, Menou's attempts at reassurance only deepened it.

However, in Captain Moiret's eyes, thereafter Menou proved himself a remarkable administrator, and became a firm favourite with some of the army who believed he genuinely cared as much for the lowest ranks as the highest, and managed to sort out many abuses of the existing systems in the months to come. Even his enemies had to admit he had solved problems apparently beyond Kléber's powers. But much of this success was due in no small part to the steady flow of tribute coming in from Murad Bey, the fair-weather ally won over by Kléber, who now protected Upper Egypt for the French. This gave Menou delusions of grandeur and he crowed over his achievements and Kléber's evident inability. With subordinates he was personally tyrannical and without hesitation dismissed those who objected to his measures, earning himself a wealth of enemies.

After the Cairo uprising and Kléber's bombardment to re-capture the city, a significant portion of both residential and civic property had been rendered dangerously unstable – the young savant Villiers du Terrage was set the task with a group of engineers of assessing the damage and condemned a consider-able number of buildings to demolition; with the aspiration of Nero, Menou set about rebuilding Cairo in a grander style, knocking down whole sections of the city, firmly convinced of the permanence of French power in the country.

He instituted administrative reforms on a scale so vast that he became equally as unpopular with the Muslims as with the French, changing the tax system and, according to Al-Jabarti, mistreating Egyptians of all creeds from Muslims to Greek Christians and Copts – the Muslim Egyptian, he claimed, suffered more under Abdallah Menou than under Bonaparte or Kléber.

Subversive mutterings were conveyed to Menou by a cadre of obsequious supporters, or 'partisan fanatics' as the savants called them, fuelling his growing paranoia. When Sidney Smith, now fully authorized by London, offered peace terms similar to those ratified by Kléber in the Convention of El Arish, Menou judged them dishonourable and refused them, going so far as to accuse Smith of taking a hand in Kléber's murder. Ever sensitive to the slightest suggestion of a lack of patriotism born of his noble rank, he wrote endless letters to subordinates and senior officers alike protesting his republicanism, seeking their approval. This, compounded by his limited and undistinguished military record, made him the very worst type of posturing, petty tyrant, suspicious of all, particularly of the gallant, smirking and decorated generals about him.

Although Kléber was not entirely devoted to the members of the Scientific Commission, it was Menou who created the great rift between the military command and the savants, a rift which was to widen as the fight with Britain worsened. As Saintine reported,

> The Commission of Sciences and Arts especially had grounds for complaint against him. Knowing that few of its members held much sympathy for him, he struck the corps as a whole, pouring contempt and humiliation upon them.[20]

His first act was to separate the engineers from the other ranks of the Commission – they had been together since the outset, but no longer; the engineers would now be more closely linked to the army, their routines governed entirely by Menou. Through his appalling inertia he thwarted a major archaeological expedition to Nubia planned since the return of the savants from Upper Egypt under Kléber, delaying it for three months, sending the civil engineers out on odd, punitive excursions to record canal levels and similar details for his administrative records.

There is an apocryphal tale that within a short time of his arrival in Cairo he ordered the Rosetta Stone be taken from the Institute and placed in the palace in Ezbekkiyyah Square, into which he moved with Zobeida, Madame Menou, apparently demanding the stone be placed under his bed for safekeeping. Conté, Marcel, Raige and others must have been astounded, as well as offended, and would have been prevented from further work on the relic. Saintine's history has little to say on the matter,[21] but the story is nonetheless a reflection of the contemporary attitude towards the new and unquestionably infuriating commander-in-chief. Of all the places the Rosetta Stone has been, beneath the bed of General Menou would probably be the most extraordinary.

With his daily prayers, harem, Egyptian wife and, later, children, and his unfortunate lack of military bearing, he became the laughing stock of the army, a joke to his senior colleagues who began plotting his removal. He was later nicknamed '*le cochon-général*' by the men. To the dismay of the general staff, Menou was confirmed in his new command by despatches received in late 1800. It seemed *général en chef* Jacques-François Abdallah Menou, Baron de Boussay, would now decide the fate of the French colony.

7

Castle Keep

According to his personal secretary, Louis-Antoine Fauvelet de Bourrienne, Bonaparte had never forgotten his 'cherished conquest in the East', and it remained dear to his heart, though he seems to have done little to support it since his elevation to First Consul. After the fall of Malta to the British in September 1800 and Sir Sidney Smith's offer of peace terms to the obstinate Menou, it became very clear that time was running out for the fledgling colony. In the second half of 1800 Bonaparte sent over the first convoy of supplies to reach Egypt since the outset of the expedition. It was not great, consisting of despatches (one of them confirming Menou's command), ammunition, newspapers, medicines and spirits, and a small group of surgeons and craftsmen. This was, however, more than Bonaparte had ever received from the Directory.

The British worked fast. Over October and November troops were assembled on the newly acquired island base of Malta to form Admiral Keith's invasion force. News of this reached France, and Bonaparte doubtless began to regret Menou's confirmation as commander-in-chief in Egypt. As Bourrienne noted:

Bonaparte's indignation was excited when he became acquainted with Menou's neglect and mismanagement, when he saw him giving rein to his passion for reform, altering and destroying everything, creating nothing good in its stead, and dreaming about forming a land communication with the Hottentots and Congo instead of studying how to preserve the country.[1]

Meanwhile, Admiral Keith's operations went forward. A veteran of the British landings in Puerto Rico and Holland years earlier, the heroic and universally admired Sir Ralph Abercromby[2] was given command of 17,000 men, supported by 5,000 sepoys from India and 2,000 men picked up from the Cape, as well as an indeterminate Turkish force, to effect a simultaneous three-pronged attack. The future of Britain's lifeline to India and her influence in the Levant resting upon his shoulders, Sir Ralph and the invasion fleet set sail from Malta in December 1800, heading not for Egypt, but first to Rhodes and the bay of Marmorice, on the coast of Turkey.

Here, Sir Ralph first rested his army from the sea voyage then drilled the men time and again in practice landings – he had no wish to send his troops into an unfamiliar environment. While the British trained, word reached them of the true nature of the Turkish army that was to support them; General Sir John Moore[3] had been staggered to discover that the Grand Vizier, Yussuf Pasha, was a venerable old man and his 'army' no more than an undisciplined mob, less than half the size it had been a year earlier. Sir Ralph accepted that tactical land support would not be forthcoming from this quarter – although it had been this same army which had confidently marched halfway across Egypt to the gates of Cairo, largely unopposed, it was also the army which had been chased back to the border by Kléber; the British knew their enemy and it was more than likely that the vizier could be forced into yet another defeat like Heliopolis.

Instead, Sir Ralph relied upon the seaborne forces entrusted to him by the sultan, led by Hassan, the Kapudan Pasha. 'Kapudan Pasha' was a title comparable to 'High Admiral' or 'Sea Lord' and in many contemporary accounts has become adulterated to 'Caputan', 'Capitan', 'Capitano' and even 'Captain'. Unlike the aged Grand Vizier, the Kapudan Pasha was an altogether different sort of ally, and would later prove to have a strategy known but to him and the sultan, and certainly not in accord with that of the British High Command. Meanwhile Menou continued building his Egyptian utopia apparently unconcerned with shore defences or his military disposition, patriotically confident in his army's ability, come what may.

Even as battle brewed in the Levant, the work of the Institute continued vigorously, and the savants enjoyed a minor success in their search for linguistic clues to hieroglyphs. In September 1800, one of the savants found what promised, at first glance, to be another Rosetta Stone.

The civil engineer Philippe Caristie discovered another black granitoid stele – it was being used as the top step to a local mosque in Nasriyah. The mosque was very close, if not next door, to the Institute. It is ironic that though the savants were combing every inch of the Egyptian sands from Aswan to the Delta, a large engraved stele lay hiding in plain sight yards from their door, its daily use understandably letting it pass unnoticed. It was very large but barely legible – it bore three scripts and was more complete than the Rosetta Stone: it included the top hieroglyph section displaying an orb with outspread wings.[4] There must have been uproar in the mosque as the savants clustered round the threshold examining the worn surface, desperate for any further clues. With scarcely a nod to his Muslim faith, Menou gave permission for the Institute to remove it. One can imagine the reaction of the congregation of the mosque when the savants returned to carry off their top step. Unfortunately, it would prove so poor a sample it served only to highlight the extraordinary condition of the Rosetta Stone itself.[5]

Negotiations with Britain continued through the end of 1800. Bonaparte was determined to retain Egypt in spite of British insistence to the contrary. He did not grasp that it was this that caused the greatest fear for Britain – with Egypt in French hands, there could be no safety for India and thus no peace. Facing British refusal to agree terms, it now became imperative to reinforce the Armée de l'Orient. Receiving reports of the British massing first in Malta and practising landings in Turkey, Bonaparte ordered Admiral Ganteaume to take 5,000 men with a squadron from Brest. When eventually Ganteaume did leave Brest after weeks of delay, he continued to dither. Rather than making straight for Egypt, he judged the risk too great and diverted to Toulon instead. Bonaparte was outraged. 'What the devil is Ganteaume about!' he demanded.

Once again, Ganteaume tried to sail from Toulon, got a good distance away, but encountered the British squadron under Sir John Warren and returned to Toulon. Ganteaume was roundly condemned for this indecision. Bourrienne refers to his 'creeping about the Mediterranean' and how Bonaparte, in Ganteaume, had 'confidence in mediocrity', which alas 'did not obtain a suitable return'. In one of the reports sent to Bonaparte was included a mildly insulting poem:

> Vessels all laden, but naught in his brain,
> Away went Admiral Gantheaume,
> He travelled from Brest to Bertheaume,
> And from Bertheaume to Brest back again![6]

Bonaparte 'laughed heartily' at this, but he later wrote angrily to Ganteaume on 25 February that the reinforcements must reach Egypt 'whatever the cost'. By this time, it was too late.

Four days earlier, Sir Ralph had set sail from Marmorice, bound for the Nile Delta. French intelligence reports reached Bonaparte quickly, for on the 20th he issued a proclamation to the Armée de l'Orient warning them of the imminent attack.

Despite having 17,000 British soldiers, now well rehearsed in amphibious assault, surging through the waves towards Egypt, Menou was the very picture of masterly inactivity: his response, not entirely out of character, was apparently to do nothing. Consequently, history has painted him as a second Ethelred the Unready; but his reasoning was based on simultaneous reports of the Grand Vizier's Turks on the Syrian border and the arrival of General Baird with his 5,000 sepoys from India, on the Red Sea coast – his strategy, according to his biographer Rigault, was to remain in the centre, at Cairo, and send troops as required. This was in direct contravention of Bonaparte's parting instructions which stated that, if Egypt were ever to be attacked, the army must reunite immediately.

Admiral Keith's invasion fleet anchored near Aboukir Bay on 26 February 1801 – near the same spot, remarked Colonel Robert Wilson[7] in his account of the campaign, as the sunken wreck of *L'Orient*, left from the Battle of the Nile. But the troops could not storm the shoreline; the weather prevented an immediate landing and the fleet waited a full week for the winds to ease. Every moment gave Menou precious time to prepare. Still he failed to marshal the army. He did not consider the English ships much of a threat. For this, General Friant at Alexandria should carry some of the blame: Friant sent a note to Menou that a small English squadron was arrayed before him and that 'if they effect a landing, I shall crush it.' Disastrous for French Egypt, Friant's only request in these invaluable moments of preparation was, 'Swiftly send me one regiment of cavalry, and put your mind at ease.'[8]

Not surprisingly, Menou was not as concerned as he should have been about the British landing. He could have had

20,000–25,000 men standing ready at the coast by the time the first British boats came ashore, or at least with time enough to orchestrate a counter-attack, but he did nothing in response. The generals under his command were maddened by the situation and this friction came close to revolt. According to Moiret, the army was well aware of the difference of opinion among the generals. Bonaparte's exclamation regarding Ganteaume would have been even more apt in the circumstances: 'What the devil is *Menou* about!'

Bourrienne is even more concise. Egypt, he says, was conquered by a genius 'of vast intelligence, [but] fatuity, stupidity, and incapacity lost it'.[9] As well as Friant's overconfident communiqué, Menou also received reassuring news just as the British invasion forces arrived off the coast. According to Colonel Wilson, an unknown frigate slipped away from the fleet and made a sudden dash for Alexandria. At the last moment, it flew the French tricolour and sailed triumphantly into safe harbour – its daring captain had coolly sailed with the British for some days, utterly unnoticed. The news they brought their beleaguered compatriots was that Ganteaume had been despatched with reinforcements – although this offered hope to an abandoned army, this doubtless served them ill, as Menou now had ample excuse for doing nothing but wait.

It was not the British plan to overrun the country but to seize Alexandria as a bargaining counter in negotiations for a French withdrawal from Egypt. They had not brought sufficient men for a full conquest: their estimates of French strength were based on intercepted despatches, particularly Kléber's letter to the Directory begging for reinforcements, which suggested the French in Egypt were barely able to continue. There were at least 25,000 French to the main British army of 17,000 – Sir Ralph was about to land a force in precisely the same place as had the Turks in 1799, a force which Bonaparte had then thrown into the sea with roughly half the number at Menou's disposal. Luckily, this time, there was no Bonaparte waiting on the shore.

On the 27th, a single British ship, the *Penelope*, boldly went in to reconnoitre the beach – but was attacked and captured by a French gunboat alerted by spotters, and her officers sent to Cairo. Still Menou did not gather his forces. With a sudden improvement of the weather on 7 March, Sir Ralph made a personal reconnaissance of the beach with Sidney Smith. Colonel Wilson recounts that, after a mix-up with signals, there was a brief skirmish ashore and an ambitious officer returned to the fleet with the first British prisoners of the Egypt expedition, a brandy-besotted ferryman and several chickens.

With this inauspicious start, the preparations began. At two o'clock in the morning of 8 March, a force of 5,500 men as assembled with landing-craft, over a subsiding swell, and readied for a pre-dawn assault. At the time there were few operations in British military history to compare with the dash and daring of that attack; it stands today as one of the British army's finest moments. After terrible delay the boats were launched an agonizing seven hours later, at nine in the morning, in broad daylight.[10] At once, says Colonel Wilson, the boats 'sprung forward' – the French artillerymen looking down on the scene from the heights could not believe their eyes. Only temporarily protected by flanking Turkish ships, the British troops were utterly exposed, all hands striking desperately at the swell to make for the shore. The boats soon came within artillery range, and the French guns opened up simultaneously in a hail of fire, the surface of the water fizzing with grape and musket-ball.

General Sir John Moore recounted that the first wave lost over 600 men. Awaiting the British were towering sand hills, some nearly vertical – when the boats crashed on to the beach the men staggered, soaking and winded yet with a 'preter-natural energy' and swarmed up the choking dunes under constant fire. Almost without loosing a shot they drove out the French 'at the point of the bayonet', overwhelming the heavily out-numbered defenders. Friant must have been mortified as he watched, but sent down the regiment of cavalry he had requested from Menou – the French dragoons charged the beaches, making a valiant attempt to slow the British advance, but were driven off by the Guards, who snapped into formation with lightning speed and forced the dragoons into retreat. Within several hours, Aboukir Bay and the beach area belonged to Sir Ralph.

With one decisive blow, Menou could have destroyed the paltry landing-force, stranded and waiting for reinforcements to come ashore – and Egypt would have remained French for some considerable time. As Friant sent panicked messages to Cairo, Sir Ralph secured the beach-head, landed his artillery and left forces behind to besiege the small French garrison at Aboukir Fort on the peninsula. Unlike Mustafa Pasha in 1799, the British then moved into the interior, heading for Alexander's capital.

The savants had been working steadily on their projects even as the enemy approached – in February, just prior to the sighting of the British fleet, the engineers Le Père and Coutelle were engaged in excavations at Gizeh, and Édouard de Villiers du Terrage continued working on his maps for the army, at Le Père's order. Although British raids of a year earlier at the Red Sea port of Kosseir had been easily repulsed, the invasion fleet standing off Aboukir for a week was taken much more seriously by the savants.

The Institute met for the final time on 7 March 1801. Recalling the events of El Arish, which nearly led to their safe return home but ended with the advance of the Grand Vizier to the gates of Cairo, it was agreed to evacuate the collections to Alexandria, the only other stronghold in Egypt capable of with-standing a siege. Here they might also take advantage of the first ships to sail for France and safeguard their work. With some luck, it was hoped, they could get to the fortified city before the British.

Hearing the news of the Aboukir landings, Menou finally issued his orders and led the army north on 12 March[11] – a full three weeks after the British fleet had been first sighted and four days after Abercromby had landed. It was here that Menou made the calamitous strategic blunder of splitting his forces. Possibly mistaking Bonaparte's successes for the invincibility of French arms, he headed north to Alexandria with only half the army, his troops numbering a mere 12,000. It could be argued that Menou wisely left behind a sufficiently strong force to defend the capital, but a more compelling argument suggests that, had he taken his full army of roughly 25,000 to smash the British, he could then have moved to meet any threat posed by the Turks as well, returning to Cairo as successful as Kléber after Heliopolis. Instead, he created two numerically inferior armies. On the 21st, Menou met Abercromby at Canopus, with disastrous results.

Just as the Battle of the Pyramids decided the fate of Cairo and thus the fate of Egypt, so did the Battle of Canopus herald the doom of the French expedition. Contemporary accounts consider it a horrendous affair with unnecessary losses on both sides. At three in the morning on 21 March, Menou pitched his 12,000 men against Abercromby's 15,000, the opposing forces clashing in the fire-lit darkness, the blaze of musket-volleys and cannon flaring against the deserted ruins of ancient Canopus. Anecdotes of the battle rank with those of Waterloo – Colonel Wilson, Sir Sidney Smith, Sir John Moore, all have their tales; Sir John wrote that he had never seen a field so littered with the dead. Smith, though a naval officer, mounted a horse and fought with distinction with the army. Of them all, Sir Ralph Abercromby's end is the most poignant: struck in the thigh by a bullet, after both sides withdrew he was draped in a soldier's cloak and, ever aware of the lot of the common man, in the midst of his anguish he insisted an aide ensure the valuable cloak's prompt return to the soldier who had so gallantly offered it. He died within the week, mourned by all, high and low.

Menou, who had already lost General Roize, unwisely tried to play the part of the concerned commander and visited the mortally wounded General Lanusse, a victor of Aboukir Bay under Bonaparte. The months of pent-up frustration under Menou's command, the bungling of a battle which could so nearly have been won, all pushed Lanusse to vent his anger: according to witnesses, Lanusse gasped with his last breath, 'Never should a man such as you have commanded the armies of France – you were fit only to run the kitchens of the Republic.'[12]

Colonel Wilson wrote that Menou's great mistake had been to engage the English when it would have served France better to wait upon the enemy in fortified Alexandria. Menou took this advice too late, after over 4,000 men had been killed, wounded or captured. He retreated to the great walled city, rather than returning to Cairo, and slammed the gates shut. His enemy was now free to roam at will over the countryside and attack the heart of Egypt.

It is here that sight of the Rosetta Stone is temporarily lost. Although Menou left Cairo on 12 March, the savants bound for Alexandria did not go with him. Rather than abandoning the Institute in Cairo, they stayed to organize the withdrawal, seeking Menou's permission to come north after his defeat and join him in Alexandria – they were refused.

Not only was the Commission refused permission to rejoin him, but he gave the order that all of its members should be locked up in the citadel [of Cairo], and he arrested and returned to

Ramanieh four or five of them who had temporarily found themselves in Alexandria for their research.[13]

Villiers du Terrage implies they were 'moved' rather than impelled to the plague-infested citadel, possibly even for their protection, but certainly Menou's order suggested they should be treated like common criminals. Over the following days, with death and sickness raging all around them, they demanded that the commander in Cairo, General Belliard, let them depart for the Delta; he wisely agreed, ignoring Menou's orders.

Parting from those colleagues who had elected to stay in the capital with the army, the savants also bade farewell to their palatial Platonic Academy, to its colonnades and gardens, and three years of exploration, uprising and adventure – which, for many, had transformed their lives for ever. They transported their precious cargo to the port at Bulaq. According to Villiers du Terrage, they left Cairo on 6 April and sailed downriver, by chance with an escort guarding provisions for the embattled fortress of Alexandria. Gliding down the Nile they would have looked upon the Pyramids for the last time. Although they had left the pestilential citadel of Cairo behind, their fortunes were not set to improve.

After the death of Abercromby at Canopus, Lieutenant-General Sir John Hely-Hutchinson took command of the combined Anglo-Turkish forces.[14] He was not a universally popular choice, considered rather dour and possibly lacking in panache; he was, however, the most senior officer, and moved quickly about his task. On 25 March, the Kapudan Pasha landed 6,000 Turkish janissaries at Aboukir;[15] Hutchinson subsequently deployed these among the British at Alexandria while also despatching an allied Anglo-Turkish corps across the Delta to take Rosetta on 2 April. Rosetta fell within a week, Fort Julien, home of the Rosetta Stone for centuries, holding out to the last; it was defended in part by the promoted Captain Pierre

Bouchard, and was captured by a company including a contingent of the 3rd Foot Guards – commanded by one Colonel Tomkyns Hilgrove Turner, the man who would later return the Rosetta Stone to Britain.

On the 13th, the British found a note by Menou in the pocket of the late General Roize, concerning his fears that the British might cut the sea-dyke protecting the Alexandrine canal. From that moment, the British could think of little else. Stretching southward from Alexandria the canal ran along a narrow dyke wall, on its western side the partially dried-up bed of Lake Maryut,[16] some six to eight feet lower than the seawaters of Lake Maadiyeh on the other. Hutchinson reluctantly agreed to breach the dyke on 13 April, and a torrent of Mediterranean seawater rushed through a number of cuts, destroying the canal and flooding Lake Maryut – with the flooded plain to the south of the city, the British had isolated its defendants. The siege of Alexandria had begun; it was to last a gruelling five months.

With the British in Rosetta the savants sailing down the Nile had to disembark at Ramanieh and make the very difficult cross-country journey to Alexandria through the now flooded Lake Maryut region. The first spectre of danger they encountered was not from the enemy but from the troops of *chef de brigade* Lacroix, commandant of the nearby fort. It seems that Lacroix, 'a creature of Menou', cared little about science, art or the savants, and curtly refused to let them pass to besieged Alexandria – Menou had given orders that all 'useless mouths' were to be ejected from the city, and Lacroix obeyed unswervingly. His troops, on their ceaseless hunt for gold and booty, took a keen interest in the mysterious packing crates, forcing the savants to defend their cargo, as well as their own dignity, as they were insulted and reviled by many of the men.

Unable to retreat to Cairo, the savants were stranded, until the timely arrival of the celebrated *chef de brigade* Jacques Cavalier, of 'the Dromedaries'. Despite Lacroix, despite Menou, and to the lasting pride and gratitude of the future of French Egyptology and science, Cavalier and his camel-mounted cavalry 'plucked them from Ramanieh', carrying the savants and their priceless collections to Alexandria on a punishing journey of nearly ten fraught days – much to the detriment of his 300 overburdened dromedaries. They crossed the flooded plain at night, feeling their way along the now treacherous dyke of the canal. In the darkness, Villiers du Terrage lost one of the crates in the lake – it had been filled with mineralogy samples and priceless antiquities.[17]

The paranoiac Menou, still involved in bitter recrimination with his senior officers, refused to let them in. The savants spent their first night at Alexandria sleeping under the walls of the city. They were let in the next morning for Menou's five-day quarantine period – in this time, one of the savants, Lerouge, died of the plague. The flower of French academic science and art, ex-members of the Institut d'Egypte, hand-picked by Monge, Berthollet and the First Consul himself, had been abused, arrested, threatened and abandoned by their military protectors in the moment of their greatest need, saved only by cavalier's chivalry, initiative officer's gallantry and generosity of spirit. Bonaparte would have been appalled.

It is widely supposed that the Rosetta Stone went with the savants on this final journey from Cairo to Alexandria, but this is not necessarily the case. It is thought that, after its return from the first attempt to escape Egypt in 1800, it would once again have been taken to Bulaq for loading, but Saintine, Marcel and Reybaud's detailed multi-volume history of the campaign makes no mention of it specifically on this occasion. It is clear that a large amount of sculpture was transported down the Nile via Ramanieh to Alexandria for shipment to France, but whether the stone was one of these is uncertain.

Judging by Menou's later attachment to the relic and judging by its location when it was discovered in Alexandria, it is possible that the stone left Cairo not with the savants, but with the possessive Menou – safely wrapped in mats, tucked into his personal baggage.

The unexpected ease with which the British took Rosetta led General Hutchinson to press home the advantage – with the French commander-in-chief sealed inside Alexandria, and with the promise of a further 6,000–7,000 men landing with General Baird on the Red Sea coast at Koseeir further south, Cairo seemed a ready target.

On 9 May, Hutchinson and the Kapudan Pasha moved south along the left bank of the Nile to Cairo. This was considered by many in his command to be unwise, if not reckless, and in many ways the detractors were right: the British then suffered the same exhausting march endured by the French three years earlier against an enemy of unknown disposition or size. At Ramanieh they clashed with General Lagrange's troops, and pushed them back to the capital where they joined General Belliard's forces, bringing the Cairo garrison up to 12,000.

The army of the Grand Vizier, previously discounted by General Sir John Moore and Sir Ralph Abercromby as medieval, crossed the border into Lower Egypt. Though numbering now only 15,000, just over a third of its original strength in 1800, the army made steady progress. Hutchinson and the Kapudan Pasha met them, supported now by Mamelukes and the Bedouin, and encamped before Cairo, where a British pontoon bridge was quickly thrown across the Nile.

Within the city walls, Belliard considered his position carefully: the mightly Murad Bey, on whom he might have relied against the Turks, had died of the plague. Belliard was very much on his own. Menou's appalling manner had so alienated his generals that they retained not one shred of loyalty to his command or to his dreams of a French colony on the Nile. Cut off, with water supplies dangerously low and the potential of another civil uprising, Belliard took a dramatic decision – on 22 June, he sent out riders to the British positions and offered terms of surrender.

With memories of General Kléber, Belliard had no wish to continue a senseless defence which would inevitably have led to surrender, after causing the deaths of thousands of his men and innocent civilians. On 27 June, Belliard's army was offered roughly the same terms as those agreed with Sir Sidney Smith at El Arish in 1800 – they were permitted to leave Cairo with full honours, armed, and with all their possessions. In the first week of July, almost precisely three years after they had arrived, the French forces began the two-week evacuation. With equal ceremony, the coffin of General Kléber was carried with them in awesome and moving spectacle.

Alexandria meanwhile held out bitterly, Menou's final belated message to Belliard arriving a week after Cairo's surrender – declaring that they should defend the capital 'or perish'. The savant Captain Malus later questioned the sanity of the officer who could issue such an order. Many would question Menou's sanity in the days to come: such blinkered obstinacy was to prove the keynote to Menou's swansong in Egypt.

Herein lies the greatest irony in the story of the Rosetta Stone: had it remained in Cairo, it might very easily have been taken back to Rosetta and there shipped to France with the repatriated troops, courtesy of the Royal Navy. Rather than standing in the British Museum in London, it would today be displayed in the Louvre in Paris. Instead, it became embroiled in what was to be the most curious expedition of all the learned excursions in Napoleonic Egypt, conducted, on this occasion, not by the savants but by three Englishmen – two of whom just happened to be passing.

Though Cairo had fallen, Menou clung on to what remained of French Egypt, from his castle keep in Alexandria. As Colonel

Wilson recounts, on 7 July Menou received the news of Belliard's surrender 'with much vexation' and later 'resolved to bury himself in the ruins of Alexandria'. Menou had been hoping for several eventualities: reinforcement from Admiral Ganteaume; the Nile flood, which would have made Anglo-Turkish operations almost impossible; and Belliard holding out for an overall peace that might allow France to retain Egypt.

His hopes were unrealistic, as were his expectations of Ganteaume's 'succours', as Wilson calls them – Menou's subordinates would undoubtedly have tried to impress upon him that, with the fall of Cairo and the loss of Belliard's army, any reinforcements would have to be of sufficient number to reconquer the country. To Menou this defeatism was tantamount to sedition. The garrison learned this to its cost: Menou blamed his generals for the defeat at Canopus, in particular his second-in-command, General Reynier. Colonel Wilson refers to Reynier's exaggerated accounts of battles for Alexandria as 'grotesque and malevolent' – it was perhaps these characteristic traits that led to his fall from grace with Menou, who would not countenance any criticism.

One night in mid-May, Menou led a large force of infantry, cavalry and grenadiers through the streets of Alexandria to Reynier's house, arrested the astonished general on charges amounting to mutiny and treason, and had him marched from his home at gunpoint. In July, Reynier and his subversive companions Damas, Daure, Boyer and various aides were sent back to France to await court-martial. Reynier later wrote that he was pleased to go and to leave the company of a man whom he heartily despised, a commander who ran his divisions like the Paris Terror. As he had in Cairo, Menou now succeeded in alienating the remainder of his officers in Alexandria.

Knowing they were surplus to requirements and considered by Menou no more than a nuisance, the savants requested permission to return to France with their collections. The savants, at last, had severed their ties to the military. They had suffered enough – yet worse was still to come.

They were granted permission, says Rousseau, on 14 May but did not receive their passports from the procrastinating Menou until 5 June. However, Menou's puzzling fear was that the collections of sculpture, rare bird species and insects could fall into the hands of the enemy and somehow aid the war against France: therefore, if the savants were to leave, they would leave empty-handed. Menou explained his actions, as ever, in a letter to Fourier, the secretary of the Institute, on 21 May in which he stated, like the good administrator he was, that the collections 'belong to the government and must be deposited', though it is also likely this was partly a spiteful act of bureaucratic malice.

Once they had signed an undertaking that they carried nothing with them that could be of military or political advantage to the enemy should it be captured, on 5 June the savants once again boarded the brig *L'Oiseau*, in Alexandria harbour – the very ship on which a number had already been immured in the aborted evacuation of a year earlier. There is some question of the precise nature of its cargo and whether the Rosetta Stone was loaded with the other monuments and sculptures; a commission was set up to oversee the loading of antiquities but there are few details and neither Saintine nor Villiers du Terrage specifies which pieces went aboard. For reasons which will soon be made clear, it is unlikely the Rosetta Stone was among them.

They sat aboard, waiting, delayed by contrary winds. With a sickening repetition of their previous ordeal, they waited an entire month on board until their departure on 15 July, content at least to be free of Menou and the army. During the delay they received a copy of the Cairo surrender treaty. Article 11 stated that the members of the Commission for the Sciences and Arts 'will enjoy the same conditions stipulated for the French troops'. They were convinced this would allow them free passage by the British, cargo included. Flying both French and British colours for safety's sake, the small ship finally made its way out to sea in broad daylight – but Menou had refused to warn the British fleet that the savants were coming out.

L'Oiseau sailed towards the British squadron, and HMS *Cynthia* moved in to attack; she fired two warning shots, eventually escorting *L'Oiseau* to the British fleet lines in Aboukir Bay. Admiral Keith was furious – his anger directed more at Menou – as he claimed that, had he been warned of the savants' plans, he would most likely have let them pass. Instead, he pointed out to Fourier that the Convention of Cairo, whereby Belliard's entire army, civilians, savants, servants and all, were to be repatriated to France, did not apply to the savants in Alexandria. He ordered them back to port.

When *L'Oiseau* reached Alexandria harbour the next day, the two French frigates which had been anchored in the port for months, *La Justice* and *L'Égyptienne*, threatened to open fire; *L'Oiseau* was ordered to go about and head for open sea within fifteen minutes or be sunk. In this shocking interval, a pilot was sent out to the savants with yet another long-winded letter from a disgusted Menou, berating them for their unpatriotic and cowardly conduct, evidently believing they should have engaged the Royal Navy with *L'Oiseau*'s four tiny cannon. They drafted a reply and sent it back to Menou, Villiers du Terrage writing that 'they counted the moments'.

The fifteen minutes passed, but the guns of *La Justice* and *L'Égyptienne* remained silent. Yet Menou still did not allow them ashore. Sir Sidney Smith came to the rescue, and acted as intermediary between Menou and Keith; to guarantee their safety and to lift their sinking spirits, he slept aboard *L'Oiseau* with the miserable savants as they sailed back out to the relative safety of the British fleet.

Keith was dumbstruck by Menou's conduct and wrote that unless Menou let the savants return, they would be put ashore and their ship set ablaze – further, that the 'behaviour of the French general exposed him to the reprimand of his own government and the reprobation of all civilized nations'.[18] When the savants finally received permission from Menou to return, they did not trust him – still uncertain that they would be allowed to disembark, they stayed where they were. Sidney Smith once more appeared that night to tell them he had won a brief reprieve for them from Keith's ultimatum.

When the ship headed at last for Alexandria, alarm and confusion reigned and several savants jumped overboard into Smith's longboat drawn up alongside, one of them, the young sculptor Castex, plunging into the sea. Smith, convinced by this obvious distress, had him brought aboard his own ship HMS *Tigre* and offered him safe passage. After Smith's indefatigable mediation with Keith, the others returned to Alexandria where they were allowed to dock, after several days of quarantine, on 31 July. Villiers du Terrage wrote:

> the anxiety being so great, placed as we had been between the cannons of the English and the commander-in-chief, some of us began raving and, I believe, would have gone mad should the test have lasted longer. The physical harm [we had endured] was incomparable to the effect on our morale.[19]

Thanks to Menou, it had been a debacle. It would not be his last.

Keith had taken a very deliberate step in refusing the savants passage to France. He believed that a hundred men (the savants and their 'suites') was a considerable number and would certainly have relieved some of the pressure on the provisioning and water supply of Alexandria. For this same calculating reason, he allowed Bonaparte's pledge to Kléber in 1799 to pass: quite literally, Lord Keith sent in the comedians.

Bonaparte's comedians (or rather, performing artistes) had been despatched along with sundry other horticulture experts and engineers aboard one of five transports in Ganteaume's fleet, and had been intercepted by the British off the African coast. These hardy troubadours were conveyed by the British to Alexandria, partly in the benign hope they would indeed cheer the French garrison, but also in a clever attempt to increase the population of a city under siege. Wilson wrote that Menou 'perversely rejected the reinforcement, so considerately and patriotically furnished by the Consuls of France'.

Menou grew obsessed with rescue by Ganteaume, and paced the shoreline daily, peering vainly at the horizon for the tricolour flying from the admiral's battleships – but of Ganteaume there was no sign. In their history of the campaign, the savants paint a sorry picture of the besieged French commander driven almost beyond his limits:

> This hope absorbed him so much that he had forgotten all the other matters of defence. The details of the service, administrative orders, all was forsaken. He neglected his office; he forgot the most important things, to delude himself with chimerical dreams and disappointing illusions. Each evening he ended his watch with the thought that his luck would be better the following day.[20]

Hutchinson began his Alexandria offensive in mid-July, the army refreshed with troops returned from the victory at Cairo, and sporadic battles for positions continued through August in the struggle for the heights around the city. Although 4,000 British had successfully contained Menou's 7,000 French, the British had been in no position to attack; the full-scale siege had partly been prevented by the lack of boats to ferry supplies to the allies – as salt to the wounds of the Alexandria savants, many craft were to be used to transport Belliard's army and their colleagues from Cairo back to France.

Alexandria was in a deplorable state, says Villiers du Terrage, with dysentery and scurvy rampant in the city and the ranks of the army. For want of manpower the savants were incorporated into the national guard. However, the conditions of the siege wore as badly on the allies as on the French, and it was here that a British soldier, Lieutenant T. Marmaduke Wybourn of the Royal Marines, gave his first comments on Egypt in a letter to his sisters:

> This plain is the most miserable of any in Egypt, not a tree or even a bit of grass, all sand and scorching as a furnace. Vermin of all sorts but most fleas and ants, scorpions and beetles crawling over one in the night and getting under the clothes, and no man is permitted to undress or even take off his sword, and in this manner, and under Tents only, have the Army been ever since they came (21 March), not a house, or a hut to be seen anywhere.[21]

Some days an ominous stillness hung over the plain, punctuated two hours before dawn by the British beating to arms in case of surprise attacks, and then returning to their tents. In a quiet moment Wybourn and three of his brother officers ventured close to the enemy positions one day and heard the French point of view:

> While we were talking to their Dragoons a French officer came up and was extremely polite, asked us the news and said they were all heartily tired of the place . . . after some civilities we all rode along the Videos and upon our turning off to return, all took off their hats.[22]

Pickets and enemy dragoons apart, one popular victory was hailed by both sides when the army mules were moved to some distant corral, their constant nightly braying driving the British and French alike to madness.

By the end of August, the tactical situation had become intolerable for Menou and the French garrison. Lieutenant Wybourn wrote joyously to his sisters: 'At length a flag of truce was sent out when we all knew it was over with them.'[23] This flag came out just in time: 'When we told the French of our intention to send the Turks in as soon as a breach was made in the Walls, they were motionless with terror.'[24] Wybourn's flag of truce arrived on the evening of 26 August, brought by Menou's aide-de-camp. The next day, General Hutchinson sent this communiqué:

> Head Quarters, Camp before Alexandria
> August 27th, 1801
> From Lt-Gen. Sir John Hely-Hutchinson KB, to the Earl
> of Elgin

> . . . I just seize the opportunity of a messenger going to Constantinople, (despatched by the Captain Pasha) to inform your Excellency, that General Menou offered last night to capitulate for the town and forts of Alexandria, and demanded an armistice of three days for the purpose of arranging the terms of the capitulation; this I have granted accordingly.[25]

The armistice did not begin until the firing of three 'unshotted' French guns, to be answered by three English, followed by the lowering of the colours of both armies. At noon on 27 August 1801, the cannons roared for the last time, and the armistice came into effect. The battle for Egypt was over. The battle for the antiquities, and the Rosetta Stone, was about to begin.

Stone Cold in Alex

In early 1801, the tireless Cambridge mineralogist and antiquary Edward Daniel Clarke[1] and his equally dogged student
companion, John Marten Cripps,[2] reached Constantinople as
part of their marathon tour across Europe and Asia. Their
adventures together would last several years, which Clarke later
recorded in his great work, *Travels in Various Countries of Europe,
Asia and Africa*.[3] He once wrote to a friend that Cripps would
follow him to 'the mountains of the moon'. He was not far
wrong – the young student rarely left his tutor's side.[4] Now the
famed art and antiquities of the Nile beckoned them from the
ancient plains of Troy, the war with the French doubtless adding
to the thrill of discovery: the pair boarded a provisions boat in
Cyprus and headed for Egypt.

They caught sight of Alexandria and the British fleet in
Aboukir Bay on 17 April before meeting with Clarke's brother,
George, captain of HMS *Braakel*. Clarke wrote, 'It was the
grandest naval sight I ever saw . . . Innumerable masts, like an
immense forest, covering the sea, swarms of sailing boats and
cutters, plying about in all directions between the larger vessels.'

When eventually the pair went ashore to Alexandria they
toured the British lines, dining with the dragoons in their 'mess',
no more than a pit dug into the sand lined with palms, and

were often close enough to watch the French cavalry change the guard at their outposts – on many occasions, just as Wybourn found, the French were close enough to ask the British for water. They visited Rosetta, their naval connection and reputation securing them the home of none other than Sir Sidney Smith.

In late May they parted for Cyprus and later that summer toured the Holy Land, returning on 1 August to witness the spectacle of Belliard's army being evacuated from Egypt.[5] Bound for home at last the troops were evidently in great spirits: 'All animosity was laid aside,' wrote Clarke, 'singing, dancing and acting, became the order of the day.' Clarke remarked on the number of Egyptian women who had accompanied the French, for fear of the retribution awaiting them – upon retaking Cairo, Sheikh Al-Bakri had assented to the beheading of his own daughter for her association with the French.

Clarke and Cripps made it to Cairo by 11 August, just as Menou was approaching his final weeks of command in Alexandria. Equipped with letters of introduction and recommendation by General Hutchinson and Admiral Keith, the pair were welcomed by notable scholars and dignitaries in the city, including the renowned orientalist 'Mr Hammer',[6] the Imperial Consul Carlo Rosetti[7] and the Grand Vizier of the Turks whom they met through Colonel Holloway of the artillery. It was through Holloway they made an unexpected discovery.

Holloway had been billeted in the old headquarters of the Institut d'Égypte in Nasriyah and pointed out to the pair of travellers several pieces that had been abandoned in the court-yard gardens, one of which Holloway allowed them to take away, a stele of hieroglyphics on red porphyry, later donated to Cambridge University Library.[8] The other was the large stone discovered in the threshold of the local mosque by the savant Philippe Caristie in 1800. In the course of departure the savants had evidently considered the stele too large and of insufficient quality to warrant a place with the rest of the collections heading for Alexandria. For much the same reason, Clarke and Cripps reluctantly left it behind. (When it was rediscovered by James Burton in 1826, it had been reinstated into the mosque steps. It was the pro-French antiquary Giovanni Drovetti and Jean-François Champollion himself who orchestrated its acquisition for France – as if, in the eyes of some commentators, in compensation for the loss of the Rosetta Stone; thus the mosque suffered its threshold to be excavated yet again.)

Clarke and Cripps were welcomed also by the Indian sepoy army commanded by General Baird and toured the area in search of relics and sites to record. One particular success was a very special Arabic manuscript. Clarke wrote in a letter from Cairo to his good friend and former travelling companion, the Reverend William Otter in England:

> The French sçavans [*sic*] searched for it all the time they spent in this country; and an Arab student from Vienna has orders to find it if possible. What will you say, if after all these staunch pointers have ranged the stubble, such a pug-dog as I should start the game and bear it home to my masters? 'Toe-ho!' you exclaim, and level your piece – bang!!! – we have it snug – the whole work complete – One Thousand and One Nights.[9]

Clarke and Cripps had found one of the most sought-after literary marvels in the East. They were to continue with such startling good fortune.

It was while seeking out antiquities in Cairo that Clarke and Cripps encountered their old friend and fellow antiquary, the young William Richard Hamilton,[10] whom they had met on their journey through Constantinople in November 1800. Hamilton was no less than the attaché and later personal secretary to Lord Elgin, British Ambassador to the Ottoman Empire in the Sublime Porte at Constantinople. He is often confused with Sir William Hamilton (1730–1803) the British Ambassador to the Kingdom of Naples, equally well known to Clarke and Cripps – a vulcanologist, avid collector and antiquary, more famed for being the aged husband of that other celebrated Hamilton, Lady Emma, the scandalous mistress of Horatio Nelson.

William Richard, however, at just twenty-four years old in 1801, was usually described as a gifted 'diplomatist'. Hamilton rose to historical prominence through his association with the Elgin Marbles[11] – it was Hamilton who, on behalf of Lord Elgin, arranged the excursion for the artist Lusieri to visit the Athenian Acropolis and record the statuary on site for the first time. His duties in Egypt involved a report on the commerce, government and nature of the country and would have included an unofficial request to note any historical sites for His Excellency.

General Hutchinson continually kept Lord Elgin abreast of developments through despatches, from the fall of Rosetta and Cairo, to Alexandria. As an embassy official and attaché of the ambassador to the ruling government of Egypt, Hamilton had been sent as Lord Elgin's agent to oversee the settlement of affairs with both the French and Britain's Ottoman allies, just as the Kapudan Pasha himself represented the sultan. Hamilton's presence was to prove crucial in negotiations.

Escorted by the Dragoon Guards, Clarke, Cripps and Hamilton went on an excursion to the Pyramids – they climbed Khufu's monument and, like the savants before them, took measurements and made observations. It was while inside the Great Pyramid they discovered that British soldiers and sailors had taken sledge-hammers to the granite sarcophagus in the King's Chamber, with the intention of breaking off pieces for souvenirs. The local commander, Colonel Stewart, was outraged by these actions and threatened to punish any man, regardless of rank, should anything similar be attempted again. Clarke comments, with a deep sense of shame and disappointment:

> This beautiful relic was entire when our troops were landed in Egypt. Even the French had refused to violate a monument considered by travellers of every age and nation as consecrated by its antiquity; having withstood the ravages of time above three thousand years, and all the chances of sacrilege to which it was exposed during that period from wanton indiscriminating barbarity. It is therefore painful to relate it is now no longer entire . . . Yet, as a proof of the difficulty which attended this worse than Scythian ravage, the persons who thus left behind them a sad memorial of the British name, had only succeeded in accomplishing a fracture near one of the angles.[12]

Just as Menou's last stand was drawing near, Hamilton left the two travellers for Alexandria, but the trio was destined to meet again within weeks. Clarke and Cripps had been given lodgings in Cairo with Mr Hammer, not far from those of the Imperial Consul, Carlo Rosetti. Rosetti had been of great value to the pair and had been well employed by the French in their dealings with the Mamelukes. Now, with the arrival of the English, he adroitly welcomed the new conquerors, doubtless with some genuine gratitude to the armies that had defeated the forces of his own country's arch-enemy. Rosetti informed them that the majority of antiquities compiled by the French had been moved to Alexandria ready for shipment to France – but this was the least of the startling information Rosetti had for them. On 31 August, during what was to be their final audience with the *Reis Effendi*, the Turkish Secretary of State at Cairo, a messenger arrived with the news of Alexandria's capitulation:

(top) The Battle of the Pyramids, 21 July 1798, the decisive engagement with the Mameluke army, which yielded the prize of Cairo and command of Egypt to Bonaparte. *(bottom)* Murad Bey, the Mameluke leader, from the *Description de l'Égypte*.

(clockwise from top left) Nicolas Jacques Conté, (1755–1805) *directeur des mécaniciens* engineer and inventor, depicted after the laboratory explosion which damaged his eye. Gaspard Monge (1746–1818) mathematician, engineer, scientist, and co-founder of the *Institut d'Égypte*. Édouard de Villiers du Terrage (1780–1855) one of the youngest members of the Commission. Étienne Geoffroy Saint-Hilaire (1772–1844) naturalist and zoologist whose defiance at Alexandria saved the savants' personal collections.

A View of Rosetta, by artist Vivant Denon, from his book of 1802, *Travels in Upper and Lower Egypt.*

Bonaparte's flagship, the 118-gun *L'Orient* exploding in the Battle of the Nile, 1 August 1798, by George Arnald.

The Rosetta Stone. Discovered July 1799, in the foundations of Fort Julien, Rosetta, by Lieutenant Pierre François Xavier Bouchard.

British troops landing under heavy fire at Aboukir Bay, 8 March 1801, by Philippe Jacques de Loutherbourg.

(left) Edward Daniel Clarke, LLD (1769–1822), scholar, mineralogist, antiquary and explorer. His travel journals give a unique account of his mission to recover the Rosetta Stone from within besieged Alexandria. *(right)* The list of T. Marmaduke Wybourn, RM, citing Item 8 as 'A stone with three inscriptions, hieroglyphics, gobic and Greek – black granite from Rosetta'.

(clockwise from top left) General Jacques-François Abdallah Menou, Baron de Boussa
(1750–1810). Sir William Richard Hamilton (1777–1859), antiquary and diplomat
in 1851. Jean-François Champollion (le Jeune) (1790–1832), Egyptologist and
linguistic genius, the decipherer of hieroglyphs. Sir Thomas Young (1773–1829),
physician, physicist, linguist and pioneer contributor to the study of hieroglyphs.

With this welcome information we took our leave, and determined instantly to hasten to the British camp, and to make Lord Hutchinson acquainted with some particulars that had come to our knowledge respecting the antiquities collected by the French in Egypt, all of which we knew to be deposited in Alexandria.

Previous to our departure it was necessary to collect as much additional information as possible, and especially with regard to the Rosetta Tablet, as there is no doubt but every artifice would be used to prevent our Commander in Chief from becoming acquainted with the place of its concealment. A report had already been circulated that this stone had been sent to France. We therefore waited upon the only person capable of furthering any views in this respect.[13]

Clarke first gave a brief account of the affair of the Rosetta Stone in a footnote in an earlier work of 1805, but had kept the name of their informant secret. He had wished to protect any sources from reprisal should the French return to Egypt; in 1805, this was not an impossibility. But in his *Travels* of 1810 this was no longer a concern, and he declares:

This person was no other than the intelligent Carlo Rosetti, whose inquisitive mind and situation in the country had enabled him to become acquainted with every thing belonging to the French army. In the course of a conversation with him on the subject of the Rosetta Stone, which he maintained was still in Alexandria, he informed the author that something even of a more precious nature was contained among the French plunder: that they had removed by force, a relic long held in veneration among the inhabitants of Alexandria, after every entreaty had failed for that effect; and that they entertained considerable apprehension lest any intelligence concerning it should reach the English army: that Menou, and some other of his officers had used every precaution to prevent the people of Alexandria from divulging the place of its concealment before it could be conveyed beyond the reach of our forces.[14]

This mysterious artefact was 'of one entire piece of stone, of astonishing size, and of a beautiful green colour'.[15] Rosetti finished by giving Clarke a sealed letter of introduction addressed to one of the principal merchants of Alexandria, who, Rosetti promised, would give them any information he could on the matter. Clarke and Cripps were in a unique position. Until this point, no one had any idea what precisely might be found within Alexandria's walls: 'I then intended to write to General Hutchinson and Lord Keith on that subject [the Rosetta Stone], to beg it might be obtained for the University of Cambridge or the British Museum.'[16]

Though delayed by a final audience with the Grand Vizier, and the tumult accompanying the procession in Cairo of the tapestry to cover the *Qa'aba* in the holy shrine of Mecca, Clarke and Cripps lost little time. Aware that they might be the only Englishmen in Egypt who knew this vital information, the resourceful Hammer, disguised in Arab dress, smuggled them out of Cairo on 2 September, just after Menou had signed terms for surrender in Alexandria.

It is evident, however, that William Richard Hamilton had more than an inkling as to what lay within the French camp, but it is possible Rosetti did not confide as much to Hamilton as to Clarke – Clarke clearly liked Rosetti, but Hamilton is unusually condemnatory of the consul:

By prudence and caution he has always succeeded in ingratiating himself with the ruling power; and though concerned, either voluntarily or by compulsion, in most of the intrigues and negotiations carried on among the contending parties, he has known so well how to time his assistance or his desertion of his friends, as to ensure himself the gratitude rather then the anger of each successive conqueror.[17]

The question for Hamilton was, could Rosetti be trusted?

Events at Alexandria had overtaken the pair of travellers hurrying downriver to meet General Hutchinson. When Menou had surrendered on 26 August, he had promised to prepare a list of 'articles of capitulation' within the three-day armistice, but it was not as simple a task as he had first imagined. A year earlier, Menou had rejected the generous peace offer of the Convention of El Arish, so ably won by General Kléber in 1800 and so foolishly lost by circumstance; now Menou was obliged to draft an entirely new treaty.

On the evening of the 29th, with only that night and the following morning remaining, Menou sent out his aide, Habert, to ask for an extension of the ceasefire by an extra twenty-four hours. Hutchinson refused, threatening to resume hostilities. General Coote was ordered by Hutchinson to stand by to attack. Having informed Menou of this, there were mutinous rumblings in the French camp, the men demanding an end to the affair; Habert returned to the British lines immediately, promising that a treaty proposal would be delivered the following day. At one o'clock on 30 August, Habert, accompanied by *chef de brigade* Lhullier, handed over the proposed terms, as agreed by Menou and his generals. This was the first draft of the Articles for the Capitulation of Alexandria.

Hamilton was sent the articles for his official inspection. According to Clarke, Hamilton then suggested several amendments to Menou's proposals, and made radical changes to one clause in particular: Article 16 was to become the single greatest bone of contention in the weeks to come. Menou's proposed version had read:

Those individuals composing the Institute of Egypt and the Commission of Arts shall carry with them all papers, plans, memoirs, collections of natural history, and all monuments of art and antiquity collected by them in Egypt.

Menou was demanding that the French forces should be accorded the same rights freely exercised by the dedicated and efficient Gaspard Monge, five years earlier in the conquest of Italy, when his Commission sent back to France any and all works of art he so desired.[18] Concerned that the British would simply do likewise, Menou had hoped to prevent this eventuality, believing, as had Fourier and the savants on *L'Oiseau*, that what had applied in the surrender of Cairo would apply in Alexandria – Menou had lost Egypt, the very least he could do was try to save the fruits of the expedition. However, had Menou been more of a sharp lawyer he might have fudged the issue more artfully and attempted a general reference to 'baggage' or 'belongings', but raising the specific instance served to highlight the matter: without realizing it, he had reminded the British of the savants' collections of antiquities and, indirectly, the Rosetta Stone.

But Hamilton needed no reminding, and advised Hutchinson how best to redraft the article. It was returned to Menou, striking a very different tone; one can imagine his reaction to this change:

ARTICLE 16:

The members of the Institute may carry with them all the instruments of arts and science which they have brought from France; but the Arabian manuscripts, the statues, and other collections which have been made for the French Republic, shall be considered as public property and subject to the disposal of the generals of the combined army.

The reference to Arabic manuscripts indicates that Hamilton might have been advised of the looting and desecration of the Al-Azhar Mosque in Cairo after the uprising in 1798, and the subsequent actions of the savants in preserving priceless treasures from the rampaging soldiers. Although not wishing to confiscate the savants' personal property such as valuable instruments, the harshly redrafted Article 16 would force the savants to quit Egypt empty-handed.

The savants were devastated by this news. The collections 'for the French Republic', though made under the auspices of the expedition, were more the personal accomplishments of explorers caught in the political machinery of the surrender – they included stuffed and preserved animals, rare entomological collections, observations on the nature of molluscs and amphibians, and research on a bewildering variety of Nile species hitherto unknown in European academic circles. To carry these off in the name of victory would have been a heinous act striking the savants personally and would in no way have brought glory to British arms.

In Hamilton's defence, the British did not know the extent of the collections gathered by the savants. It is likely that, aware of the activities of the Institute over the past years, Hamilton designed Article 16 as a catch-all to prevent great works of art from escaping to the confines of an enemy capital.

Menou was not overly sympathetic to the savants' case, even when they demanded he make changes to the article. Once again, the scholars were proving a nuisance to the army: 'Menou had certainly received some timid representations [by the savants] but he stopped these by the simple act of not receiving them.'[19] It was deeply felt among the savants that Article 16 had been passed by the military as merely another aspect of the surrender and nothing of any particular importance – whereas to the savants, the idea of their cherished collections being taken from them was nothing short of anathema.

General Hope entered the city on 31 August to sign the terms and explained that he had not the authority to rewrite the clause. Menou acquiesced and signed the treaty. Having signed a legally binding document, he then made an attempt by letter to Hutchinson the following day to change it, and convince the British commander-in-chief of the savants' case. As Clarke had suspected, this attempt involved some considerable 'artifice'. It would be the first in a long line of wearisome correspondence on the matter. Although Menou had already written to Fourier in May to say that the prized collections of the Institute were the property of the French Republic, on 1 September, Menou now wrote to Hutchinson that in fact the opposite was the case:

> As to the collections, none of those which exist here in such small number belong to the French Republic; all of them were made at the cost and expense of individuals. I know of no objects which could be considered property of the French Republic other than two sarcophagi, one taken in Alexandria, the other coming from Cairo.[20]

This 'small number' amounted to a shipload of sculpture including such pieces as the giant granite fist of Memphis, two large statues found in Alexandria, Rosetti's mystery treasure, and of course the Rosetta Stone, which Menou neglected to mention, perhaps trying to maintain the illusion that it had already gone back to France – he might have been wiser not to refer to the sarcophagi either. It was a desperate gambit, but possibly the only way he could see to save the antiquities for France and keep the Rosetta Stone, the greatest prize of them all.

Hutchinson wrote back, with some rhetorical style, that France had plundered the treasures of Rome and all of Europe, wherever it had waged war, and that he was merely following the example set by Menou's compatriots on the Continent.

'I demand,' he wrote, 'all these objects, and you may be sure I shall not let a single part of them leave for France.'[21] So began a war of words between the commanders, what Menou later referred to in one of his many messages as '*la guerre de plume*'; though he complained, he engaged in it with some fervour – certainly more than Hutchinson.

The next day, on 2 September, just as Clarke and Cripps left Cairo, Lord Keith came ashore to ratify the treaty, Menou's complaints thrust aside. On the same day Anstruther, the quartermaster general, went into the French lines to be shown the two forts that the British were soon to occupy. Later that morning, the Grenadier Guards, with colours flying and the bands playing, marched forward to take possession of these outer positions.

Although surrendered to the British, Alexandria had not been fully secured and Hutchinson refused to enter and relieve the city until the terms of the capitulation were met – he wanted the antiquities. Menou did not seem to have understood this, for his letters referred to vague locations of some pieces and to whom they belonged, and how expensive their excavations had been as if in search of recompense should they be confiscated – without any thought for his sick and wounded or the wretched inhabitants of the city.

Hamilton believed that the Rosetta Stone was in Alexandria, and possibly had feared it had been loaded aboard *L'Oiseau* when the savants tried to pass through the blockade. This might have given rise to the fanciful tale of Hamilton rowing out to a French transport to intercept the stone which had been 'stealthily shipped out'.[22] It was possibly Hamilton who suggested to Lord Keith that the savants be returned to port for just this reason. On 6 September, a week after terms had been signed, Menou wrote back to Hutchinson and admitted to the stone's presence:

I have in my possession a stone, which I had unearthed at Rosetta, and which bears three different inscriptions. It is my property, but I declare to you that I truly hoped to offer it to the Republic upon my return to France. You want it, Monsieur le général? You can have it, because you are the stronger but I shall not be sorry to publicise it in Europe that my property was taken from me on the orders of Monsieur the English general.[23]

As to the story of the savants trying to steal away with it in broad daylight, Menou set the record straight, and made a surprising revelation:

You were misled when you said that this stone was on board *l'Oiseau*: for a long time it has been in storage in Alexandria. I had it brought to me, I will have it taken out and you may take it when you wish.[24]

This generous offer never materialized, for Hutchinson made it very plain that he wished it very much indeed, immediately in fact – but no Rosetta Stone appeared, and no antiquities were forthcoming. Hutchinson was beginning to experience the same frustration with Menou as Lanusse, Reynier, Marmont and Kléber had before him, drowning in a sea of Menou's protestations. It was to continue for another week. As Colonel Wilson later wrote, with some considerable respect, 'In the whole of this correspondence, General Menou displayed much ability and ingenuity of argument.'[25]

After still further adventures aiding a group of fleeing Egyptian women whom they found hiding in their riverboat, Clarke and Cripps sped along the torrent of the Nile in the grip of the annual flood, so powerful it virtually launched their *djerm* into the Mediterranean out of control. They sailed out to Aboukir and joined another ship to meet Lord Keith and acquaint him with their vital information. He explained an aspect of the Anglo-French exchange of antiquities often overlooked in the story of the capture of Alexandria:

> The next morning, Wednesday, September the ninth, we waited upon Lord Keith, to thank him for the civilities he had shewn [*sic*] to us and to take our leave. [But] he told us that no vessels would be permitted to sail into the port of Alexandria, until the French had evacuated the city, and the magazines been properly secured by our army; as he knew that there were not less than fifty or sixty ships, manned by Greeks and Turks, waiting for the sole purpose of plunder.[26]

The fear was that if Menou did not hand over the antiquities, they might soon be snatched away by the piratical Ottoman crews waiting in the bay, and sold off piecemeal on the markets of the Mediterranean, probably never to be seen again. This could also have precipitated another armed confrontation in the moment of victory, forcing the Royal Navy to blockade the port once again.

Obliged to make a tiring overland journey from Aboukir that night, Clarke and Cripps arrived at the British camp on Thursday morning, 10 September, and hurried through a dazzling maze of white canvas tents to find Hutchinson. The general was out, inspecting the lines:

> We waited in his tent until he returned, when he received us with his usual condescension and kindness. He told us that our friend Mr Hamilton had also reached the camp that morning, and had been furnished with a passport to enter Alexandria.[27]

It would seem that Hutchinson had already tired of Menou's delays and sent for Hamilton – as Hamilton later wrote in his account of the affair, he went to Alexandria to assist in the recovery of the antiquities, at Hutchinson's request.[28] Clarke and Cripps had arrived at just the right moment. The general explained the situation:

> The capitulation for the surrender [of Alexandria] had been protracted by the contumacy of the French General Menou, who was unwilling to deliver up the Antiquities demanded by the English; his reluctance was considerably augmented by observing the increasing nature of these demands.[29]

It seemed that Hutchinson received occasional reports from within Alexandria of yet more treasures hidden by Menou; he would then write, demanding the latest piece.

> Thus finding himself stripped of the Egyptian trophies with which he had prepared to adorn the Museum at Paris, Menou gave no bounds to his rage and mortification . . . the valuable Tablet found near Rosetta, with its famous trilinguar inscription, seemed to be, more than any other article, the subject of his remonstrances.[30]

As if this were not enough to consider, Clarke and Cripps then told Hutchinson about Rosetti's hidden artefact, 'for the possession of which the French were more anxious than even for this Tablet [the Rosetta Stone]'. This would add yet another to the list of treasures to be demanded from Menou. But Hutchinson recognized the good fortune which had brought Clarke and Cripps to Alexandria, and seized the opportunity without hesitation:

> making known to him the nature of our errand, [we] received his orders to set out instantly for Alexandria, and endeavour to discover not only where the particular monument was hid . . . but also whatsoever other antiquities the French might have secreted in the city.[31]

And as to the Rosetta Stone, Clarke and Cripps received instructions even more specific than these:

> He gave us also the authority from himself to receive the Rosetta Tablet, and to copy its inscription; fearful lest any accident might befal [*sic*] it, either while it remained in the possession of the enemy, or in its passage home.[32]

Sitting and waiting in the heat of the plain outside the great walls of Alexandria, Hutchinson must have considered the eventuality that the French might destroy the works they had collected rather than surrender them. Menou had already threatened to bury himself in the ruins of the city. In the continual stream of information coming from Alexandria regarding the antiquities would also have come reports of the garrison's demoralized state and their attitude towards Menou 'whom they detested', as Clarke observed. Judging by the behaviour of the French troops later reported by Clarke, Hutchinson's fears were justified: one could argue that, if the French rank and file had known that the Rosetta Stone was delaying their evacuation and return home, there could well have been another army revolt – the stone might easily have been summarily tumbled through the gates to the British lines or, worse, in their justifiable rage and in a final act of defiance, the troops might also have tried to smash it to pieces. They had already done worse in the Al-Azhar Mosque.

Beyond the city gates were Edward Daniel Clarke and John Marten Cripps, two men who would help bring the matter to its ultimate conclusion. On the success of their mission depended the lives of the starving inhabitants of Alexandria, the French garrison, the British soldiers who would be forced to storm the city if necessary – and some of the finest treasures of antiquity, including the Rosetta Stone. Without delay, the pair were issued with passports and horses.

'Thus provided,' wrote Clarke, 'we left the British camp, crossing the valley which separated the two armies, and drew near to the outworks of Alexandria.'[33]

The greatest scavenger hunt of the art world was about to begin.

9

Scavenger Hunt

Though Colonel Wilson argued in his account that Alexandria had been well stocked with food, the scenes witnessed by Clarke and Cripps suggested otherwise. On the morning of Thursday, 10 September, the travellers gave the password to the last British sentinels near the city walls and crossed over to the French line.

> As we approached the gates of the city we saw a vast number of Arabs, who were stationed on the outside of the walls with baskets of poultry and other provisions, waiting for permission from the English to supply the inhabitants who were then greatly distressed for want of food.[1]

Showing their passports to the French outposts, they entered the outer defences. What greeted them did not augur well for their stay:

> In the desolate scene of sand and ruins which intervenes between the outer gates and inner fortifications we met a party of miserable Turks, who were endeavouring, literally, to crawl towards their camp. They had been liberated that morning from their dungeons. The legs of these poor creatures, swoln [*sic*] to a size that was truly horrible, were covered with large ulcers; and their

eyes were terrible from inflammation. Some too weak to advance, had fallen on the sand, where they were exposed to the scorching beams of the sun.[2]

The Turks begged Clarke and Cripps for water, and it was only then they realized that in their eagerness to get into the city they had not brought any provisions of their own. They called over several Arabs who took the men to the Turkish lines – Clarke learned later they had reached them safely. With this ominous start to their task, at eleven o'clock they passed through the inner gates and into 'the great square' of Alexandria.

Many of them [the inhabitants] had not tasted meat or bread for several months. The French who were better supplied for some time, were now driven to such straits, that they had put to death fifteen horses every day for many days past to supply their own soldiers with food. The families to whom we brought letters were in a state of misery hardly to be described.[3]

They went first to the house of the Austrian Imperial Consul of Alexandria and found the family in an advanced state of malnutrition:

Every individual beneath the Consul's roof exhibited proof of the privation which his family had sustained, fallen cheeks; clothes hanging loose, as if too large for their bodies . . . They asked us eagerly when the English were to enter the city: and being told that some days would elapse before this could take place they burst into tears.[4]

The French army had taken everything in the city, from meat to plate and merchandise, pulling down houses for use as fuel. Here Clarke hears the first negative report of Menou in the siege; the consul said that: 'Upon the landing of our army, most of the inhabitants were under the necessity of making biscuit for the support of their families; but as soon as this was known to Menou, he ordered the whole of it to be seized for the use of the garrison.'[5] Every two weeks the French army made a regular collection of goods and provisions, paying for their purchases with republican banknotes, of questionable value to the inhabitants.

The French army's treatment of the Turks was equally reprehensible to Clarke. They had put their Turkish prisoners to work 'like horses' making them draw water and work the mills like beasts of burden – nearly forty Turks died each day. It is small wonder that Wybourn heard the French were 'motionless with terror' at the prospect of seeing Turkish janissaries pouring in through a breach in the walls – not a single French soldier would have been left alive. Clarke reported further that the Turks were also forced to bear arms for France, and that those who refused were imprisoned. Despite these remarks Clarke refuses to indulge in jingoistic anti-French generalizations:

[this] perhaps might have been expected from any troops similarly situated; neither would it be altogether fair to judge of Frenchmen in general by the sample which their army in Egypt afforded.[6]

Clarke soon learned that Hutchinson had been right to question the safety of the antiquities inside the city – the troops were not on the verge of mutiny, but they did not seem sufficiently motivated to make a last stand for the republic – and certainly not for Menou:

So desirous were the French of abandoning Alexandria, notwithstanding the obstinacy of the General, Menou, whom they detested, that they had been seen to seize Arabs by the beard, who arrived by stealth with provisions, and beat them, in order that supplies of food might not be the means of protracting the surrender of the place.[7]

It was a curious situation; Clarke and Cripps were enemies in an enemy camp, sent to root out items which had been deliberately hidden, and were surrounded by a soldiery desperate to leave – had Clarke been a military man he might well have considered rounding up a platoon of French soldiers to help him find what he was looking for, and end the siege. It is by no means certain they would have refused.

As soon as Clarke and Cripps reached the house which had been set aside for their stay, they were visited by a party of merchants who had heard of their arrival from the Imperial Consul, and had come to congratulate them on the successes of the British army, and to offer 'any assistance in their power, for expediting the entry of the English'. It must have been a large group – Clarke wrote that some hung back cautiously from the rest. Within moments it was clear their secret mission was running:

> Some of these waited until the room was cleared of other visitants, brought by curiosity, before whom they did not think proper to make further communication. But when they were gone, speaking with circumspection, and in a low voice, they asked if our business in Alexandria related to the subject of contention between Lord Hutchinson and Menou; namely, the Antiquities collected by the French in Egypt.[8]

When Hutchinson issued Clarke and Cripps with passports, he had also given them an extraordinary object, an impression of the inscription on the Rosetta Stone. Other than those copies made by Marcel and Conté and circulated by General Dugua upon his return to France in 1800, this could have been the only copy of the inscription in British hands.

> Lord Hutchinson had already obtained an impression from the stone, made with red chalk upon paper, by some member of the French Institute; but the characters so impressed were too imperfectly marked to afford a faithful representation of the original: this he consigned to our care, as likely to assist us in [our] undertaking.[9]

Clarke does not specify where this copy came from, nor whether it had been brought from Europe and was a copy of one of the early lithographs or, more intriguing, whether it had come from one of the forty-seven members of the Institute still confined within the city walls. It is unknown who made this copy, and whether it was officially sanctioned. In light of the events which were soon to take place, the latter is not unthinkable.

Poor though it was, the copy certainly assisted Clarke and Cripps, who showed it to the merchants as proof of their intentions. It had the desired effect. But rather than discussing its possible location, the merchants instead asked a surprising question: 'Does your commander-in-chief know that they have the tomb of Alexander?'

> We desired them to describe it; upon which they said, that it was of one entire and *beautiful green stone*, shaped like a cistern and taken from the Mosque of St Athanasius, that, among the inhabitants, this cistern had always borne the appellation of Alexander's Tomb.[10]

Within their first hours of being in the city, Clarke and Cripps had stumbled across Rosetti's mystery treasure.

it was evident that this could be no other than the identical monument to which our instructions from Cairo had referred. We produced the confidential letter entrusted to us upon this subject. The person to whom it was written was not present but they offered to conduct us to his house. We had hitherto carefully concealed the circumstance of its being in our possession; and, for obvious reasons, we shall not mention, even now, the name of the individual to whom it was addressed.[11]

The merchants promised they would 'put it in their power to get possession of it'. This particular antiquity was of far greater value to the Alexandrians, for local religious reasons, than an inscribed tablet. As liberator of Egypt from the Persians and later crowned pharaoh, Alexander had been made a god in Egypt; despite the Islamic revolution and the Arab invasion, this piece, his sarcophagus (or *soros* as Clarke prefers) held great importance to the Alexandrians. It had been reverently placed in the Mosque of St Athanasius, and there worshipped for centuries. Bonaparte would not have approved officially of its removal from the mosque, and neither indeed, could General 'Abdallah Pasha' Menou, the Muslim convert, though he never once commented on the rights or wrongs of its acquisition. The merchants told Clarke and Cripps what had happened.

So eager were they [the French troops] to obtain it, that the most solemn treaty was infringed, whereby they had guaranteed to the Moslems the inviolable possession of their sanctuaries. The Mosque of St Athanasius was forcibly entered by a party of their pioneers, with battle-axes and hammers, and the 'Tomb of Alexander' was borne away amidst the howling and lamentations of its votaries.[12]

They were taken through the winding streets of the city to visit Rosetti's informant, and handed him the letter of introduction.

He confirmed all they had heard about the relic, and told them it had been hidden in the bowels of a hospital ship.

> After its removal the most cautious measures were used to conceal it from observation. With prodigious difficulty and labour, they had placed it in the hold of a crazy vessel in the harbour which, being converted into an hospital, might on that account escape examination and in either respects was not likely to become an object of attention.[13]

Without any delay the merchants obtained a boat and Clarke and Cripps rowed out into the inner harbour to the mouldering hulk *La Cause*. 'We there found it, half filled with filth and covered with rags of the sick people on board.' William Richard Hamilton himself was later rowed out to *La Cause* and commented in his own account: 'It had been for months in the hold, and was intended to be sent to France [at] the first opportunity. This monument was resigned to us not without much regret, as it had long been considered one of the most valuable curiosities in Alexandria.'[14]

Having found this particular treasure by covert means, Clarke and Cripps now began work in the open. It is here a British officer makes his first appearance in the search for the Rosetta Stone, Colonel Tomkyns Hilgrove Turner of the 3rd Foot Guards.[15] His identity and testimony often confused with Hamilton, he is otherwise the man most usually credited with the capture of the Rosetta Stone.

Turner was no ordinary guards officer. He had seen extensive action in Holland and France in the Revolutionary Wars, where he had served under Abercromby; he had also fought at Alexandria and later Rosetta – but with regards to the search for the French antiquities, in the eyes of General Hutchinson he had one particular qualification: since June 1798, Turner had been a member of the Society of Antiquaries of London. Consequently, it was Turner whom Hutchinson had appointed to oversee the recovery of the French collections. As Hamilton wrote,

> My first visit to Alexandria in the autumn of 1801 had been occasioned by a request of the Commander in Chief of our army to accompany to the French headquarters the British officer under whose direction the monuments of Egyptian antiquity . . . were afterwards conveyed to England.[16]

Colonel Wilson spoke very highly of him as 'Colonel Turner, of the Guards, whose learning and particular attention to this branch of science justly selected him as the proper person to have charge of those valuable monuments'.[17]

Clarke wrote that Hamilton and Turner had entered Alexandria an hour before he and Cripps did, specifically 'about the Hieroglyphic Tablet'. As Clarke and Cripps were questioning the merchants about the Rosetta Stone, Turner and Hamilton were in the midst of their own interview with Menou – it was to be the first of several – but Menou was evidently as evasive as ever. Pressure was brought to bear, perhaps by the threats of the red-coated Colonel Turner, which later gave some satisfying results, as Clarke reported:

> Our proposals were made known, and backed with a menace from the British General that he would break the capitulation if the proposals were not acceded to . . . In the evening of the same day, about five o'clock, we waited upon Monsieur Le Roy, Ordonnateur de la Marine, in consequence of receiving, by Menou's Aid-de-camp, an order from the French General to see the other antiquities.[18]

In his account of the events in Alexandria, Turner also mentions Monsieur Le Roy (referring to him as the Prefect

Maritime). It must be presumed the four antiquity-hunters had gathered forces at some point during that afternoon, as it was Clarke and Cripps who led the party to *La Cause* and the tomb of Alexander; upon learning that the sarcophagus was aboard the vessel, Turner 'procured a sentry on the beach from Monsieur Le Roy'[19] to guard access to the hulk and prevent locals from rushing the ship to retrieve their holy artefact.[20] The four now followed Le Roy, who 'treated us with great politeness', wrote Clarke, on a tour of Alexandria's warehouses and magazines where most of the antiquities had been deposited. Clarke and Cripps had not been prepared for what awaited them.

The group was shown into an Aladdin's cave of treasures: another *soros* (sarcophagus), from Cairo, and the giant granite fist of Memphis were found lying on the beach near the port ready to be shipped to France; three seated figures, with lions' heads, holding the *ankh* or Crux Ansata; the colossal head of a ram, 'or of Ammon, whose name and worship, derived from Æthiopia',[21] wrote Clarke; two oblong slabs adorned with hieroglyphics; a stone coffin 'adapted to the human form'; a fragment of another *soros* from Upper Egypt – 'Also, other antiquities, the description of which might afford very pleasing employment: but a volume rather than a chapter, would be required for the undertaking.'[22]

The tour concluded at the house of General Friant, where they were shown the two large white marble statues which Hutchinson had specifically demanded, uncovered during earthworks to Alexandria's defences; it was these that Menou had tried to apportion as personal property to Friant, the commander of the unit which had discovered them. One piece was of Marcus Aurelius, the other of Septimius Severus – they were both earmarked for the British.

Clarke makes no mention of how or when these colossal pieces were taken away, suggesting they were not touched until the final French evacuation. It seems that the disclosure of their whereabouts was sufficient for Turner, who could then orchestrate their embarkation from Alexandria's own harbour when the time came.

On their first day within the city, Clarke and Cripps had discovered a prize of the French expedition and the bulk of the French antiquities. But Menou still refused to hand over the Rosetta Stone.

Neither Hamilton, Turner, Clarke nor Cripps had any way of knowing how many pieces represented the French antiquity collection. At some point in the negotiations, it is not clear when, Fourier, the secretary of the Institut d'Égypte, composed an inventory of the collection for the British which was given to Turner by the senior savant, Le Père, head of the engineering branch. It was much more than a simple list however, and was designed to reinforce Menou's claim that most pieces were personal property, in particular the Rosetta Stone which, apparently, was his. Fourier wrote a clear description of each artefact, specifying to whom it 'belonged' and, ostensibly, its location. The Rosetta Stone was Item 8:

8: 'Une Pierre d'un granit noir, chargées de trois Bandes | chez le général Menou
de caractères, hyèrogliphiques, Grecs, et Égyptiens, |
trouvée à Rosette. |

'Chez le général Menou' was a very loose expression, for it was still nowhere to be found.[23] List in hand, the four set about Alexandria, hunting down the remainder of the antiquities while awaiting news of the stone. As Clarke wrote to William Otter,

We found much more in their possession than was represented or imagined, Pointers would not range better for game than we have done for Statues, Sarcophagi, Maps, MSS, Drawings, Plans, Charts, Botany, Stuffed Birds, Animals, Dried Fishes &c.[24]

It was the latter that caused the greatest furore within the city. This was the moment the savants had been dreading – the confiscation of their natural history collections. The news that Clarke and Cripps had found these exhibits was to send panic through the academics of Alexandria. The timing of the following event is uncertain but, judging by Clarke's letter to William Otter, it must have been the following day, Friday 11 September, just as Clarke and Hamilton were enjoying a brief respite, inspecting Pompey's Pillar and Cleopatra's Needles. At this moment Menou fell under an entirely new siege:

> The whole corps of sçavans [*sic*] and engineers beset Menou, and the poor old fellow, what with us, and them, was completely hunted.[25]

The savants wrote a blistering letter to Menou, no longer afraid of the commander's influence within Alexandria; they defied the jurisdiction which claimed their collections, concluding their note with the thunderous assertion that,

> [although] the Commander in Chief [Menou] had been able to have at his disposal the fate of the army, his implements of war, [and] a conquered country, he exceeded his powers when he made himself the master and donor of a private property, of a property of science and art, the holiest of all.[26]

Possibly stung by this unexpected attack on his artistic sensibilities, the very measure of a gentleman, and doubtless contemplating the repercussions upon their return home, Menou wrote back that they were right, and that he would have the matter addressed at once. Unfortunately, after his previous conduct over the surrender, Menou's word carried little weight with General Hutchinson. Menou's protest was ignored.

After months of humiliation and abuse at Menou's hand, which had nearly resulted in their destruction by their own forces, the savants dispensed once and for all with Menou's dubious services as intermediary. They sent their own delegation direct to Hutchinson in the British camp. According to Saintine, Marcel and Reybaud this delegation consisted of Geoffroy Saint-Hilaire, Delile and Savigny – although according to Colonel Wilson it was Fourier, Nouet and Redouté.[27] Wilson related that, with 'great politeness and good reasoning', the savants explained to the general that their work was to be published in France, for the world to see – the planned masterwork, *Description de l'Égypte* – and should their specimens be taken prematurely it would deny European science of their extensive efforts for years to come, if not for ever. Although surrounded, in the depths of what seemed a Philistine army, possibly even flanked by musket-bearing guards, they declared:

> What do we find, here, on this frontier: a camp of soldiers transformed into a corps of customs men, to confiscate the product of observation and intelligence![28]

Determined to resist, they promised that, should their pleas not be accepted, they would scatter their collections into the 'sands of the Libyan desert'. Hutchinson listened 'coldly'. After a moment he said he would consider their words and that Hamilton would bring his answer.

Unwilling to interpret the legally binding Articles of Capitulation, Hutchinson remained inflexible and Hamilton returned to the savants with the news. In the savants' account of this moment, Hamilton is at first portrayed as the sum of all evil, an envious man who had come to steal their research to impress the learned societies in London, Oxford or Cambridge. Having suffered so much in the course of their three-year expedition, the savants were not about to surrender lightly, and protested once again. Hamilton however, clearly on their side, interrupted: 'No, Messieurs . . . I believe that all new steps would be useless: they would lead to rigours that for my part I would like to spare you; they would expose you to being detained as prisoners of war.'[29] To this Geoffroy Saint-Hilaire famously exclaimed:

No, we will not obey: your army will not be able to enter this place within two days. Very well! By then the sacrifice will be made. You can then dispose of our persons as seems fit to you: we will *burn* our treasures ourselves . . . So trust to the remembrances of history – you too will have burned a library in Alexandria![30]

This dark allusion to the work of Caesar and Caliph Umar was not lost on the appalled Hamilton. Recovering from his horror at such a suggestion, he replied, 'Count on me gentlemen – I shall return to the British camp and plead our cause – if I cannot do it, no one can.'[31]

Hamilton now bore a very grave responsibility. Added to this came the latest news regarding the Rosetta Stone. Without the aid of the diplomat, Clarke and Cripps had confronted Menou.

At just before midday – possibly as the savants were challenging Hamilton – Clarke and Cripps tried to discover the secret location of the Rosetta Stone. Once known, they could first take a more detailed impression of its inscription, then report the find to Colonel Turner, who would march in and take it. First they had to outmanoeuvre Menou.

In the forenoon of this day, the author [Clarke] waited upon General Menou, requesting a passport, that might enable him to pass and repass the outer gate, to and from the British camp;

and at the same time made application for permission to copy the Inscriptions upon the Rosetta Tablet, which was still carefully concealed.[32]

One of Menou's aides conducted Clarke and Cripps to a small tent, 'pitched in a spacious area, or square, near the inner gates of Alexandria, where the parade of the garrison was daily held'.[33] This detail is of crucial importance when comparing the two versions of events as told by Clarke and Turner. Turner later described going to Menou's house; Clarke only ever mentioned a tent.

This tent, small as it was, had been separated into two parts by a curtain, behind which Menou had his harem; giving audience in the outer part, near to the entrance, where there was hardly room enough to stand upright. Having waited some time, during which women's voices were heard in conversation behind the partition, the curtain was suddenly raised, and Jacques Abd'allah made his appearance.[34]

It must have been something of a shock to Clarke finally to come face to face with the man about whom he had heard so much. On the whole, he was not immediately taken with the *général en chef*:

A more grotesque figure can hardly be conceived. He wore a flowered embroidered waistcoat, with flaps almost to his knees, and a coat covered with broad lace. Elevating his whiskered face and double chin, in order to give all imaginable pomp and dignity to his squat corpulent figure, which, covered with finery, much resembled that of a mountebank, he demanded in an imperious tone of voice, '*Que souhaite-t-il, Monsieur Clarke?*'[35]

Considering the raging famine that had left the family of the Imperial Consul to Alexandria with sunken cheeks and clothes hanging from skeletal frames, this description of a rotund Menou suggests he suffered little privation in the siege. If Clarke had noticed it, the miserable troops would have as well.

Clarke explained his search for a passport – which perhaps he did not need, since he had one from Hutchinson, but it was a useful pretext – and was directed to enquire of General René for this document. Cripps looking on, Clarke then tentatively raised the small matter of the Rosetta Stone, and how they might go about copying its inscription.

> At the very mention of this Stone, Menou gave vent to his rage; and, ready to burst with choler, exclaimed, 'You may tell your Commander in Chief he has as much right to make this demand as a highwayman has to ask for my purse! He has a cannon in each of my ears, and another in my mouth; let him take what pleases him. I have a few embroidered saddles, and a tolerable stock of shirts; perhaps he may fancy some of these!'[36]

Clarke replied courteously that he could be the bearer of no such message, but that whatever Menou wished to put in writing he would be more than happy to convey. Clarke and Cripps waited by the tent while General René arranged the passes, and after a few minutes, received a note to Hutchinson from Menou. They took it gladly. This had been the first Menouesque tirade Clarke had witnessed – the following day would see another.

Clarke and Cripps joined Hamilton either on their way out of the city or later that Friday in Hutchinson's tent, learning of the contretemps with the savants and their dire threat. As appalled as Hamilton, and certainly sympathizing with the French in their awkward position, Clarke and Cripps did their utmost to intervene on behalf of the savants with Hutchinson.

As Clarke relates, with Hamilton's help the three devised a temporary solution which appealed to the general:

> Savigny, who has been years in forming the beautiful collection of Natural History for the republic, and which is the first thing of the kind in the world, is in despair. Therefore, we represented it to General Hutchinson, that it would be the best plan to send him to England also, as the most proper person to take care of the collection, and to publish its description, if necessary.[37]

Hutchinson agreed to their proposals. The collections of the savants were saved – thanks to Hamilton, Clarke and Cripps. There would have been no question that the learned societies of England would have welcomed Savigny and his colleagues, not only for their spectacular scientific achievements, but also for their triumph in the face of harrowing adversity, and surviving the malice of Menou and their own military.

It had been a busy two days. In that time Clarke, Cripps and Hamilton had tracked down nearly all the French antiquities and the savants' collections, and uncovered the famed tomb of Alexander – but they had still been denied access to the Rosetta Stone. Hutchinson was running out of patience. He glanced at Menou's note brought by Clarke and Cripps, but his only reply was to tell Menou to stop sending any more messages or letters and 'to obey the conditions proposed for the surrender of Alexandria, upon pain of having not only his own baggage, but that of all the officers of the French army, submitted to an examination'.[38] To suggest that brother officers, be they friend or foe, would not tell the truth and force a search of their belongings was a terrible slight, impugning the honour of Menou and the French army – but Hutchinson cared little for Menou's selective sense of honour or dignity;

he had been playing this game for nearly two weeks. Pride and propriety being what they were, this last threat would be the unkindest cut of all.

That evening, Hutchinson invited Clarke and Cripps to dine. Having supped with General Baird's sepoys near Cairo in the plush silk pavilions of the East India Company, complete with chandeliers and brocaded servants, Clarke was astounded to find Hutchinson's offering to be no more than 'the remaining half of a cold pie, made by one of the privates the day before, containing some lumps of meat encased in a durable crust above an inch thick'. It was apparently the general's daily diet. Over this meal they resolved the next morning to place the general's final threats before the obstinate 'Abdallah Pasha' Menou. They gathered the fresh provisions and horses which Hutchinson had provided, as well as a groom, who presumably joined them on their return to the lion's den. Late that night, they headed back to the darkened walls of Alexandria.

Saturday, 12 September brought an unexpected turn of events. Neither Clarke nor Hamilton recorded the day precisely, but Hamilton visited the savants and conveyed the glad tidings that Savigny was welcome to accompany his collections to England. With some mixed relief, others agreed to do likewise – it was not the best outcome but, for the grateful savants, the news was set to improve even further in the following days, and Hamilton was honourably received as the discerning antiquary and scientist that he was, who had intervened on their behalf with the enemy general. Despite their earlier confrontation, Hamilton, Clarke and Cripps had been the savants' truest allies.

The matter of the stone still loomed. Ready to throw down the gauntlet at Menou's feet, Clarke and Cripps left their house and ventured to the French headquarters once again, making their way to the general's tent near the parade square. This time, Hamilton went with them.

Regardless of their orders from Hutchinson, Clarke and Cripps were civilians who had no legal authority to parley with an enemy officer, let alone agree terms – Hamilton, however, was the skilled ambassadorial official. Perhaps still glowing from his meeting with the savants, he had sufficient experience to know that Menou would not be so gracious. He went inside the tent. Clarke and Cripps waited, and listened:

Mr Hamilton . . . undertook to mention to Menou the result of our visit to Lord Hutchinson.[39] We remained near the outside of the tent; and soon heard the French General's voice elevated as usual, and in strong terms of indignation remonstrating against the injustice of the demands made upon him. The words '*Jamais on n'a pillé le monde!*', diverted us highly, as coming from a leader of plunder and devastation.[40]

Clearly to take antiquities from Menou was far more unjust than the acts perpetrated by the French army in Egypt; Clarke was evidently much amused by Menou's cry of 'Never has the world been so pillaged!' This hypocrisy is even more astonishing in light of the brutal removal of Alexander's tomb from the Mosque of St Athanasius.

Having had little success, Hamilton appeared at the tent entrance. As he did so, the blustering general's final bolt burst through the tent flap after him: he challenged Hutchinson to a duel. '*Nous nous verrons, de bien près – de bien près, je vous assure!*' (We shall see each other, up close – up close, I assure you!)

Menou never did fight his duel. It is doubtful whether Hamilton or Clarke ever passed on the threat to Hutchinson. What was more important to Clarke and Hamilton was that at some point that same day, they received a message: a French officer, a 'Member of the Institute' wished to meet them near the warehouses, in the backstreets of Alexandria.

The British were about to receive the Rosetta Stone.

10

Splendid Plunder

There is no consensus as to what happened over the next few hours on Saturday, 12 September 1801. It is here, outside the tent of General 'Abdallah Pasha' Menou, that the only two detailed accounts of the recovery of the Rosetta Stone, by Clarke and Turner, diverge. This discrepancy caused some minor controversy among the parties concerned several years later, and has created considerable confusion ever since. Saintine and the savants recorded no French account of the recovery of the stone, and neither did Édouard de Villiers du Terrage. Georges Rigault, Menou's biographer, related only matters between the generals and the armies, and makes little mention of antiquities. It is the two existing British accounts that have caused the problem.

In 1812 the Society of Antiquaries of London published volume 16 of its review, *Archaeologia: or, Miscellaneous Tracts Relating to Antiquity*. In the extended section entitled 'An account of the Rosetta Stone, in three languages, which was brought to England in the year 1802', the editors outline how the Society came to possess the stone before the British Museum and their academic efforts to date; as part of this section they published a letter which they had requested from Colonel Turner, a member of the Society and by then promoted to major-general, to relate how he had brought the stone to Britain. Dated 30 May 1810, the letter was read out at a meeting of the Society on 8 June. This letter is often mistakenly attributed to Hamilton.

Turner claimed he went to Menou's house in Alexandria, where he saw the stone for the first time, 'covered with soft cotton cloth, and a double matting'. He continues with a shocking tale of Menou's behaviour:

> When it was understood by the French army that we were to possess the antiquities, the covering of the stone was torn off and it was *thrown upon its face*, and the excellent cases of the rest were broken off.[1]

His comments are clearly an abridgement of events – it had been understood by Menou for nearly two weeks that the British were to confiscate the antiquities, and was by no means a revelation on the very day the stone was recovered. Turner does not specify whether this fit of pique took place in Menou's house, before Turner's eyes or elsewhere, nor who the perpetrator was. After this display he goes on, curiously, to describe Menou as 'civil'. Few would have agreed with him. Turner then apparently left the stone where it was and reported to Hutchinson, who was a good distance off in the British camp.

> When I mentioned the manner in which the stone had been treated to Lord Hutchinson, he gave me a detachment of artillerymen, and an artillery-engine, called, by its powers, a devil-cart with which, that evening, I went to General Menou's house, and carried off the stone, without any injury, but with some difficulty, from the narrow streets, to my house, amid the sarcasms of numbers of French officers and men.[2]

Turner then adds that several of the savants appeared that same evening on the doorstep of his billet in Alexandria and asked to take a plaster-cast of the stone for posterity, which he readily allowed, 'provided the stone should receive no injury'. It is perplexing to hear such concern from a man who had that same day lashed the relic to a gun-carriage.

Turner's statement seems very much that of a man seeking the plaudits of his peers, both as an antiquary and as an officer of the British army dealing with a defeated and hated enemy. He makes references to the care he exercised with the stone, how he carried it away 'without any injury' and admonished the savants to be equally cautious, as if they had never handled it before, and finished by adding that the plaster-cast was made 'leaving the stone well cleared of the printing ink, which it had been covered with to take off several copies to send to France, when it was first discovered'. This comment suggests he felt that Conté and Marcel's brilliant use of the stone as a printing-block had been an act of reckless vandalism, proof of French ineptitude in caring for such a rare artefact. As with many instances of antiquarian cultural imperialism, the implication is that Turner had *rescued* it.

In 1809 Hamilton published *Ægyptiaca: Remarks on Several Parts of Turkey*, his report and memoirs of his time in Egypt, a year before Turner's letter, but he gives no account of the stone's recovery in any great detail. All he says is

> much greater reluctance was manifested by General Menou when the claim was made for the Trilinguar, or Rosetta Stone, nor was it given up without frequent remonstrances on his part.[3]

However, the first detailed account of the recovery of the Rosetta Stone was published much earlier, in 1805,[4] by Edward Daniel Clarke, in a footnote to his dissertation, *The Tomb of Alexander*: Clarke, Cripps and Hamilton attended their secret rendezvous at the warehouses in the quiet backstreets. They were met by a somewhat nervous French officer, apparently an anonymous savant of the Institut d'Égypte. After weeks of nego-tiation, threats, and Menou's *guerre de plume*, this 'gem' of the French collections, according to Clarke, was finally presented. There, covered by mats, most probably in some sort of cart, was the Rosetta Stone:

> This invaluable monument was afterwards delivered up in the streets of Alexandria (Mr Cripps, Mr Hamilton, and myself being present,) by a Member of the Institute, from the ware-house in which they had concealed it, covered with mats. The officer who surrendered it, expressed at the same time his appre-hension, lest the indignation of the French troops should cause its destruction if it remained there . . .[5]

It appears Hutchinson had not been alone in his fears of French troops venting their rage upon the antiquities. Appre-ciating the officer's concerns, Hamilton and Clarke would then have guarded it as best they could; wanting to keep its pres-ence secret they would not have entrusted any passer-by with a message to Hutchinson – using his new passport to repass the gate, young Cripps would most likely have been sent as a runner to give Hutchinson the word: 'We have the Stone.'

> We made this circumstance known to Lord Hutchinson, who gave orders for its immediate removal, and it was given in charge to Colonel Turner under whose care it came safe to England.[6]

This account of 1805, confined first to this footnote in *The Tomb of Alexander*, was later expanded in Clarke's multi-volume work *Travels in Various Countries of Europe, Asia and Africa*, published in 1810. An added clarification was made as if in emphatic response to Turner's conflicting account, read out at the meeting

of the Society of Antiquaries that year and doubtless circu-
lating for some time before as academic gossip:

> The Rosetta Tablet was taken from a warehouse, covered with
> mats, where it had been deposited with Menou's baggage; and
> it was surrendered to us, by a French officer and Member of
> the Institute, in the streets of Alexandria; Mr Cripps, Mr
> Hamilton, and the author, *being the only persons present, to take posses-*
> *sion of it.* The officer appointed to deliver it recommended its
> speedy conveyance to some place of safety, as he could not be
> answerable for the conduct of the French soldiers, if it were
> suffered to remain exposed to their indignation. We made this
> circumstance known to Lord Hutchinson, who gave orders for
> its immediate removal, and it was given in charge to General
> Turner.[7]

According to Clarke, Turner was not present at the hand-
over. More than this, he specifies in both versions of his account
that Turner appeared only once the stone had been delivered
up – Hutchinson had to send for him. It also appears from
Clarke's *Travels* that the hand-over contained a certain ambiguous
detail: the 'officer and Member of the Institute' who brought
them the stone could, by some interpretations, be either one or
two men; but comparison with the obscure footnote in *The Tomb
of Alexander*[8] of 1805, in which the relic is handed over 'by a
Member of the Institute' who is then referred to as 'the officer
who surrendered it', suggests that only one man presented the
stone to Clarke and his companions.

Clarke's more detailed version of events seems more plausible
than Turner's because he shared credit with colleagues, whereas
Turner claims he had seized the Rosetta Stone himself, single-
handed, from the clutches of an enraged enemy; neither Clarke,
Cripps nor Hamilton play any role in his tale whatsoever, while
Clarke credits Turner fulsomely.

Clarke also took pains to portray the French in a positive light where possible; in 1810, when he published the first edition of his *Travels*, this would have been unpopular in some quarters, certainly within Turner's Brigade of Guards. Further, describing the stone's surrender by an officer and 'Member of the Institute' suggests a greater degree of accuracy than does Turner's story of confronting Menou 'in his house' – indeed, Clarke never wrote of Menou's house but made elaborate observations of Menou's *tent*.

Having related the excesses of the French army in Egypt, and without hesitation those of the English, Clarke's writings step beyond the bounds of war between nations and speak of an international respect for the arts and sciences.

> We visited the Members of the French Institute, at the house where they held their sittings, and found them assembled round a long table, inspecting and packing a number of drawings, plans, and maps. We were very politely received, at our entrance, by Le Père, Architect, Director of the Class of Civil Engineers . . . We assured them, that although our business in Alexandria related to the literary acquisitions made for their nation by their army in Egypt, it had nothing whatsoever to do with the private collections or journals of individuals; and therefore we hoped they would allow us to compare notes with them upon certain points of observation, in which we might be mutually interested.[9]

However, the savants felt compelled in this instance to decline this exchange, fearing that any further revelations might lead to yet more demands from Hutchinson. Clarke, though saddened, understood – once again, war had intervened. There is certainly no question that Clarke, Cripps and Hamilton were welcome after the three had secured the safety of the natural history collections – Saintine, Marcel and Reybaud recorded how Hamilton later paid a personal call, welcomed as one who would appreciate what they had gathered 'from the four corners of Egypt':

> Later, this moment of error [the attempted confiscation of collections] was nobly rectified . . . Reconciled with our savants, Hamilton was allowed then to visit their rich personal collections; and he was silent, filled with wonder at what passed beneath his gaze.[10]

Although Clarke later assumes it was the case, it is by no means certain that Menou had ordered the hand-over of the Rosetta Stone to the British at all, or was even aware of it. Had he sanctioned it, Turner's story of his intemperate vandalism makes little sense, but Clarke's version could still stand: crushed, Menou could reluctantly have ordered the stone to be removed from the warehouse and handed over – but, also possible, he might have wanted to wash his hands of its surrender and blame the act on treacherous subordinates, as he had done with his defeat at Canopus. Such seemed to be his style.

There is one piece of evidence that could suggest the stone was handed over without Menou's knowledge. According to Clarke, they received the stone on Saturday the 12th.[11] In a letter to Hutchinson dated the 13th, Menou expressed his exasperation for the last time, pleading again to retain Friant's Roman statues and the Rosetta Stone. He added laconically that Hamilton had the goodness not to take Menou's personal copies of the Koran even though it was an 'Arab manuscript' – ('As to Arab manuscripts . . . you know very well, I say, that when you buy an Arab book in Egypt it is always a manuscript, because no printing-presses exist.' Despite his gross faults, most would admit that Menou was not without some wit.) This final blast in the *guerre de plume* must surely decide Menou the winner of the contest:

I finish my last letter to you, praying that I may have persuaded, etc. P.-S. – Messrs Hamilton and Turner are free to do all you have ordered them. I have just learned this moment that several of our collection-makers wish to follow their seeds, minerals, birds, butterflies or reptiles wherever you direct their crates. I do not know if they wish themselves stuffed for the purpose, but I can assure you that if the fancy should take them, I shall not prevent it.[12]

With this parting shot, *général en chef* Jacques-François Abdallah Menou, Baron de Boussay, brought the matter to an end. Yet his continued protestations about the antiquities and his hopes that he may have persuaded Hutchinson seem to have come too late. His postscript that Hamilton and Turner may do as Hutchinson ordered suggests that, as yet, he had no idea that Hamilton, Turner and Clarke had already done just that the day before, on the 12th, and carried off his beloved Rosetta Stone on a devil-cart.

If this is the case, then it must follow that the 'French officer and Member of the Institute' had acted without Menou's orders. This is not altogether impossible. The savants had only just heard that their collections were safe and would not be parted from them. Since they would have learned from Le Roy that Clarke, Hamilton and Turner had found the tomb of Alexander, and seen the other antiquities in the warehouses, as well as Friant's Roman statues, the only matter delaying the relief of Alexandria and their return to Europe was the surrender of the Rosetta Stone.

After their treatment at Menou's hands, it is hardly surprising that they should bear little personal loyalty to him or, worse, might have suspected that the general would not, as he declared in his letters to the British, hand over the stone to the museum authorities in Paris upon his return to France. It had been stored, after all, in his personal baggage. The savants would have had no guarantee that Menou's attachment to the stone might not have led it, however temporarily, to the grand foyer of his ancestral home, his only success from the ruins of the Egypt campaign.

In defence of Menou, judging by the bureaucratic and officious manner he displayed throughout his command in Egypt, the idea that he might try to appropriate 'government property' or behave in any way that might compromise himself personally, would be most unlikely and, perhaps, unjust to his memory. Whether the savants in Alexandria would have been prepared to grant him such benefit of the doubt is another matter. If they had agreed to do this, recognizing that the British would not yield and that they themselves were bound for England, the sacrifice of the stone for the sake of scholarship to the three English antiquaries, Clarke, Cripps and Hamilton, would have been far preferable than waiting for the procrastinating Menou to make up his mind. The anonymous savant was doubtless happier handing the stone to three distinguished scholars who had intervened on their behalf with Hutchinson, than to the brute British soldiery of Colonel Turner. In which case it would seem the Rosetta Stone was handed over almost in an act of preservation, rather than seized in an aggressive act of victory.

The identity of the 'Member of the Institute' is another matter. Clarke referred to him as an officer, and it is possible that he was, like Bouchard, an army officer in the technical branch of the engineers and part of the Commission. It seems strangely fitting that the Rosetta Stone was both discovered and handed over by a man of the same stamp. Clarke clearly respected his privacy – the academic future in France of the man who gave up the Rosetta Stone to the British would have been more than tarnished. Doubtless for this reason, as he did originally with Rosetti and the merchant of Alexandria, Clarke maintained the anonymity of this mysterious savant.

* * *

In his account of May 1810, Turner says nothing of Clarke, Cripps or Hamilton's part in the stone's recovery, nor of their involvement in the acquisition of any of the other antiquities – the picture he paints is of his personal achievement with regular bows to General, then Lord, Hutchinson. There is some suggestion that the Society of Antiquaries was curious about his account, with which they would certainly have become familiar in the time since the stone's arrival in Britain eight years earlier. This curiosity might have been sparked by one of the Society's events: they were to be presented with a copy of William Richard Hamilton's 1809 publication, *Ægyptiaca*. As we have seen, Hamilton does not confirm Turner's version of events in this work. In the flyleaf of the volume was an intriguing inscription:

> Presented to the Society of Antiquaries of London
> By the author, 31ˢᵗ May 1810

Turner's statement is dated 30 May 1810 – the day before Hamilton presented the book. The question arises whether the Society, equally familiar with Hamilton's account since the previous year, asked Turner to clarify those points in Hamilton's work that reveal little detail and in fact do not mention Turner by name anywhere. This should not be construed as necessarily suspicious: one could argue that Hamilton's lack of detail regarding the antiquities is not surprising since his book deals chiefly with the political events of the time; but it could also suggest that the diplomatic Hamilton, aware too of Clarke's version of the hand-over, wished to remain on neutral ground – consequently, corroboration of Turner's story does not appear. It is possible that members of the Society of Antiquaries, baffled by this discrepancy, pressed for Turner's clarification in the days surrounding the presentation of Hamilton's book.

Clarke verifies that Colonel Turner was called to take charge of the stone, and there should be little doubt he arrived with his squad of artillerymen and devil-cart to carry it away under armed escort.[13] Given the situation, this would have been imperative – after so long a struggle they had no intention of losing it to the blows of an angry mob of French soldiers. Turner was clearly happy to undertake this task and describes it as an action performed with great satisfaction by his men. Perhaps too, as he suggests, he had a preliminary interview with Menou, not in the general's tent by the inner gate but in the official house which Menou, as commander-in-chief, would have warranted; in that interview he might well have seen some packing crates smashed in Menou's anger. But had he seen the Rosetta Stone in Menou's house, it is doubtful he would have left it in order to report to Hutchinson. Instead, surely Turner would have called on a squad of men – any men – from the recently occupied outer defences perhaps, to take it away that very instant.

The only possibility for the two stories of Clarke and Turner to converge comes when Clarke, Cripps and Hamilton 'conveyed it to a place of safety' – they might have taken it to Menou's house, where Turner later called to collect it. But Clarke, who described his meetings with Menou in some detail, does not mention this, and neither would it make sense for them effectively to return the stone to Menou, who had been the chief obstacle in acquiring the relic – they would have wanted to keep it as far from him as possible.

Turner's account, though vague in places, should not necessarily be interpreted as a deliberate falsification, but possibly one where the details of the matter carried little importance for a consummate soldier who had lost patience with Menou's evasions. He tries very much to emphasize that this was a success for the British army and no one else, although none of the antiquities would have been secured without the help of the scholars Clarke, Cripps and Hamilton. Turner had been in a difficult position. As a member of the Society of Antiquaries, at the forefront of the expedition, he might have seen his chief task to be the liberation of the Rosetta Stone and all other relics plundered by an enemy, as he saw it, for their own gratification. Consequently, his account must be questioned closely and contrasted with that of Edward Daniel Clarke, which ascribes justifiable credit to the French savants who had cared so well for the precious artefact.

As soon as the antiquities had been recovered and accounted for, there was little delay in evacuating the French, the first regiment of which marched out with full honours on Monday, 14 September. Over the following days the armed camps of Alexandria were in a state of celebratory uproar:

> Even in the British camp, might be seen a French officer joining in conviviality with our troops; drinking toasts for the health of King George, the success of the capitulation, and a speedy deliverance from the government of Menou.[14]

The Turks, however, were not quite as jubilant as the French or British. The French ships in the harbour, *L'Égyptienne*, *La Justice* and numerous others, including Clarke's 'crazy vessel' *La Cause*, were considered prizes, and worth specific sums of money to be divided between those men who had shared in their capture – it is uncertain how precisely this was done in this instance, but *La Cause* had been put down as a prize for the Turkish Kapudan Pasha, Hassan.

When Hassan Pasha learned that the great green sarcophagus tomb of Alexander had once been aboard, and had since been removed by Colonel Turner, he was infuriated. It was a priceless relic and would have conferred more honour to its saviour than any other piece in Alexandria. Turner and Hamilton had to use all their powers of persuasion, and possibly the copious purse of His Majesty's Government, to loosen the Pasha's hold on the item. The Kapudan Pasha, as the British learned later, was not a man to be denied.

High Admiral of the Turkish fleet, the pasha had promised Clarke and Cripps passage on a Turkish frigate on the next leg of their journey to Greece. They left Alexandria for his camp to confirm these arrangements but, instead, were asked by the pasha whether they could convey a query to Rear Admiral Sir Richard Bickerton on HMS *Madras*: the Kapudan Pasha wanted permission to allow the Turkish ships to enter Alexandria harbour before the British. Clarke deduced this was to be the Sublime Porte's method of paying the Greek and Turkish 'galeongies' waiting on the edge of the harbour – by way of Alexandrian plunder.

Obliged to the pasha for their forthcoming free passage, Clarke felt he could hardly refuse to bear his message, and made the laborious journey back to the city and out to Sir Richard aboard the *Madras*. Bickerton denied permission to the pasha, annoyed that the Turkish admiral persisted in asking for it, and threatened to sink any Turkish vessel moving in before the town was fully surrendered and occupied.

Clarke and Cripps hurried back to the pasha, fearing that, with this news, they would forfeit their promised berths. Colonel Wilson portrayed the Kapudan Pasha as an honourable nobleman, possessed of natural majesty, and one who displayed concern for all. Clarke, however, did not believe he could be trusted, and his description varies significantly from Wilson's. He would later prove quite correct in his estimation. They returned to his tent and found the pasha's fool larking on the cushions to the merriment of sundry advisers:

This unusual facetiousness on the part of the Turks was soon put to flight by the arrival of the great man himself, with his Interpreter; who no sooner heard the answer to his message, than, acting with much less dignity than his buffoon, he *spat* on the ground, stamped, and, abruptly quitting the tent, hurried on board a covered boat upon the lake, in which he was accustomed to pass the night, and made his appearance no more on that evening.[15]

Frustrated twice, first over the tomb of Alexander, and now over the plunder for his naval forces, the Kapudan Pasha would not have been well disposed to the English for some time.

Over the next few weeks the French were quickly evacuated – Menou had demanded to take one of his captured frigates to convey himself to France but was refused. The savants set sail, but not for England. Perhaps to simplify operations, or as a gesture of sympathy, Hutchinson had relented still further, and rather than convey them to Britain, had allowed the savants to take their natural history collections, drawings, journals and plans home to France. It was a final note of humanity to end such a protracted and otherwise unhappy association.

The problem then came of how best to despatch the antiquities to safety in England, for ever out of the reach of both the French army and possibly Hassan Kapudan Pasha himself.

In the 1950s a folio of private papers and journals was found by the descendants of Major T. Marmaduke Wybourn of the Royal Marines. Among these papers, was a list proudly entitled 'Relicts bro.ᵗ down from Egypt & now in the British Museum, by me, in the Madras, 50 guns'. The list is something of a relic in itself, and raised certain questions. Item 1 is the famous 'tomb of Alexander' described in the list as a sarcophagus 'from the Mosque of St Athanasius'; further down the list, Item 8 seems even more familiar:

> 8. *A stone with three inscriptions, hieroglyphics, Gothic and Greek, black granite from Rosetta.*

At first glance the list appears to be an inventory or cargo manifest. In the hands of a Royal Marine officer this would be the most likely explanation. Marines had a number of duties aboard ships of the Royal Navy; they were to maintain security, act as amphibious infantry, guard prisoners and, in certain circumstances, watch over precious cargo. Nor was Wybourn any ordinary officer: he was the protégé of the Earl Spencer, First Lord of the Admiralty, and hero of a remarkable action in Helder Town during the Holland campaign two years earlier – in this he had led a bayonet charge of seventy-five Marines against several hundred French infantry, putting the enemy to flight and saving the inhabitants of the town. Rear Admiral Sir Richard Bickerton had a very special consideration for him and included him on a diplomatic excursion to meet the Kapudan Pasha. It would not have been surprising that such an important cargo should be consigned to the care of so distinguished a junior officer.

However, Turner wrote in his letter to the Society of Antiquaries that Item 8, the Rosetta Stone, had not been loaded with the other antiquities into the belly of HMS *Madras*.[16] Instead, he took it aboard the captured French frigate *L'Égyptienne*. *L'Égyptienne* was a fine prize and still seaworthy; she was to transport many officers and men back to England after the successful campaign, among them General Hutchinson and his staff. In search of an explanation and to authenticate the list, it was presented to the British Museum. The museum authorities believe Wybourn's list to be a translated copy, almost verbatim, of the list made by Fourier for Turner, used to collate the treasures within Alexandria.

The objects on Wybourn's English list are in much the same order as on Fourier's, with similar descriptions. It would have been common sense to use the same list as a cargo manifest, and it has been suggested there were possibly several of these lists passed round to quartermasters and men supervising the loading of the *Madras* in October and November of 1801. It might also have been the official ship's copy for the *Madras*, possibly given to Rear Admiral Bickerton, or to Wybourn for his records as the Marine officer in charge of a valuable cargo. If it were such a manifest the question remains why Item 8 had not been stricken out, and thereafter added to the list of *L'Égyptienne*.

Once the British had at last secured the forts and the city of Alexandria, the Turkish and Greek sailors among the Kapudan Pasha's fleet would have come ashore and begun looting, albeit under the watchful eyes of their British 'allies'. News of the Rosetta Stone's whereabouts and value would certainly have travelled. It is not beyond the realms of possibility that the loading of the ships at the dockside was done in such a way as to confuse the eye and deceive any onlookers bent on rich pickings further out to sea. It is also not inconceivable that the Kapudan Pasha, denied Alexander's tomb by the British, denied the honour of first entry to the city and fresh plunder for his men, might have had designs on the prized tablet himself – with the Rosetta Stone in his possession he would have had a sufficiently strong hand to negotiate an exchange for the tomb.

With unmarked crates swinging from the overhead booms of British and French ships, captured Venetian men o'war and Greek merchantmen, each being loaded with supplies, munitions or ancient relics, it would have been virtually impossible to establish the true location of the Rosetta Stone – especially as an easily available list claimed it was to be loaded on to the wrong vessel. However, Turner mentions no such deception scheme, though a word to the loadmasters on the quay to include the three-quarter-ton crate with officers' baggage as anonymously as possible would have been a simple matter:

Having seen the other remains of ancient Egyptian sculpture sent on board the Admiral, Sir Richard Bickerton's ship, the Madras, who kindly gave every possible assistance, I embarked with the Rosetta Stone, determined to share its fate, on board the Egyptienne frigate, taken in the harbour of Alexandria.[17]

Proof of this can be found in the ship's logs, which reveal that *Madras* was certainly heaving with relics, some loaded by the transport HMS *Ann*:

HMS MADRAS

Thursday 29th October 1801

Mod[r]. Breezes & Pleas[t]. W[r]. People Emp[d]. Stowing Cleopatra's Bath in the Main Hold. Broach'd a Cask of Pork N°358 . . .

Friday 30th October 1801

. . . People Empld. Pumping Water aft in the Main Hold to receive another Bath. AM Hot & Sultry W[r]. Several Sail in the Offing . . .

Saturday 31st October 1801

Mod[r]. & clear W[r]. Rec'd 19 Casks of Pork from the ANN transport at 6 the Launch came alongside with the Bath and several large pieces of Statues . . .[18]

The Rosetta Stone was not among them: *L'Égyptienne* set sail for Malta long before the *Madras* and Admiralty records confirm she arrived in Portsmouth while *Madras* was still being overhauled for repairs on Malta. *L'Égyptienne*'s voyage was not without incident; had there been a deliberate effort to conceal the stone's true location it could possibly have failed. It is a matter of record that when *L'Égyptienne* set sail for Malta, she was followed, as the ship's log of HMS *Madras* reveals:

HMS MADRAS

Saturday 7 November
Mod^r. & Fair W^r . . . AM D^o We made the Signal for all Midshipmen
Sailed hence HMS LA EGYPTIAN . . . Recd. Per *Genn* 3 Leag^{rs}.
6 Butts 7 Punch^{ns} & 5 Pipes of Water. Sailed Hence a Turkish Man
of War . . .[19]

This Turkish warship was not an escort provided by the
Kapudan Pasha – Captain Stevenson of the *L'Égyptienne* kept
a wary eye on the vessel, caring little for her proximity. If
there had been a clumsy plan of the Kapudan Pasha to intercept the Rosetta Stone and delay the *L'Égyptienne*, it was
executed in plain view and nearly succeeded, as Stevenson
recorded himself:

HMS L'EGYPTIENNE

7 November
PM light and inclining to calm came on board Genl. Hutchinson
and suit ½ past 7 weighed and made sail out of the harbour. Owing
to the Ship not Wearing Quick ran on board a Turkish line of
Battle Ship which carried away our Spritsailyard. Bumpkin.[20]

What with only a partly fitted-out prize ship which did not
'wear quick', filled with a live lumber cargo of British and French
soldiers, as well as the commander-in-chief and his entourage,
Stevenson could well have done without the embarrassment of
this very public collision – if it were indeed a simple accident.
Had it been otherwise, *L'Égyptienne* escaped relatively lightly.

HMS *L'Égyptienne* was recorded as arriving at Malta on the
23rd whereupon Captain Charles Ogle took command and sailed
her to England on the 25th, arriving in Portsmouth in February
1802. According to Turner, *L'Égyptienne* sailed round the Kent

coast, and carried the Rosetta Stone up the River Thames:

> When the ship came around at Deptford, it was put in a boat
> and landed at the Custom-house; and Lord Buckinghamshire,
> the then Secretary of State, acceded to my request, and permitted
> it to remain in the apartments of the Society of Antiquaries
> previous to its deposit in the British Museum.[21]

The editors of volume 16 of *Archaeologia* prefaced Turner's
account with details of a surprise delivery within several weeks
of *L'Égyptienne*'s arrival:

> On the eleventh of March, in the year 1802, the Society of
> Antiquaries received a letter from Granville Penn, Esq., informing
> them that by the desire of Lord Hobart, he had forwarded two
> cases for the inspection of the Society, and to remain in their
> custody till further directions for the removal of them to the
> British Museum.[22]

One of the cases contained the Rosetta Stone. It was displayed
within the halls of the Society of Antiquaries of London (at
the time located in Somerset House), until its formal donation
to the British Museum, along with the other antiquities, in June
that same year. Other than a brief trip to Paris 170 years later,
it has stayed there ever since. Turner, the veteran soldier of the
3rd Foot Guards, pronounced it

> a proud trophy of the arms of Britain (I could say *spolia opima*[23]),
> not plundered from defenceless inhabitants, but nobly acquired
> by the fortune of war.[24]

So the 'splendid plunder' was suitably marked. After the
savants' careful preservation of the stone from bombardment,
destruction and theft, and Turner's own concerns about the

ravages of ink and plaster of Paris, the left side of this 2,000-year-old relic was daubed with the legend 'CAPTURED IN EGYPT BY THE BRITISH ARMY 1801' and on the right, 'PRESENTED BY KING GEORGE III'. These are still visible today.

At the time, the most suitable epilogue to the tale of the stone's discovery, its travails, concealment and eventual hand-over must have been the words of the man who orchestrated its acquisition, William Richard Hamilton. His remarks, merely a footnote in his *Aegyptiaca* of 1809, would echo for years to come:

> The Trilinguar Stone, which was found by the French army at Rosetta . . . is now one of the most interesting of the monuments deposited in the British Museum. Hitherto, however, all attempts to decipher the hieroglyphics or Coptic inscriptions by the help of the Greek translation have proved fruitless.[25]

It stood, a mute block of stone, promising everything to its captors, but yielding little. Its decipherment would be another struggle altogether.

11

The Key

Egypt herself continued to suffer after the defeat of the Armée de l'Orient. Clarke and Cripps left Alexandria on Wednesday, 16 September, with the compliments of the Kapudan Pasha, 'who had regained his composure', though even with such apparent civility, Clarke still did not trust him. His fears were well founded: 'The Capudan Pasha was a person upon whom no reliance could be placed, although he had not then manifested all the atrocity of his character.'[1] This atrocity was the finely orchestrated mass-murder of the heads of the Mameluke leadership, known as the Murder of the Beys.

The Kapudan Pasha contrived to lure the beys of Cairo, including the eminent Kashif, to visit him at his camp near Alexandria in late September, getting them into boats on the vast inland lake, heading to the walled city for a pleasure-trip – thus separating the Mamelukes from their personal body-guard, which had been sent on ahead. Minutes after the small flotilla set off across the water, a messenger rowed out to them with an urgent despatch from Constantinople. The pasha then play-acted an entire scene for the beys, opening the letter, supposedly distressed at the interruption, but sadly regretting that he must answer the message immediately. He promised to catch them up shortly, and was taken back to shore. The Mamelukes were now in the hands of the pasha's own men – who were hired killers.

The boat carrying the beys changed course. Instead of heading westward for Alexandria, it slowly turned east, towards the moored anchor-ropes of the fleet lines in Aboukir Bay and the grand Turkish battleship, the *Sultan Selim I*. Recognizing at once what was happening, the Mamelukes cried out in alarm, whereupon the pasha's men in the escort boats surrounded them and opened fire at point-blank range. The blast of gunshots mingling with their shrieks echoed across the lake as the attackers set upon the survivors with scimitars. In all only two were left alive, the murder having taken place under the horrified gaze of the British on the far shore. Colonel Squire witnessed the entire episode. He wrote to his brother:

> Sir J. (now Lord) Hutchinson … immediately waited upon the Pasha at the head of his troops, and, after calling him, to his face, *liar, coward, villain, assassin*, and using every menace and other opprobrious expression until the mean traitor burst into tears.[2]

The same plot was tried at Cairo by the aged Grand Vizier, Yussuf. Hutchinson hurled a similar thunderbolt to the capital declaring that unless the Turks released the captured beys immediately, the British army would march on Cairo and destroy the vizier's forces. The British had agreed to cooperate with the Mamelukes and, in their capacity as the beys' protectors, Hutchinson meant it. Squire realized that this threatened their uneasy alliance with the Sublime Porte, but wrote with emphasis:

> Whatever may have been the policy of England, OUR GENERAL HAS CONDUCTED HIMSELF WITH HONOUR AND PROPRIETY. He could not have remained an inactive spectator of such base transactions.[3]

The great falling-out with the British was another example of the shifting alliances continually at play in this period – only a short while later, the sultan allied himself once more with France, as Squire said, 'as if the invasion of Egypt were virtually forgotten'.

Clarke and Cripps were spared this last sour taste of the Egypt campaign, having departed only several days before. They eventually made their way, not without incident, to Rhodes and the islands of Greece. Their adventures, certainly not over, had been wearying; as Clarke wrote to Otter:

> Ah! Why did fate his steps decoy
> In stormy paths to roam,
> Remote from all congenial joy!
> Oh take the wanderer home![4]

Having moved on to Greece, Clarke missed an unusual ceremony involving the tomb of Alexander, his favourite piece of sculpture. Some time later, the promoted General Turner wrote a letter of explanation to a colleague of Clarke's relating the scene as he had heard it himself. Just before its departure in late November, HMS *Madras* had received an official visit – the Kapudan Pasha had gone aboard with his retinue and each knelt before the sarcophagus:

> the Capitano Bey, with his suite and many Turks of distinction . . . all solemnly touched the Tomb with their tongues. The privilege to render this act of adoration from the *Iman* of the Mosque, by a contribution of six *paras* or *medins*, for each individual. On taking his leave, the Capitano Bey declared, that Providence would never suffer the Tomb, in our hands, to go safe to England.[5]

Lieutenant Wybourn of the Royal Marines was there as well, and lived to recount the almost tragic fate of the statuary which they had acquired with such difficulty. En route to Malta, the *Madras* nearly sank as she was hit by a sudden violent storm and kept from their island destination for weeks: 'our leak increased from one to four feet of water in an hour',[6] he wrote, despite pumps which could drain three tons of water per minute. The superstitious sailors were terrified and the Inspector General was 'melancholy with fear' at the dark words of the pasha. It was possibly the first incidence of a 'Curse of the Pharaohs'. They reached Malta after twenty-one days.

Nevertheless, in spite of the Turks' worship of the great green sarcophagus, it was later labelled that of Nectanebo III, much to Clarke's heartfelt disappointment. It still bears this description today – though recent research has gone some way in suggesting the sarcophagus was also used for the remains of Alexander the Great.[7] It is immediately obvious in the collection in the British Museum, as Clarke said, for its astonishing size and 'beautiful green colour'.

Clarke and Cripps had no more scruple than did others of their day with regard to collecting antiquities; Clarke's concern seems to have been that pieces were treated with the respect and care they deserved. Possibly for this reason he maintained an objective attitude to the French savants throughout his time in Alexandria:

> we experienced from all of them that urbanity, which, in despite of the impressions and prejudices caused by the consequences of hostility, and the lawless deeds of a promiscuous soldiery during the ravages of war, must yet be considered as the distinguishing characteristic of the French people, in their conduct even towards their enemies.[8]

But in his work on the tomb of Alexander, he berates the French army for removing the sarcophagus from the Mosque of St Athanasius, and sees its place in the British Museum as the result of fortune, and no more; Alexandria and Egypt were in the grip of a military empire, its precious antiquities having survived only out of good luck. Much as he decried the removal of the sarcophagus from the mosque in Alexandria, he had this to say about one particularly famous episode on the Acropolis of Athens, the tremors from which still reverberate today:

> In this satisfaction I must lament the plan pursued by the agents of Lord Elgin in this place. Under pretence of *rescuing* the arts from the hands of the Turks they are pulling down temples that have withstood the injuries of time and war, and barbarians for ages, to adorn a miserable Scotch villa [Elgin's home]. The fine bas-reliefs of the Parthenon are embarking for Constantinople, and Minerva blushes for the asylum to which her altars are to be conveyed.[9]

Clearly there was a difference between preserving relics and cutting them from temple pediments. Watching the work in Athens, it is said the faces of European onlookers streamed with tears. In a footnote to the letter above, William Otter wrote happily:

> It is pleasing to reflect that one ground of Dr. Clarke's lamentation has proved to be erroneous; and whatever difference of opinion may still exist with respect to the propriety of the spoliation here deprecated, there are few, we believe, who are not disposed to rejoice, that the fruits of it are now permanently deposited in the British Museum.[10]

Clarke held no particular affection for Elgin and has been accused of spreading defamatory remarks about the earl to Lord

Byron, who also took against this 'rescue' of the Acropolis. Although, as Otter points out, the relics were saved from languishing in Lord Elgin's Scottish home, there were, and still are, a significant number who did not rejoice at their removal to London.

Upon their return, Clarke and Cripps went their separate ways to pursue their antiquarian interests and were honoured for their achievements. Each married, Cripps settling in Sussex, Clarke remaining in Cambridgeshire and later moving to Essex to take up the post of vicar in a parish, where he continued his own studies in mineralogy. His great work, *Travels in Various Countries of Europe, Asia and Africa*, was very popular; printed between the years 1810 and 1823, it went through several editions, the final volume published posthumously by Clarke's friend, the Reverend Robert Walpole.

Jacques-François Abdallah Menou, Baron de Boussay, erstwhile *général en chef* of the Armée de l'Orient, was not pilloried in the quads of the Paris Academies upon his return to France for having 'lost' the expedition antiquities to the British. Instead, he was admitted to the Légion d'honneur and in 1802 appointed Governor of the Piedmont region of Italy by Bonaparte, who was still very much aware of Menou's capabilities as an administrator. Menou went on to become Governor of Tuscany and later of Venice, raised to the honour of Comte de l'Empire in 1808, taking the title Comte de Menou. The 'eccentric lunatic' of Marmont's description died in 1810, his correspondence with Hutchinson a unique record of this moment in military history, his memory for ever linked to the great expedition to the Nile and the Rosetta Stone.

General Hutchinson was made Baron Hutchinson of Alexandria for his victory; he later succeeded his brother as the 2nd Earl of Donoughmore. Colonel Turner continued to produce papers for the Society of Antiquaries, was later knighted, and rose through the senior ranks to general, serving a term as

Lieutenant Governor of Jersey and later as Governor of Bermuda before being appointed Groom of the Bedchamber to the Royal Household. He finished his days at his home in Gorey, on the island of Jersey. He died, immortalized by his account of the recovery of the Rosetta Stone in Alexandria, the man who had returned the 'proud trophy' to England.

William Richard Hamilton went on to explore Egypt with Colonel Leake, and later performed much the same service in the liberation of Italy as he did in Alexandria – returning those treasures taken by the defeated French since their conquest by Bonaparte. His work *Ægyptiaca, or Remarks on Several Parts of Turkey* was published in 1809; intended to be the first of two parts it was never followed by a second volume. Hamilton's career continued in the civil service and he became involved in the Elgin petition regarding the Parthenon Marbles – it is widely supposed it was he who wrote an anonymous defence of his former employer's actions.

Examining the chronology of events of August and September 1801, there can be little doubt that, without Hamilton's intervention in Alexandria, the Rosetta Stone and the Egyptian artefacts currently in the British Museum would have sailed for France and might possibly be standing in the Louvre today. Whether the one is more suitable than the other is another matter.

With the defeat of the French in Egypt, the Treaty of Amiens was signed in May 1802, and peace temporarily blanketed Europe. Many British scholars took this opportunity to visit Paris and acquaint themselves with the latest academic developments, having heard reports of the savants' return.

The first public mention of the Rosetta Stone in England was made in the *Gentleman's Magazine*, a monthly paper covering subjects from horticulture and architecture to antiquarianism, with a special news and intelligence section, which contained despatches from fighting officers in the field. In volume 71, for 1801, the following was reported, with reasonable accuracy, by the editors:

> General Dugua, lately returned from the Egyptian expedition, brought home two copies of a remarkable inscription found on a piece of black and extremely fine-grained granite . . . The rare and valuable collections of plants, medals etc. etc. made by the French Sçavans with so much toil and care in Egypt, having been captured by the English army, will no doubt be brought to this country by General Lord Hutchinson. This is what Virgil would have said, 'Sic vos non vobis'.[11]

Having reached Britain, the Rosetta Stone was not hoarded by the Society of Antiquaries or the British Museum. The first British work on its inscription was begun by the Reverend Stephen Weston, a member of the Society, who presented numerous papers over the years. In April 1802, within a month of the stone's arrival, he gave a brief translation of the Greek inscription. In July 1802 four plaster-casts were made of the relic, one copy sent to the universities of Oxford, Cambridge, Edinburgh and Dublin, and a facsimile engraving of the Greek inscription made for numerous learned bodies across the world listed by the Society in *Archaeologia* 16: the Vatican, Cardinal Borgia in Rome, the Imperial Society at St Petersburg, and academies, universities and libraries in Venice, Berlin, Copenhagen, Uppsala, Madrid, Lisbon, Leiden and Philadelphia. A copy was also sent to the National Institute library in Paris.

The remaining antiquities recovered from the French made slow progress to England and eventually came to rest at the British Museum in June 1802. As reported in the *Gentleman's Magazine*, the streets of London's Bloomsbury were witness to an astonishing sight as the antiquities were delivered:

The various Egyptian antiquities collected by the French army and since become the property of the conquerors have been conveyed to the British Museum and may be seen in the outer court of that building. Many of them were so extremely massive that it was found necessary to make wooden frames for them.[12]

The writer then describes the pieces with great interest, remarking on 'a hand clenched, the statue belonging to which must have been 150 feet high' and finishes with 'the smallest bath weighs about 11 tons and there were 11 horses to draw it to the Museum . . . the whole weight of the collection is calculated at about 50 tons.'[13] Writing in 1805, Clarke seemed disappointed by the display:

[The Egyptian antiquities] were placed in the open court of the British Museum, and considered as curious but unimportant monuments of Egyptian art, glorious to the nation as trophies of its valour, but whose dark and mystic legends, impervious to modern inquiry, excited despair rather than hope of explanation.[14]

This despair continued for some time. The Society had spread its news far and wide, but evidently not far enough for those amateur scholars not privy to such releases of information. In August 1802 the *Gentleman's Magazine* once again raised its voice in comment, to report French progress: the brilliant linguist Silvestre de Sacy had been at work on the stone since the introduction of those first copies brought to France by Dugua in 1800, and had apparently found the name 'Alexander', unusually with a capital, in the fourth line of Greek and in the third line of the 'Egyptian' text. The writer grimly looked forward to a full facsimile of the inscription to be produced by the Society of Antiquaries, and ends on a competitive note:

I have only to observe on the subject that the Frenchman has undertaken the explanation of the most difficult inscription before the English Literati are in possession of a single copy of the easiest.[15]

With the advent of peace, a new war seemed to have broken out: the race to solve the riddle of the stone.

Having dispersed what they could around the world, the Society seemed aggrieved that they received no response or contribution on the inscriptions in return – the Reverend Weston therefore read his own more lengthy translation to the gathered members of the Society on 4 November 1802. However, a week later, the secretary received a letter written in French, accompanied by a Latin version of the Greek inscription, 'with a considerable number of learned remarks thereon, from Professor Christian Gotlob Heyne, of the University of Göttingen'.

It was not precisely the same as that of Weston, but such was the thirst for information that the Society generously printed both in full. However, in December 1802 the first full English translation of the Greek inscription was published by Plumptre, and printed in the *Gentleman's Magazine*.[16] The remaining work by the Society involved a contribution in December by Taylor Combe, Keeper at the British Museum, on the Memphis Decree itself, and Reverend Weston and Professor Porson's efforts on the missing section from the broken bottom right corner of the Greek inscription, in the New Year of 1803. In summing up their efforts in *Archaeologia* 16, the editors write with some lament:

Seven years having now elapsed since the receipt of the last communication to the Society on this subject, there is little reason to expect that any further information should be received.[17]

In 1812, when this was written, they could not have anticipated the work of Thomas Young and a certain young linguist
across the Channel, Jean-François Champollion.

The story of the decipherment of hieroglyphs has been dominated largely by two key figures, Thomas Young and
Jean-François Champollion.[18] Consequently it has often been
portrayed as a bitter Anglo-French academic conflict. This is a
simplistic view and obscures the efforts of other notable scholars
in Europe.

Initial work focused on the Greek inscription, considered 'the
easiest' by the correspondent in the *Gentleman's Magazine*. The
first translation of the Greek performed outside Egypt was
accomplished by Citizen Ameillion of the Institute in Paris,
using the copies brought by General Dugua who had left Egypt
in the spring of 1800. On 6 January 1801, Ameillion presented
his Institute colleagues with his version of the Greek text and
later accompanied it with a Latin translation comparable to
that of Heyne of Göttingen, who sent his version to the Society
of Antiquaries in London in 1802. It was Ameillion who cast
doubt on the accuracy of the engraving sent out by the Society.
When he compared it to the copies of the stone taken by Marcel
and Conté in Cairo, there were clearly certain differences – to
the extent that the engraver, so Ameillion suggested, had 'tidied'
some of the Greek characters. As a result he apparently worked
from the original copies made by the savants of the Institut
d'Égypte.

The first scholars to make strides with the demotic inscription were the famous orientalist and linguist Baron Antoine
Isaac Silvestre de Sacy,[19] who had been asked by the Minister
of the Interior to study the stone, and the Swedish diplomat
and orientalist Johann Åkerblad.[20] The popular fascination with
hieroglyphs has tended to overshadow the importance of the
demotic text on the Rosetta Stone, which provided immensely

valuable information. As Marcel and Raige had recognized in Cairo in 1799, the demotic inscription was complete – more so even than the Greek – and its study suffered no prejudicial associations with symbology, which continued to plague the early work on hieroglyphs.

De Sacy made the first great breakthrough. Unlike Marcel and Raige in 1799, who had made their attempt by means of geometry, pinpointing where in the demotic they thought certain words should appear, De Sacy used his knowledge of Coptic to identify names such as 'Ptolemy'. Although he was later proved incorrect in his conclusions about the meaning of individual demotic glyphs, he successfully went beyond Marcel and Raige and identified 'Alexander', 'Alexandria' and 'Epiphanes' among others.

Johann Åkerblad published a letter he sent to De Sacy in 1802, *Lettre sur l'inscription égyptienne de Rosette, addressée au Silvestre de Sacy*, containing his efforts on several features of the demotic text. Using his limited understanding of Coptic, he had identified third-person pronouns and the demotic equivalents to 'Egypt', 'many', 'the king', 'the temple' and 'Greek'. However, he mistakenly believed that demotic was alphabetical, and went so far as to establish a putative alphabet for the script – this was superseded by later discoveries and his conclusions did not lead to any greater understanding of the hieroglyphs, nor dispel any of the prejudice surrounding their application.

Despite the combined efforts of Marcel, Raige, Ameillion, Weston, Heyne, De Sacy, Åkerblad and others, the two names most associated with the decipherment of hieroglyphs and the Rosetta Stone are Thomas Young and Jean-François Champollion, neither of whose efforts were obtained wholly independently without reference to the achievements of those who had gone before.[21]

A gifted linguist and scholar, Champollion had conquered Latin and Greek at a very early age and soon developed a fascination for Egyptian history and culture. His elder brother, Jacques-Joseph,[22] had delivered a paper about the Rosetta Stone in 1804, and the pair had been in regular contact with the savant secretary of the old Institut d'Égypte, Joseph Fourier, since made Baron and Prefect of the Isère. At the age of sixteen the young Champollion presented a paper to the Académie in Grenoble asserting that Coptic was the original language of ancient Egypt, and a year later, in 1807, his elder brother suggested he examine the Egyptian texts of the Rosetta Stone itself. The pair went to Paris and Champollion studied Arabic under De Sacy, as well as Sanskrit and Chinese, all with a view to understanding both cursive demotic Egyptian and hieroglyphs. He also studied Coptic, joining a congregation of the Coptic Church. De Sacy, who had already struggled for some years with the inscriptions of the Rosetta Stone, later tried to dissuade Champollion from a similar path, convinced that success with the stele would come only through luck rather than persistence.

Among many British scholars who attempted the puzzle of the inscriptions was Thomas Young. A scientific genius of international renown, Young was the Secretary for External Affairs to the Royal Society, a polymath physicist, mathematician, linguist and practising physician who made a pioneering study on the nature of colour in light and visual optics. In 1814 he was shown an Egyptian papyrus by a collector friend, Sir William Rouse Boughton. Fascinated by the script, he began work on the Rosetta Stone that same year, during his summer vacation, in Sussex.

Although he laboured under the centuries-old misapprehension that hieroglyphs were purely symbolic ideograms or 'logograms', he believed phonetic glyphs would have been used to write foreign names. Young had based his hypothesis on the knowledge that this very principle was evident in certain Chinese manuscripts, where foreign names or words were spelt out by phonetic characters rather than being ascribed an ideogram to symbolize their meaning. Earlier scholars had suggested that royal names lay within the six oblong 'cartouches' of the Rosetta Stone's hieroglyphs, but it was Young who made the first breakthrough in this respect.

After some two years, Young was able to identify one of the six hieroglyphic cartouches as 'Ptolemy'. Believing the demotic shared a similar structure to hieroglyphs, he used the demotic text as a guide, and assigned the phonetic values of P, T, M (or 'Ma'), I and S to five separate hieroglyphic 'letters' in the cartouche correctly, but made errors with a further eight. This was no mean feat, as the cartouches contained additional glyphs which did not readily correlate to recognizable letter-values; it was later discovered that these were descriptive royal epithets, such as 'autocrator' which Young's methods incorrectly identified as other proper names.

Young accomplished similarly impressive work on the demotic text, recognizing that the script consisted not only of phonetic, 'alphabetical' characters but symbolic logograms as well. Although he identified a substantial number of word groups in the hieroglyphs, he was unable to conceive that the same principle which applied to the demotic might also apply to hieroglyphs. He concluded that only foreign names could be rendered phonetically in hieroglyphics, and that all other hieroglyphs were purely symbolic signs. Young published his findings in 1819 in his *Supplement to the Encyclopaedia Britannica*.

The popular conception of an Anglo-French decipherment contest is confounded by Young's correspondence. He did not work in isolation but wrote to De Sacy, exchanging information on his work in progress, pleased to receive the opinion of the respected orientalist. At the same time, however, in his capacity as Secretary for Foreign Affairs of the Royal Society, he was contacted by Champollion. Much as Ameillion had complained over ten years earlier, the young linguist was concerned about the discrepancies between the exported English copy of the stone and the version created for the *Description de l'Égypte*, and consequently sought a cast of the stone to clarify certain details. Young checked the various passages for Champollion against his own copies of the inscriptions, and began a correspondence with him that was to last until Young's death in 1829.

The year 1815 was to bring fresh political turbulence to France, with the return of Bonaparte and the onset of the Hundred Days, which culminated in the Battle of Waterloo. The Champollion brothers were known Bonapartists, and with the defeat of the emperor, fell out of favour themselves. That same year, De Sacy, aware both of the academic interchange between Young and his pupil, and the advances Young had made, warned him: 'If I had one piece of advice to give you, it would be not to communicate your discoveries too much to M. Champollion. It could happen that he might then claim to have been first.' Further aspersions followed: 'He is prone to playing the role of a jackdaw in borrowed peacock's plumes.'[23]

An understandable misconception is that the Rosetta Stone alone was used to solve the riddle of the hieroglyph – this is not the case. For years the keenest observers had gazed at its inscriptions, driving some, like the great De Sacy, to frustrated surrender, or the savant Rémi Raige, to the edge of obsession, still struggling with demotic transliterations on his deathbed. It was as if the proximity of success was more torturous than the hieroglyphs themselves. The irony was, it was not the stone that blocked them at every turn, but their own prejudices concerning the nature of the ancient signs. They needed fresh material and a new approach – but without the extraordinary advances with the Rosetta Stone made by scholars in France, Sweden and Britain, the final piece to the jigsaw would never have fallen into place.

Faced with only fourteen fragmented lines of hieroglyphs by which to decipher the entire script, the general feeling was that further multilingual texts were needed – certainly Champollion wanted more material, feeling he had exhausted the resources of the Rosetta Stone. William John Bankes, the gentleman scholar, historian, artist and explorer,[24] provided the final piece to the puzzle. Since 1812, Bankes had travelled the Mediterranean in the wake of Wellington's victories in the Peninsular War, searching for art treasures. He made the crossing to Egypt, exploring sites along the upper reaches of the Nile in September to December 1815. On the island of Philae he found a fallen obelisk, which bore two inscriptions, one in Greek and the other in hieroglyphs.

Unable to return the piece to England immediately, he recorded both texts accurately, the relic not finding its way to Bankes's Dorset home until 1821.[25] Bankes, Young and Henry Salt,[26] the British Consul who had joined Bankes on a second excursion up the Nile in 1818–19, believed that the inscription on the obelisk was actually bilingual, which put the monument momentarily on a par with the Rosetta Stone. Although he could not read the individual glyphs, Bankes was able to identify one hieroglyphic cartouche on the obelisk as that of Cleopatra III, queen of Ptolemy VIII – her name also figured in the obelisk's Greek inscription. Although this was never published, Young used this hypothesis in his own work. It was this added information from Bankes and the Philae Obelisk inscription that was to inject a new vigour into the decipherment of hieroglyphs.

By July 1821, Champollion's political leanings had cost him dear, and he lost his post in Grenoble for his outspoken admiration for Bonaparte and his policies. He moved to Paris to live with his brother, who had become the private secretary to Joseph Dacier, secretary of the Académie des inscriptions et belles lettres. A month later Champollion read a paper to the academy on the hieratic script,[27] in which he demonstrated that hieratic was a form of hieroglyphics – but he also reaffirmed his belief that hieroglyphs were purely symbolic.

Subsequently, however, it is not clear when, he came to doubt this assertion, either through his own work of the previous years or through an analysis of Young's efforts. He tested his own theory: if hieroglyphs were 'logographic', that is, each glyph representing a single word or concept, then the number of glyphs on the Rosetta Stone should correspond roughly to a proportionate number of words in the Greek inscription. In December 1821, Champollion counted both texts of the stone. Curiously, no one had thought to do this before. Working on the assumption that its fourteen lines of hieroglyphs were equivalent to eighteen lines of Greek, he concluded there were 1,419 individual hieroglyphs to only 486 words of Greek. Therefore hieroglyphs could not be purely logographic – there were simply too many of them on the stone.

This dramatic realization led directly to the solution all scholars had been seeking. Yet there seems little explanation why Champollion began to accept the possibility of phonetic hieroglyphs when he did – all that is known is that at some point after the presentation of his paper in the autumn of 1821, he had begun to question his own certainty that hieroglyphs were only symbolic. Further suggestion of this phonetic potential was to follow.

William Bankes published lithographs of the Philae Obelisk inscriptions in 1821. The following year, at a crucial moment in his studies, a copy reached Champollion. Although he could see that the inscription was not bilingual, as Young, Bankes and Salt had hoped, Champollion concurred with Young's analysis of the phonetic glyphs in the name of Ptolemy – and of Cleopatra. 'Cleopatra' was a vital piece of deduction. Just as the names Cleopatra and Ptolemy shared Greek letters, the cartouche of Cleopatra from the obelisk shared hieroglyphs with the cartouche of Ptolemy on the Rosetta Stone. Before Champollion's eyes were the beginnings of a phonetic hieroglyphic alphabet. Yet Young had taken it no further.

It was Champollion, not Young, who applied this invaluable information. The two names provided him with fourteen alphabetic hieroglyphs which he used on other texts from Karnak, translating the names of Ptolemaic kings and Roman emperors, the alphabetical list expanding rapidly as he progressed. In this process he identified homophonic glyphs – interchangeable characters that produced the same sound.[28] He translated a host of names, each expanding the new alphabet. The greatest leap was still to come.

Jean-Nicolas Huyot, an architect and draughtsman who had explored the Nile with Bankes's party, had sent Champollion copies of inscriptions from the temple of Abu Simbel. Among the hieroglyphs was the cartouche of a king, featuring a sun-like disc. He recognized the two final glyphs in the cartouche as 'SS' and, using his knowledge of Coptic, he ascribed the Coptic word for the sun, 'Re', to the circular glyph. This gave him 'Re . . . SS' which immediately suggested the name 'Ramses', or, as the historian Manetho had transliterated it, 'Ramesses'. Taking each glyph to be a single consonant he supposed the central sign to represent 'M'. He had translated the most famous name of pharaonic Egypt:

In another text he found a cartouche featuring the image of an ibis, the animal traditionally associated with the ibis-headed god 'Thoth', appropriately enough, the deity who had brought writing to man. The other two glyphs in the cartouche were comparable to those of 'Ramses'. If he was correct, the cartouche was that of the Pharaoh 'Thothmes'. This was an important step, proving first that phonetic hieroglyphs could be applied to pharaonic Egyptian names as well as foreign, and second that hieroglyphs were a *combination* of phonetics and logograms: the ibis represented an entire concept, 'Thoth', rather than a single sound. This was the greatest breakthrough in the decipherment process to date. With this last revelation, the exhausted Champollion supposedly leapt up from behind his desk at the academy and burst into his brother's office next door, whereupon he cried, '*Je tiens l'affaire!*' (I've got it!) and collapsed. It was 14 September 1822. He lay unconscious for five days.

Two weeks later, on Friday, 27 September, he presented his findings in a landmark paper, his famous *Lettre à M. Dacier*, at the Académie des inscriptions et belles lettres, where he set out the basis of his hieroglyphic alphabet. However, he did not expand on all his hypotheses, but concentrated on the application of phonetic hieroglyphs in Greco-Roman names and the potential use of phonetic signs in pharaonic Egyptian hieroglyphics.[29] Among those in the audience was Thomas Young.

The nationalistic controversy that brewed over the following years had far more personal roots. Young's earlier success in identifying the first phonetic hieroglyphs played little part in Champollion's paper: it appeared that Champollion had arrived independently at his conclusions. Though relegated to a position of obscurity similar to Clarke at the hands of Turner in the recovery of the Rosetta Stone, Young's reaction was remarkably gracious. On the following Sunday, the 29th, he wrote a letter to William Richard Hamilton:

I have found here, or rather recovered, Mr Champollion junior, who has been living for these ten years on the Inscription of Rosetta, and who has lately been making some steps in Egyptian literature, which really appear to be *gigantic*. It may be said that he found the key in England which has opened the gate for him, and it is often observed that *c'est le premier pas qui coûte* (it's the first step that costs); but if he did borrow an English key, the lock was so dreadfully rusty, that no common arm would have strength enough to turn it; and, in a path so beset with thorns, and so encumbered with rubbish, not the first step only, but every step, is painfully laborious . . .

You will easily believe, that were I ever so much the victim of the bad passions, I should feel nothing but exultation at Mr Champollion's success: my life seems indeed to be lengthened by the accession of a junior coadjutor in my researches, and of a person too, who is so much more versed in the different dialects of the Egyptian [Coptic] language than myself.[30]

A nobler response could not have been written. Young and Champollion continued to communicate, as before, until the spring of 1823, when Champollion wrote a letter to Young bristling with indignation. He had just read a commentary of his *Lettre à M. Dacier* in Britain's *Quarterly Review*.[31] This issue announced the forthcoming publication of a work by Young which would 'reveal' the author of the original alphabet 'extended' by Champollion. Champollion was outraged: 'I will never consent to recognize any original alphabet other than my own.'[32] It would seem that this churlish salvo was typical of Champollion, who was fiercely self-promoting – Young might well have recalled De Sacy's earlier words of warning. Despite this protest, Young published the work, amid an atmosphere of mounting nationalistic rivalry.[33]

Anti-French commentators in Britain later added to the acrimony by claiming that not only had Champollion based his work on Young's without acknowledgement, but that he had further help from the Bankes obelisk lithographs. A scattered, eclectic mind, with a keen distaste for method, Bankes had apparently taken a pencil to a number of copies of the lithographs and written 'Cleopatra' beside the cartouche, which he believed represented the queen's name. It was alleged that Champollion had seen this pencilled name, which had led to the development of his alphabet. There was no evidence that Champollion had seen one of Bankes's doctored copies, but

Henry Salt later claimed that the copy sent to the Institute in Paris bore Bankes's unofficial notation.[34]

There can be no doubt that Champollion's grasp of Egyptian scripts far outstripped that of Thomas Young or any other scholar in Europe, and Young readily accepted this. Although their 'rivalry' has been emphasized by some, it was by no means of their own making, but a consequence of post-war nationalist feeling on both sides of the Channel. Although he published his *Account* with his original hieroglyphic alphabet despite Champollion's protests, Young would have been the last to suggest he had as wide an understanding of Egyptian as Champollion. His final comment on the subject of his own discovery conveyed a genuine acceptance of Champollion's extraordinary linguistic abilities:

> I sent it at that time to Champollion, as I have stated, and he acknowledged the receipt of it. To have placed more emphasis on the precise dates than I have done would have been to display more parade than the thing required, or to have shown too much hostility to Champollion, to whom I would rather give up something that is my right, than take from him anything that ought to be his.[35]

Champollion's more conclusive work on the decipherment of hieroglyphs was published in 1824, as *Précis du système hiéroglyphique des anciens égyptiens par M. Champollion le jeune*. Henry Salt later tested the precepts against materials in the British Museum and declared them sound. Though details are not well documented, in the same year the Champollion brothers allegedly travelled to the British Museum and looked for the first time upon the stone itself. The man who had cracked the code had never seen the device by which he had achieved success.

Assessing the process of the decipherment of hieroglyphs is made more difficult by the nationalist leanings of contemporary commentators; Champollion was seen in Britain very much as the arrogant upstart who had marginalized the British underdog Thomas Young, without whom he would never have made his discoveries. This oversimplification demonstrates a reluctance to accept Champollion's linguistic genius. Young might have made the first step with 'Ptolemy', but was unable to develop the potential of his decipherment beyond its use in foreign names and correctly determined only five hieroglyphic signs. Champollion, whose breadth of Egyptian linguistic knowledge was vast by comparison, formulated an entire system, leaving Young far behind. The argument that Champollion refused to acknowledge Young's contribution is further weakened by a passage in Champollion's own *Précis* of 1824:

I recognize that [Young] was the first to publish some correct ideas about the ancient writings of Egypt; that he also was the first to establish some correct distinctions concerning the general nature of these writings, by determining, through a substantial comparison of texts, the value of several groups of characters. I even recognize that he published before me his ideas on the possibility of the existence of several sound-signs, which would have been used to write foreign proper names in Egypt in hieroglyphs; finally that M. Young was also the first to try, but without complete success, to give a phonetic value to the hieroglyphs making up the two names Ptolemy and Berenice.[36]

With the decipherment of hieroglyphs, Bonaparte's bloody Egypt adventure had been vindicated, and the names of Young and Champollion for ever linked to the expedition. However, not everyone in France was convinced, or impressed, by Champollion's dramatic announcement.

Speaking with the sanction of the veteran savants, the authors Saintine, Marcel and Reybaud commented on the great decipherment in their history of the Egypt expedition:

[Champollion] knew, with this unique conquest, to make a lot of noise; to present his discovery in such a manner that it should benefit him and him alone, even if it remained partly fruitless for science; he knew to combine his system of reservations, half-proofs, vague promises and still more vague explanations so well, with so much art and spirit, so that he should enjoy, at least in his lifetime, results over which he must then haggle; to act finally in such a way that the incense of the Press should smoke for him, and that the gold of our Patrons of the Arts should discount his future revelations.[37]

A fitting memorial for the savants and their achievements in Egypt is best served by their own testament, the *Description de l'Égypte*, a work so colossal that specialized engraving machines and printing presses were devised to accommodate its enormous pages, which later filled twenty-three volumes. Little in print has rivalled this masterpiece published between 1809 and 1822. Demand for the set was so great that a second edition was necessary almost immediately. In an act of the most sincere gratitude to the man who had continually intervened on their behalf with ceaseless concern, they presented a complete set to Sir William Sidney Smith, transcending the brutal hostility between nations.

Eclipsed by the glare of Champollion's success, the savants continued their work, some returning to Egypt, others like Geoffroy Saint-Hilaire rising to Olympian heights in their field in France. It was said that after Egypt Fourier could no longer bear the European climate and could often be seen swathed in heavy overcoats in all weathers, fair and foul, insisting on roaring fires in his rooms even in the height of summer. He and his colleagues are the forgotten men who, despite tremendous odds, rediscovered the lost world of Egypt. When history recalls the Rosetta Stone 'Champollion' springs first to mind, rather than Jomard, Conté, Monge, Raffenau-Delile, Raige, Denon and

Marcel. Of the English, Hamilton, Clarke and Cripps, and Colonel Turner have faded equally by comparison to Young, Champollion and the dark face of *la pierre merveilleuse*:

> Our savants accomplished at least practical researches; they searched Egypt in every direction, reconstructed its buildings, drew them stone by stone, copied the hieroglyphic rock-walls, caskets, capitals, friezes, entablatures; ... explored from Damietta to Elephantine, from Suez to the lake of Mœris; omitting nothing in their path, neither ancient temple, nor modern monument, neither essential site, nor historic location, neither crypt, nor obelisk, nor pyramid.[38]

By 1830 and the publication of the words above, the war was long over, and Bonaparte imprisoned. The hypnotic wail of the *muezzin* calling to prayer from painted minarets, and the howling war-cries of bejewelled Mamelukes echoing only in their dreams of the Nile, the ageing savants of the first Institut d'Égypte had been displaced by the new generation. Whether they had in fact handed over the Rosetta Stone to Clarke, Cripps and Hamilton to save it from Menou or to speed their return home will remain something of a mystery. Champollion's contact with Thomas Young and his ability to move beyond Young's efforts demonstrated that, in the end, the copied inscriptions of the 'black granite from Rosetta' served both nations better as shared knowledge than it ever did as Turner's 'proud trophy'. Nevertheless, the minutely detailed reproduction of the stone in volume 5[39] of the *Description de l'Égypte* must have haunted their imaginations with thoughts of what might have been.

The code had been cracked and the stone, at last, had spoken. Not long afterwards, all Egypt would clamour for attention, its monuments and temples calling out to the new science, each demanding to be heard. Thanks to Bouchard, the savants, to Belliard and gallant Cavalier of the *Dromadaires*, to Sir Wiliam Sidney Smith, Hamilton, Clarke and Cripps, to Turner, to Young and Champollion, and the Rosetta Stone itself – they were.

Epilogue

A Proud Trophy

Despite the Rosetta Stone's public profile, historically its status as an exhibit in the British Museum has not been nearly as contested as that of the 'Elgin' or Parthenon Marbles. To many it is immediately recognizable and more memorable than the sculptures that were formerly part of the Athenian Acropolis. This is understandable; until the end of the 1990s the Rosetta Stone rested on an angled frame close to the entrance of the museum – unavoidable, it was one of the first objects to be encountered, and crowds of visitors have gathered round it for the past two hundred years. Cleaned by conservators, it now occupies an equally prominent position in the centre of the Egypt collection by the Great Court entrance, upright within a protective case, still one of the most famous objects in the world. Before the arrival of the antiquities from Egypt in 1802, the British Museum contained little grand sculpture, its halls filled chiefly with smaller curiosities. The acquisition of the Rosetta Stone and the cargo from the Alexandria victory was an important step in the development of the institution.

Since 1999 and the bicentenary celebration of its discovery, there has been a reawakening of Egyptian interest in the Rosetta Stone. In July 2003 an article in Britain's *Sunday Telegraph* newspaper claimed that Egypt was calling for its return. The feature stated that negotiations for the repatriation of the stone were under way with Dr Zahi Hawass, the Secretary General of the Supreme Council of Antiquities in Cairo. However, in early 2005 the British Museum confirmed that Britain's legal title to the Rosetta Stone was indisputable – the Articles of the Capitulation of Alexandria show that Osman Bey and Hassan, the Kapudan Pasha, leaders of the Mameluke and Turkish forces representing the recognized government of Egypt in 1801, had signed the treaty with the British and the French, thereby accepting Article 16, that Britain had the right to the antiquities collected by Bonaparte's expedition. In the circumstances, Dr Hawass apparently requested a replica of the stone, which was duly sent to Rosetta for display.

It seemed that Egypt had accepted the legality of British ownership of the stele; but at a meeting of the Intergovernmental Committee for Promoting the Return of Cultural Property to its Countries of Origin, Dr Hawass called for the return of key artefacts from around the world including the Rosetta Stone. In autumn 2007, a Bloomberg news report stated that Dr Hawass had made further representation to the British Museum for its return, be it permanent or by temporary loan, for the planned opening of the new Grand Museum at Gizeh, to be completed in 2012.

The restitution or repatriation of ancient artefacts to their native lands is a growing concern for the world's museums for obvious reasons. According to reports, Dr Hawass has succeeded in reclaiming some 4,000 items since he took up the post of Secretary General of the Supreme Council of Antiquities. It has been argued that to return the tens of thousands of Egyptian relics dispersed across the world would be virtually impossible; however, with prominent statuary, the political issues intensify through increased public awareness, stimulating powerful emotion – as witnessed by the case of the bust of Nefertiti currently displayed in Berlin, the cause of considerable public resentment in Egypt today. Such relics cease to be ancient artefacts and become instead a nebulous but much more contentious 'cultural heritage' – and there is little moral justification for any nation to possess or exploit the heritage of another against its wishes.

Technically the Rosetta Stone and all the relics confiscated by the British from the defeat of Alexandria were legally obtained, their release granted by representatives of the national government which 'owned' them. In the case of Egypt in 1801, this is not as clear-cut as that of Italian pieces from individual city-states such as Venice or Rome, whose native governments were displaced by Napoleonic conquest, their treasures looted and later restored upon liberation. The state of Egypt, as it is recognized today, took no hand in the decision to relinquish its historic antiquities because it did not exist.

The Ottoman Kapudan Pasha represented a foreign military dictatorship and Osman Bey exercised direct Mameluke rule ostensibly in the name of the sultan. Although the Mamelukes had become naturalized Egyptians over the centuries it could be argued they were still a foreign people – warrior-slaves and merce-naries from the remote plains of the Ottoman Empire, they had been rulers of the country since the Middle Ages, and contrary to Ottoman wishes exercised a rebellious independence and tyrannical military oppression of the general population. The question arises then whether Osman Bey and Hassan Pasha had the right to relinquish Egyptian antiquities. Perhaps those best qualified to dispose of Egyptian heritage in 1801 were the sheikhs of the Divan or the learned men of the Al-Azhar Mosque. However, there was no resistance to the collection of the ancient relics on cultural or religious grounds – after the tumult of the French defeat in 1801 and the accession of leader Muhammed Ali Bey similar treasures were exported with official sanction.

It would be a mistake to view past incidences of archaeological collection purely as cultural theft. In the

eighteenth century the collection of art and architectural fragments from remote rural sites in the Mediterranean was not
seen as looting or vandalism, but as rescue and preservation.
To the European antiquary, civilized nations cared for their art
treasures – to find broken statuary and religious artefacts lying
deserted in a state of ruination suggested a lack of civilized
understanding – the ruins themselves evidence of a once-great
culture since fallen into decay in the hands of a backward or
barbarian government. The French savants in Egypt were
presented with precisely this situation: the relics of a lost civilization lay neglected in the wastes of sand, ignored, if not
feared, by locals. Before the arrival of collectors in the late eighteenth century, artefacts in Egypt were certainly in danger of
destruction – as in the case of the Great Sphinx, which had
been wilfully defaced, and the Rosetta Stone, buried in foundations, or Louvre stele C122, built into the threshold of a
mosque.

The expedition had one other supreme right, internationally
recognized since war began: the right of conquest. However,
the legality of this right could also be challenged. Bonaparte
invaded Egypt under the pretext of aiding the Ottoman sultan
and did not officially declare war – far from it, he did his utmost
to avoid such an open conflict for as long as possible. Theoretically, Bonaparte could not legally claim any treasure as spoils
of war, even though he had defeated his enemies on the battlefield. Because of this, neither had the savants been able to secure
the legal rights from the ruling Ottomans to remove Egyptian
antiquities – although there was no specific opposition to their
scientific operations, the pieces had therefore been obtained
without permission. In this regard, the artefacts standing in the
British Museum from the fall of Alexandria could be considered plunder, just as Turner described them in 1810. The
document that created a legal provenance of their ownership,
and prevented Britain from becoming a receiver of stolen goods,

was the Articles of the Capitulation of Alexandria. According to Article 16, the antiquities of Egypt – and the Rosetta Stone – had been transformed into spoils of war.

The Rosetta Stone falls into a different category from the other artefacts collected by the French expedition and captured by the British in Egypt. It was not a work of art, or religious icon, taken from a temple or mosque. Unlike the other antiquities, its value upon discovery arose from the potential information it could yield as a code-key in the decipherment of hieroglyphs. Herein lies the overlapping nature of its cultural importance: although a piece of Egyptian heritage, its function was fulfilled only by the Europeans who found it. It is therefore by no means clear to which people it should by rights 'belong' – to the British, by right of arms, and the pioneering work of Young; to the French, for its discovery and the success of Champollion – or to the Egyptians, to whose ancient past it owes its origin. For this reason it has been described as an exhibit of world heritage, part of the 'universal museum', which to many implies that it makes little difference where it is located so long as it is properly preserved and accessible to the majority of people. One might expect something of universal value to be shown liberally around the world, yet in the 206 years since it was brought to London, it has left only once, in 1972, for a special exhibition in Paris celebrating the 150th anniversary of Champollion's historic 'Letter to M. Dacier' (although the French request for the stone for the occasion was initially refused by the British Museum and granted only after further consideration).

There is a strong case for rejecting the Ottoman right to dispose of Egyptian artefacts, but this is a moral judgement, not legal. However, the relevance of bills, receipts and treaties relating to the acquisition of artefacts by nations that no longer exist, such as Bonaparte's France and the British and Ottoman Empires, must be questioned in the light of today's modern world. Few historical or legal arguments address the relevant issue: it is not whether European nations *had* the right to acquire Egyptian antiquities, but whether today they should have the right to retain them.

Despite the Articles of the Capitulation of Alexandria and the binding nature of nineteenth-century Ottoman signatures, it would be difficult to argue that the Rosetta Stone belonged more in Britain or France than in Egypt. Yet, erected by the priests of the pharaoh, discovered by French savants, and preserved by British scholars, the Rosetta Stone unites two of the elder states of Europe with the most ancient of western civilizations. Two centuries later, still on the threshold of a new millennium, this unique cultural relationship could complete the cycle of discovery and decipherment, and herald a new era for the Rosetta Stone in the land of its creation. This 'gem of antiquity' could evolve beyond its original task – where once its message united a diverse culture, its renewed power could bind nations.

Appendix 1

The Inscription on the Rosetta Stone: The Decree of Memphis

The Rosetta Stone bears, in essence, a circular, a political information pamphlet carved in stone. The inscription consists of a decree issued by the Egyptian priesthood on 27 March 196 BC, roughly six months after the coronation of King Ptolemy V in the old capital of Memphis. In exchange for the adjustment of certain taxes, the priests granted Ptolemy a royal religious cult and commemorated his victory over rebel towns at the end of several years of regional revolt and national unrest. It hails him as the Immortal Ptolemy, offspring of the Gods, his name, Epiphanes, meaning 'out of heaven'.

Towns in the Nile Delta had been in revolt, as had parts of the Upper Nile, to the south. Even though it was religiously and culturally tolerant, the rule of the Macedonian Ptolemies after the death of Alexander the Great was not entirely welcomed by native Egyptians, particularly by the temple priesthood, the centre of Egyptian religious identity. Since the arrival of Alexander's Macedonian dynasty, there had been a noticeable change in the priesthood which, of all strata of society, had the greatest contact with the Greek government administration – the ancient gods had slowly become more Greek in nature, 'Hellenized', causing widespread resentment. This, combined with economic difficulty, led to uprisings and the rule of petty kings in defiance of the Ptolemaic court.

The sudden death of Ptolemy IV, who had been in his thirties, was tinged with suspicion and scandal, as was the succession – the news of the old king's passing, concealed by the authorities, came to light when the palace in Alexandria was set alight, possibly by plotters in the court, killing the widowed queen but sparing the child. Eventually soldiers joined an angry mob which stormed the palace and tore the six-year-old Ptolemy V from the arms of his nurse and proclaimed him king in 205 BC.

Although a new king was established on the throne it was clear that Egypt was badly weakened. Antiochus the Great, king of the Seleucids, attacked the eastern borders of the country while the internal revolts continued. The border campaign against Antiochus lasted more than five years and the Egyptian rebellions were not quashed until the eighth year of Ptolemy's reign. The punishment meted out to the rebels of Lycopolis became part of his corona-tion in 197 BC, when the thirteen-year-old king was crowned by the High Priest Hamarchis, in Memphis. It was the celebration of this event and its religious and economic consequences that was recorded in the Decree of Memphis and inscribed upon the Rosetta Stone. It is believed the stone was erected in the temple of Sais in Lower Egypt, and from there taken to Rosetta to form the foundations of the Tower of Sultan Qayt-Bey in the fifteenth century.

A host of scholars produced a number of translations of the Decree of Memphis since the discovery of the Rosetta Stone, and the work of decipherment continued after Champollion. Champollion had created a system, but it was by no means complete, much of it still to be tested and certain areas of hiero-glyphic script still uncertain. In 1847 Edward Hincks, who had previously deciphered the ancient script of cuneiform, tried to develop Champollion's system and published through the Royal Irish Academy '*An attempt to ascertain the number, names and powers of the letters of the hieroglyphic or ancient Egyptian alphabet; grounded on the establishment of a new principle in the use of phonetic characters*'.

However, the efforts of German scholars dominated Egyptology for much of the nineteenth century. Although Young had read out a translation of the demotic inscription of the stone at a meeting of the Society of Antiquaries of London, Heinrich Brugsch (1827–94) has been considered the first scholar who really understood the meaning of the demotic on the stone. The German Egyptologist Karl Richard Lepsius (1810–84) continued the work on hiero-glyphs, correcting and expanding Champollion's *Grammaire*, and later produced the extraordinary multi-volume work *Denkmaeler aus Aegypten und Aethiopien* (1849–59) comparable in scale and scope to the savants' *Description de l'Égypte*. Lepsius is also credited with the accurate translation of a Twelfth Dynasty papyrus which had been misinterpreted by Champollion twenty years earlier.

It was in 1866 that Lepsius was able to put Champollion's theories to the fullest test. Working at Tanis in Lower Egypt he discovered a large well-preserved stele, bearing another multilingual inscription which predated the Rosetta Stone by some forty years, from the reign of Ptolemy III (238 BC). Unlike the Rosetta Stone, the 2.2-metre-high 'Tanis Stone' (often referred to as the Canopus Stone), was virtually whole, though battered mostly to one side, and its inscription, the Decree of Canopus, was equally legible. Using the principles of the Champollion system and the developments since its inception, the hieroglyphic section of the inscription was deciphered in a dramatic vindication of the linguistic labours begun at the turn of the century.

Study of the Rosetta Stone is generally believed to have a European focus, but shortly before Lepsius started work in Tanis, a complete translation of the Rosetta Stone was presented by three young Americans of the Philomathean Society of Pennsylvania. Founded in 1813, this organization continues to this day, and is consequently the oldest literary society in the United States. In the mid-nineteenth century the society appointed a committee of three undergraduates, C. R. Hale, S. H. Jones and H. Morton, to translate the inscription using the principles laid down by Champollion. In 1858 they presented what is generally known as 'The Rosetta Stone Report', or more fully, *Report of the Committee Appointed by the Philomathean Society of Pennsylvania to Translate the Inscription on the Rosetta Stone*. This report, a magnificent combination of Victorian artistic design and Egyptian motif, was applauded at the time as one of the first marathon tests of Champollion's work, in several instances improving on certain aspects which had previously needed clarification.

The translation of the Greek inscription reproduced here is that of the Reverend Stephen Weston. Weston was the first to attempt an English version of the Greek in April 1802, giving a fuller translation in the following November. His final effort was presented to the Society of Antiquaries, just as Porson had finished his own, in January 1803. It was published by the society in 1812 in their 'Account of the Rosetta Stone', and is rarely seen in modern print.

THE SOCIETY OF ANTIQUARIES OF LONDON
TRANSLATION:
BY STEPHEN WESTON, B.D.

[N.B. The words between square brackets are restored by conjecture, and filled up where the stone is defective beginning from the second line to the end.]

A Decree of the young King (who received the kingdom from his father), Lord of kingdoms, great in glory, the settler of the constitution of Egypt, and in all things relating to the Gods of distinguished piety; superior to his adversaries, improver of the life of men, Lord of the festival of thirty years; like Vulcan; the great King, resembling the Sun; the great Monarch of Upper and Lower Egypt, the offspring of the Gods Philopators, whom Vulcan approved; to whom the Sun gave the victory; the living image of Jupiter, the son of the Sun, Ptolemy the immortal, beloved by Philia. (Aetos, son of Aetos, in the ninth year being high priest of Alexander, and the Gods Soteroon, and the Gods Adelphoon, and the Gods Euergetoon, and the Gods Philopatoroon, and the God Epiphanes, most gracious and victorious.) Of Berenice Euergetis, Pyrrha, the daughter of Philinus, being Basket-bearer of Arsinoe Philadelphus, Areia, daughter of Diogenes, being Priestess of Arsinoe, wife of Philopator, Irene, daughter of Ptolemy, being Priestess. (On the fourth day of the month Xandicus, the eighteenth of the Egyptian month Mechir, the priests and the prophets, and all those who go into the sanctuary to dress the Gods, and the pterophorae, and the sacred Registrars, and all the priests throughout the country, collected at Memphis to meet the King for the assumption of the kingdom of Ptolemy the Immortal, beloved by Phtha, the God Epiphanes most gracious, which kingdom he received from his father.) The said priests being assembled in the temple at Memphis, have on this day pronounced this decree:–

Whereas King Ptolemy the immortal, beloved of Phtha, the God Epiphanes, most gracious, son of King Ptolemy and Queen Arsinoe, the Gods Philopators has in many things benefited both the temples and those set over them and those in authority in his kingdom, being himself a God, descended from a God and a Goddess, like Orus the son of Isis, and Osiris the avenger of his father; has, being benevolently disposed towards the Gods, laid up in the temples silver and corn, and expended much revenue in order to bring Egypt into a state of calm, and established her religious worship: in doing this he has exerted all his powers, and given repeated marks of his philanthropy, by remitting some taxes in the whole, and lightening others so that all ranks of people might live in prosperity in his kingdom; but the debts to the crown, numerous as they were in Egypt, and the rest of his kingdom, he forgave, and those who had been led away to prison, he set free, and those who had been a long time under criminal accusations he dismissed. The revenues of the temples, and the annual contributions to them in corn and money, he ordered should remain as usual everywhere, together with the customary portions to the Gods from the vineyards and the gardens, and all other places belonging to them, in his father's time. With respect to the priests, his commands were, that they should pay nothing more for the completion of their order, than they had paid to the first year of his father. He remitted also the annual voyage to Alexandria, and ordered that no one should be pressed for the navy. Of the fine linen cloth manufactured in the priests' houses for the King's palace, he remitted two parts; and all other matters he settled in the order they were in before, considering how the usual service of the Gods might be perfected, as it was fit it should be. In like manner he dealt out justice to all, like the great, great Hermes. He ordered also that all men who came back to their country in arms and all disaffected persons who returned to Egypt in times of confusion, should remain on their own estates. He considered also how forces of horse and foot, and ships, might be sent against Invaders of Egypt by sea and land; making provision at the same time, at a great expense of money and corn, for the temples, and the security of those who belonged to them. He then proceeded against Lycopolis, which is in the division of Busiris, that had been seized and fortified for a siege, and largely provided with arms and ammunition; for it had been of a long time in conspiracy, and of settled disaffection, and all who were there had arrived at one uniform pitch of impiety, both against the temples of the Gods, and the inhabitants of Egypt, to whom they had succeeded in doing much mischief: and when he sat down before it, he surrounded it with walls, mounds, and ditches, of considerable extent; but the Nile rising very high in the eighth year, and according to custom drowning the meadows, he repressed it in many places, by damming up the mouths of the rivers, being provided with implements of all sorts for the purpose, and appointing a guard to watch the dykes, he took the city in a short time by assault, and utterly destroyed all the irreligious rebels that were in it [like Hermes], and Orus the son of Isis and Osiris. The rebels also, who had been sent from the apostate chiefs to his father, [and had in their way laid waste] the country, and offered violence to the temples, were worsted in these parts. And now, proceeding to Memphis to avenge his father, and his kingdom, he inflicted punishment upon all delinquents, as his office required, at the moment when he was come for the completion [of all things], and to take the government upon himself: but he remitted what was owing to the royal treasury unto the eighth year, being a large sum in money and corn, [and also] the duties on linen cloths not manufactured for the King's house, and on those which were finished for samples of different sorts, unto the same period. He discharged also the temples from [the deficient] measure by acre of the priests, land, and the vineyards according to measure of the Κεζαμιον by acre; and both to Apis and Mneusis he gave great largesses; and to other sacred animals in Egypt, much more than the Kings which preceded him. Caring also for every thing that belonged to them, he provided both for their funerals whatsoever was customary with the noblest and most costly presents, and all requisites for each of their temples, with sacrifices and assemblies, and other usual ceremonies; and this preserved the honour both of Egypt and its Gods, conformably to the law, he fitted up also the temple of Apis with costly works, having made a large provision for that purpose [of gold and silver], and no small number of precious stones. He built shrines and altars, and gave orders for their decoration; having enquired the divine will of the God Euergetes in those things [that belonged] to his service, he repaired the most venerable temples in his kingdom that had fallen into decay. In return for these things, the Gods have given him health, victory, strength; [with] the blessings of a reign continued on to him and his children to the end of time. It has been decreed by the priests, and may it prosper of all the temples of the country, as well those of King Ptolemy, living for ever, beloved of Phtha, the God Epiphanes most gracious, as those of his parents the Philopators and those of his ancestors the Gods [Energetoon], the Gods Adelphoon, and Soteroon, greatly to increase their glory;. and to set up an image of the immortal King Ptolemy, the God Epiphanes, most gracious in each of their temples in the [most conspicuous part] of them, which shall be called the image of Ptolemy the Defender of Egypt; and near it shall stand the supreme deity of the temple, presenting to the image a wreath of victory [prepared in the usual manner]: and the priest shall perform service three times a day before the image; and dress it with sacred vestments, and perform such ceremonies as are prescribed for the other Gods [in their festivals and solemn assemblies]. In addition to the statues erected to King Ptolemy, the God Epiphanes most gracious, sprung from King Ptolemy and Queen Arsinoe, the Gods Philopators, a small statue, and a shrine [of gold], shall be made, and placed in the sanctuary [of each of the temples] with the other shrines, and in the great festivals, when the Exoduses are made from the temples, [this shrine] of the God Epiphanes [most gracious] shall go forth: but in order to make it conspicuous, both now and in after times, unto the temple of the King shall be dedicated ten crowns of gold, near which shall be placed an asp [like the one on the other] crowns in form of asps in the other temples. In the middle of the sanctuary shall be the crown called Psokent, which he wore when he went [to the palace] at Memphis, for the consummation of the ceremonies at the time he was solemnly invested with the kingdom. About the square or corners of the foresaid crown, as about the others, there shall be phylacteries of gold [on which is an image of the King with his name] who has made both Upper and Lower Egypt illustrious. And when, the thirtieth day of Messori, the King's birth-day is celebrated, and on the day . . . he received the kingdom from his father, during these two days of the same name, which are the authors of many blessings to all, it has been decreed to celebrate a festival [and hold a solemn assembly throughout] Egypt, in its temples monthly, and perform therein sacrifices and libations, and all other rites of [procession and feasts in the] forementioned temples, as at other feasts and assemblies and moreover to keep a festival and hold an assembly to the immortal, beloved of Phtha, King Ptolemy, the God Epiphanes most gracious, every year [throughout Upper and Lower Egypt] from new moon of Thouth during five days, in which the priests shall wear chaplets whilst they offer sacrifices, and pour out libations, and perform all other acts of worship. Unto the names of the other Gods whom they serve [they shall add the name of the King] living for ever, the God Epiphanes most gracious, and imparting unto all the oracles, [and the most celebrated temples of Egypt] his holy priesthood. It shall be lawful also for private individuals to keep this feast, and build the forementioned temple, and to have sacrificing priests at their own temples annually, that it may be known that the Egyptians honour and revere the God Epiphanes the most gracious Monarch, as they should do. [This decree of the young King] shall be engraved on a solid stone in sacred,[1] in vernacular,[2] and Greek characters, and be set up in the first, second [third, and fourth[3] temples of the Gods of Egypt]. Farewell.[4]

Reprinted from *Archaeologia, or, Miscellaneous Tracts Relating to Antiquity*, vol. 16 (1812), pp. 220–4, by kind permission of the Society of Antiquaries of London.

Appendix 2

Recovery of the Rosetta Stone: The Account of Major-General Turner

THE SOCIETY OF ANTIQUARIES OF LONDON
Read 8th June, 1810

Argyle Street, May 30, 1810

Sir,

The Rosetta Stone having excited much attention in the learned world, and in this Society in particular, I request to offer them, through you, some account of the manner it came into the possession of the British army, and by what means it was brought to this country, presuming it may not be unacceptable to them.

By the sixteenth article of the capitulation of Alexandria, the siege of which city terminated the labours of the British army in Egypt, all the curiosities, natural and artificial, collected by the French Institute and others, were to be delivered up to the captors. This was refused on the part of the French General to be fulfilled, by saying they were all private property. Many letters passed; at length, on consideration that the care in preserving the insects and animals had made the property in some degree private, it was relinquished by Lord Hutchinson; but the artificial, which consisted of antiquities and Arabian manuscripts, among the former of which was the Rosetta Stone, was insisted upon by the noble General with his usual zeal for science. Upon which I had several conferences with the French General Menou, who at length gave way, saying, that the Rosetta Stone was his private property; but, as he was forced, he must comply as well as the other proprietors. I accordingly received from the under secretary of the

Institute, Le Pere, the secretary Fourier being ill, a paper, containing a list of the antiquities, with the names of the claimants of each piece of Sculpture: the stone is there described of black granite, with three inscriptions, belonging to General Menou. From the French sçavans I learnt, that the Rosetta Stone was found among the ruins of Fort St. Julien, when repaired by the French, and put in a state of defence: it stands near the mouth of the Nile, on the Rosetta branch, where are, in all probability, the pieces broken off. I was also informed, that there was a stone similar at Menouf, obliterated, or nearly so, by the earthen jugs being placed on it, as it stood near the water; and that there was a fragment of one, used and placed in the walls of the French fortifications of Alexandria. The Stone was carefully brought to General Menou's house in Alexandria, covered with soft cotton cloth, and a double matting, where I first saw it. The General had selected this precious relick of antiquity for himself. When it was understood by the French army that we were to possess the anti-quities, the covering of the stone was torn off and it was thrown upon its face, and the excellent wooden cases of the rest were broken off, for they had taken infinite pains, in the first instance, to secure and preserve from any injury all the antiquities. I made several remon-strances, but the chief difficulty I had was on account of this stone, and the great sarcophagus, which at one time was positively refused to be given up by the Capitan Pasha, who had obtained it by having possession of the ship it had been put on board of by the French. I procured, however, a centry [sic] on the beach from Mon. Le Roy, prefect maritime, who, as well as the General, behaved with great civility; the reverse I experienced from some others.

When I mentioned the manner the stone had been treated to Lord Hutchinson, he gave me a detachment of artillerymen, and an artil-lery-engine, called, from its powers, a devil-cart, with which that evening I went to General Menou's house, and carried off the stone, without any injury, but with some difficulty, from the narrow streets, to my house, amid the sarcasms of numbers of French officers and men; being ably assisted by an intelligent serjeant [sic] of artillery, who commanded the party, all of whom enjoyed great satisfaction in their employment: they were the first British soldiers who entered Alexandria. During the time the Stone remained at my house, some gentlemen attached to the corps of sçavans requested to have a cast, which I readily granted, provided the Stone should receive no injury;

which cast they took to Paris, leaving the Stone well cleared from the printing ink, which it had been covered with to take off several copies to send to France, when it was first discovered.

Having seen the other remains of ancient Egyptian sculpture sent on board the Admiral, Sir Richard Bickerton's ship, the Madras, who kindly gave every possible assistance, I embarked with the Rosetta Stone, determining to share its fate, on board the Egyptienne frigate, taken in the harbour of Alexandria, and arrived at Portsmouth in February 1802. When the ship came round to Deptford, it was put in a boat and landed at the Custom-house; and Lord Buckinghamshire, the then Secretary of State, acceded to my request, and permitted it to remain some time at the apartments of the Society of Antiquaries, previous to its deposit in the British Museum, where I trust it will long remain, a most valuable relic of antiquity, the feeble but only yet discovered link of the Egyptian to the known languages; a proud trophy of the arms of Britain: (I could almost say *spolia opima*), not plundered from defenceless inhabitants, but honourably acquired by the fortune of war.

I have the honour to be, Sir,

Your most obedient, and most humble servant,

H. TURNER, Major General

Nicholas Carlisle Esq.
Secretary to the Society of Antiquaries,
&c. &c.

Reprinted from *Archaeologia, or, Miscellaneous Tracts Relating to Antiquity*, vol. 16 (1812), pp. 212–14, by kind permission of the Society of Antiquaries of London.

Appendix 3

Recovery of the Rosetta Stone: The Account of E. D. Clarke, LL.D.

SATURDAY, *September the twelfth.*

Mr. Hamilton went with us to the French head-quarters, and undertook to mention to Menou the result of our visit to Lord Hutchinson. We remained near the outside of the tent; and soon heard the French General's voice elevated as usual, and in strong terms of indignation remonstrating against the injustice of the demands made upon him. The words *'Jamais on n'a pillé le monde!'*[1] diverted us highly, as coming from a leader of plunder and devastation. He threatened to publish an account of the transaction in all the Gazettes of Europe; and, as Mr. Hamilton withdrew, we heard him vociferate a menace of meeting Lord Hutchinson in single combat – *'Nous nous verrons, de bien près – de bien près, je vous assure!'*[2]

However, Colonel, now General, Turner, who had arrived also in Alexandria, with orders from our Commander-in-chief respecting the surrender of the Antiquities, soon brought this matter to a conclusion. The different forts were now occupied by our army; and the condition of the garrison was such, that Menou did not deem it prudent to resist any longer: he reluctantly submitted to the loss of his literary trophies. The *Rosetta Tablet* was taken from a warehouse, covered with mats, where it had been deposited with Menou's baggage; and it was surrendered to us, by a French officer and Member of the Institute, in the streets of Alexandria; Mr. Cripps, Mr. Hamilton, and the author, being the only persons present, to take possession of it. The officer appointed to deliver it recommended its speedy conveyance to some place of safety, as he could not be answerable for the conduct of the French soldiers, if it were suffered to remain exposed to their indignation. We made this circumstance known to Lord Hutchinson, who gave orders for its immediate removal; and it was given in charge to General Turner, under whose direction all the monuments of Egyptian antiquity, resigned to us by the articles of the capitulation, were afterwards conveyed to England. (See Hamilton's *Aegyptiaca*, p. 402, *Lond.* 1809.)[3]

Reprinted from E. D. Clarke's *Travels in Various Countries of Europe, Asia and Africa*, 4th edn, Part 2, vol. 5, *Greece, Egypt and the Holy Land*, Section 2 (London, 1810), pp. 372–3.

Appendix 4

Wybourn's List of Antiquities

The following is a transcript of the list of antiquities confiscated by the British from the French at Alexandria in 1801, found among the papers of Major T. Marmaduke Wybourn of the Royal Marines. Turner's original list, translated from the French, differs in precision, as if the copyist who created this particular version used a common form of shorthand to describe the pieces.

A copy of Turner's list was reproduced in an appendix to Robert Wilson's *History of the British Expedition to Egypt*, but according to the work of M. L. Bierbrier in the British Museum's Occasional Paper No. 123, it is by no means an exact rendering of Turner's original and should only be used for rough identification purposes (it is also signed 'W. Turner' rather than 'H. Turner' or 'T. H. Turner'). Just after the list in Wilson's book is this remarkable note:

> Several antiquities were found by the English; the most valuable were the figure of a Roman soldier, as large as life, and a large tablet, the inscription of which stated, that whatever this belonged to, was created in honour of Septimius Severus, by the veterans of the 11th Legion; which tablet is now in the possession of General Coote. A stone was also found in the camp of the 3d regiment of Guards, with hieroglyphics, of the same unknown kind as the Memnon.

The Rosetta Stone does not appear at all in this brief summary, suggesting either that Wilson did not understand its importance or, more remarkable, had heard little of it – but Wybourn makes no mention of it in his journals either, despite having it on his own list of 'relicts' as Item 8.

It is a curious experience to pass through the Egypt collection at the British Museum, using Wybourn's list as a guide: to one side lies the giant granite fist of Memphis, and further on, the deep green sarcophagus supposed by Clarke and all of Alexandria to be Alexander's tomb – there is the sense that, by some strange magic, the great pieces had only just been deposited days before, bringing us closer to their unusual story, to Clarke, Cripps and Hamilton, to Menou and the indefatigable savants, and thus the beginnings of Egyptology itself.

Relicts bro[t] down from Egypt & now in the British Museum, by me, in the Madras, 50 guns.

1. An Egyptian sarcophagus, with Hieroglyphics of brech verte, from the Mosque of St. Athanasius.
2. D°. of black granite from Cairo.
3. D°. of bazaltes, from Menouf.
4. The fist of a Colossean Statue, supposed to be Vulcan, red granite, found in the ruins of Memphis.
5. Five fragments of Statues, of lion headed women, black granite, from the Ruins of Thebes.
6. A mutilated figure kneeling, black granite.
7. Two Statues, Septimus [*sic*] Severus and Marcus Aurelius – white marble from the Ruins in Alexandria.
8. A stone with three inscriptions, hieroglyphics, Gobtic and Greek, black granite from Rosetta.
9. A statue of lion headed woman sitting, black granite, from Upper Egypt.
10. Two small fragments of lions head[s] black granite f[tm] upp[r] Eg[pt].
11. A small figure kneeling, with hieroglyphics, D°, D°
12. Five fragments of lion headed women D°, D°
13. A fragment of a sarcophagus, D°, D°
14. Two small obelisks, bazaltes.
15. A Ram's head, very large, Red grais from Upper Egypt.
16. A statue of a woman sitting on y[e] ground, black G.[t] U[r] Eg[t].
17. A fragment of a lion headed man, black granite, from Upper Egypt.

18. A stone with Hierg^{cs} in same hand as y^e Memnon, from y^e Camp of 3^d Gu^d

A Chest of Oriental Manuscripts, from Cairo —

Note:

'D^o'= 'ditto'.

'y' as used in 'y^e' was an old printing form of 'th' – consequently 'ye' is actually 'the'.

Item 18 refers to the stele described by Wilson, found in the British lines outside Alexandria by Turner's own 3rd Foot-Guards, hence '3^d Gu^d'.

Notes

INTRODUCTION

[1] Greek: *stele*; Latin: *stela*.
[2] Recorded dimensions vary. The British Museum also reports 114.4 cm high (max.) x 72.3 cm wide x 27.9 cm thick. Dimensions given in the text are from Dr Richard Parkinson, current Keeper of the Dept of Ancient Egypt and Sudan at the British Museum; see his *Cracking Codes: The Rosetta Stone and Decipherment* (London: British Museum Press, 1999).
[3] Published in *Archaeologia, or Miscellaneous Tracts Relating to Antiquity*, vol. 16 (1812), Society of Antiquaries of London.
[4] E. D. Clarke, *Travels in Various Countries of Europe, Asia and Africa*, 4th edn, vol. 5: *Greece, Egypt and the Holy Land*, Part II, Section II (London: Cadell and Davies, 1810).

CHAPTER 1

[1] Thought to be Psamtek I – or Psamtik – (r. 664–610 BC) first ruler of Egypt upon the fall of the Assyrian Empire in 612 BC.
[2] Herodotus, *Histories*, II.35, in Robin Aterfield, trans. (Oxford: Oxford University Press, 1998).
[3] He even commented on Egyptian toilet habits for passing water: women stood and men sat.
[4] See Erik Iversen, *The Myth of Egypt and Its Hieroglyphs in European Tradition* (Princeton: Princeton University Press, 1961; repr. 1993).

[5] The etymology of the word 'Copt' is debatable, but is largely accepted as a derivative of the Arabic *Qubt*, itself from the Greek name for Egypt, *Aiguptos*. *Aiguptos* is believed to stem from the Mycenaean (c. 1500 BC) whose own term for 'Egyptian' was *akupitijo* and probably derived from the Egyptians themselves, who called their nation *Hut-ka-ptah*, the Land or House of Ptah.

[6] See Jeremy Black, *The British Abroad: The Grand Tour in the Eighteenth Century* (New York: St Martin's Press and Stroud: Alan Sutton, 1992).

[7] The middle band inscription on the Rosetta Stone was mistakenly identified as Coptic, or 'Gobtic' as some English writers called it. See Major Wybourn's list of antiquities: 'a stone with three inscriptions, hieroglyphics, Gobtic and Greek . . .'.

[8] *Byzantion* to the Greeks, situated at the commercially strategic point where Europe met Asia, between the Golden Horn and the Sea of Marmara – Constantinople was the largest and wealthiest city in the ancient world, guarding both the gateway to the East and the West. Known as the Eastern Roman Empire after Constantine moved the imperial capital there from Italy, it was also known to many as the Empire of the Greeks because of the predominance of the Greek language, or, in the Islamic world, the land of *Rum* (Rome). The 'Byzantine Empire' is a traditional reference for the Eastern Roman Empire in the period following the collapse of Rome in the West, extending into the Middle Ages until Constantinople fell to the Ottoman Turks in the fifteenth century.

[9] Eight years after the victory over the crusaders, Hulego Khan's Mongols sacked Baghdad, reputedly killing nearly all of the city's inhabitants. Hulego also took Damascus, but the Mameluke general Baibars, victor against Louis IX, escaped to Egypt. The Mamelukes gathered an army and marched across Sinai to meet the invaders, destroying the khan's forces at the Battle of Yn Jalut – the first decisive defeat of the Mongols in the field.

[10] Similar to a duchy or county in western Europe, ruled by a bey.

[11] The city was known as Constantinople even after the establishment of the Ottoman Empire, not officially becoming Istanbul until the twentieth century.

CHAPTER 2

[1] France invaded Austrian territory in the Netherlands, hoping the Dutch would rise up and join them in the fight against Austrian tyranny; instead

the French forces quit the field in disarray, at least one unit turning to mutiny. The army went on, however, to defeat the Prussians at Valmy in September 1792, in the first major French success of the war.

2 Napoleon Bonaparte [Bonaparte I] (1769–1821); General, First Consul of the French Republic, later Emperor of the French, King of Italy, Mediator of the Swiss Confederation, Protector of the Confederation of the Rhine.

3 From the French republican calendar, which imposed new days, new months and new years, beginning with Year 1 in September 1792. 13 Vendémiaire, Year 4, was 5 October 1795.

4 General Jacques-François Menou, Baron de Boussay (1750–1810), later le Comte de Menou, was to become entwined in Bonaparte's military fortunes more dramatically in the Egypt campaign.

5 Barras (1755–1829) later facilitated Bonaparte's marriage to Josephine de Beauharnais, at one time Barras's own mistress. It was Barras who suggested Bonaparte for the command of the Italian campaign.

6 'The line of battle' was the predominant order of combat at sea, bringing the greatest weight of guns to bear at once in a single file, providing a continuous stream of fire. The 'line of battle ship' later became the 'battleship'.

7 It was in this battle that Nelson sealed his well-deserved reputation for almost reckless bravery, disobeying Jervis's orders and swerving from the line of battle to cut off the path of the Spanish and divide their fleet, exposing his own ship to an appalling barrage of fire. So close was the fighting that he personally led boarding parties from one Spanish ship to the next, executing what later was called 'Nelson's Patent Bridge'.

8 An expression given to the first wave of assault troops into the breach of a besieged city or fortress, almost certain to be annihilated or 'lost' to the fire of waiting defenders.

9 This had been one of the many targets of Robert Guiscard ('the Wily'), the eleventh-century Norman mercenary warlord who, among others, contributed to the Norman conquest of southern Italy and Sicily some years before Duke William's invasion of England.

10 Of this figure estimates vary from 30,000 to 40,000 combat troops; an eyewitness claims 30,000 but most modern commentators prefer 35,000 to 40,000. The likeliest figure is c.38,000. See J. Christopher Herold, *Bonaparte in Egypt* (London: Hamish Hamilton, 1962), and Paul Strathern, *Napoleon in Egypt* (London: Jonathan Cape, 2007).

11 An honour granted at Bonaparte's own request, although there is no

question of his deep interest in the proceedings of the Institute, having delivered several addresses himself.

[12] Louis Marie Maximilien de Caffarelli du Falga, known as Maximilien Caffarelli (1756–99) was in command of the engineers of the Armée de l'Angleterre, but these units were marched south to become part of the Armée de l'Orient.

[13] Baron Georges Léopold Chrétien Frédéric Dagobert Cuvier (1769–1832). A contemporary and correspondent of Geoffroy Saint-Hilaire, Cuvier was one of the most important naturalists of his day, establishing the reality of extinction and the fields of comparative anatomy and palaeontology.

[14] His full name was Dieudonné Sylvain Guy Tancrède de Dolomieu.

[15] Marie-Jules César Savigny (1777–1851) would later compile a collection of flora and fauna specimens so extraordinary it would cause Edward Daniel Clarke to call it 'the first thing of the kind in the world'.

[16] The removal of the pope by General Berthier (who served as Bonaparte's chief of staff in Egypt) later caused the sheikhs of Cairo's Al-Azhar Mosque to condemn the French as godless heathens.

[17] Madame Monge had apparently complained with some exasperation that even after an entire bottle of champagne her husband had revealed no details of the commission to her. More out of frustration, she let him go.

[18] It is worth noting by comparison that the Royal Navy's Mediterranean fleet was barely a tenth of this number.

[19] This involved dummy orders to Bonaparte in the north and the collaboration of the press, much as the Allies attempted with Patton's 'phantom army' in 1944 prior to D-Day.

[20] Troops received no desert training and their inability to carry a personal water supply led inevitably to harrowing consequences.

[21] See Joseph-Marie Moiret, *Memoirs of Napoleon's Egyptian Expedition 1798–1801*, ed. and trans. Rosemary Brindle (London: Greenhill Books, 2001), p. 1.

CHAPTER 3

[1] A further parallel to the days of Caesar, this was similar to the pension of a Roman soldier after twenty-five years' service.

[2] George John Spencer, 2nd Earl Spencer (1758–1834), First Lord of the Admiralty (1794–1801).

[3] Letter to Admiral Jervis (Lord St Vincent) from Earl Spencer, 2 May 1798.

4 Vice-Admiral François-Paul Brueys d'Aigalliers, le Comte de Brueys (1753–98), naval commander of the expedition fleet.

5 The knights had continued in their feudal practice of enslaving their enemies, as did their North African neighbours. The mob that stormed the Bastille may have liberated only a handful of prisoners, but indirectly succeeded in releasing 2,000, enslaved in the name of St John.

6 *Napoleon in Egypt: Al-Jabarti's Chronicle of the French Occupation 1798*, 3rd edn, trans. Shmuel Moreh *et al.* (Princeton, NJ: Markus Wiener, 1997), p. 20.

7 Louis Antoine Fauvelet de Bourrienne (1769–1834), a French diplomat whose association with Bonaparte began during negotiations with Austria after the victory in Italy in 1797. He accompanied Bonaparte to Egypt as his private secretary.

8 A kashiff [also kasheff, kachef and kachieff] was a powerful leader as distinct from a sheikh or amir.

9 Also transliterated as Koraim or Kuraim in some works.

10 Monge later wrote a monograph on the subject.

11 The divisional square was a tactic devised by Bonaparte for infantry faced with cavalry attack. As effective as a Macedonian phalanx, it was readily adopted by Wellington and other commanders.

12 Moiret, *Memoirs of Napoleon's Egyptian Expedition*, p. 49.

13 'Scimitar' is a derivative of *shamshir*, the damascened blades of Persia and the Middle East. Its use in Egypt and the Ottoman Empire later gave rise to the British 'Mameluke' hilt and grip, a sabre fashion popular in the Regency period.

14 *Al-Jabarti's Chronicle*, p. 33.

15 Moiret, *Memoirs of Napoleon's Egyptian Expedition*, p. 53.

16 Ibid.

17 *Al-Jabarti's Chronicle*, p. 37.

18 Cited in Moiret, *Memoirs of Napoleon's Egyptian Expedition*, p. 54.

19 Also known as Elfi Bey. His palace remained the French military HQ in Cairo until the city's fall in June 1801.

20 Pierre Charles Jean Baptiste Silvestre de Villeneuve (1763–1806) would meet Nelson later at Trafalgar.

21 The destruction of *L'Orient* was romantically immortalized by Felicia Hemans in her poem 'Casabianca', famous for its first line in reference to the son of Captain Casabianca who had been aboard with his father, 'The boy stood on the burning deck'.

CHAPTER 4

[1] En route they inadvertently became involved in the Battle of Shubra Khit on their riverboat.

[2] The French had met with no resistance, finding the residents conducting their business as ever, out in the streets, in the markets, on their doorsteps – even the shops were open. With its houses, lush gardens and fields, Rosetta was the most pleasant sight they had encountered since landing a week earlier.

[3] Menou, the disgraced General of the Interior who had failed to clear the Paris streets three years earlier on the historic day of 13 Vendémiaire, had been plucked from obscurity by Bonaparte. Menou was to prove one of his most loyal subordinates. Generals Kléber and Menou had been badly wounded in the assault on Alexandria. Bonaparte consequently reorganized the divisional structure, putting Kléber in command of Alexandria and appointing Menou the Governor of Rosetta, a task for which he was ably suited.

[4] Auguste Fréderic Louis Vienne Marmont, Duc de Raguse (1774–1852).

[5] The number fluctuated over the years as members were replaced or seats left vacant.

[6] The Institute of France was established in 1795 during the Revolutionary period to supersede the royal Academies which had been abolished, or 'suppressed'.

[7] After a lengthy survey conducted in an expedition to the Sinai Peninsula, it appeared the restoration of the canal would not be possible. Later efforts proved these first investigations contained a number of errors in the calculation of land levels.

[8] 'Courier' was a consistent misspelling evident on the paper's front page, and is often corrected to 'Courrier' by commentators.

[9] On the republican calendar, 12 Fructidor, Year VI.

[10] The title refers to the republican calendar's ten-day week, the *décade*.

[11] 22 September 1798; republican New Year fell on the autumn equinox, either the 22, 23 or 24 September.

[12] Herold, in his history of the affair, insists that in fact Bonaparte wisely did not go inside the Pyramid, the entrance to which was awkward, dangerous and, more important, undignified. Bonaparte is credited with calculating that the blocks of the Great Pyramid could make a wall one metre thick and three metres high all around the borders of France – dutifully, Monge later proved him right.

¹³ Thutmosis IV is said to have rested beneath the chin of the Sphinx on a hunting expedition, and dreamt that the Sphinx promised him he would become pharaoh if he restored the monument. He did so and placed a memorial tablet between its paws, since known as the 'Dream Stele'. Consequently Thutmosis could be considered to be the first Egyptologist.

¹⁴ Without question the Sphinx lacked its nose long before the arrival of Bonaparte – the folktale of a French cannon-ball knocking it cleanly from the face is without any basis whatsoever as no cannon were ever fired anywhere near it; the Battle of the Pyramids took place some miles away. The Sphinx was recorded in this damaged state as early as the ninth century AD, suggesting that religious fanaticism had led some to attack the sculpture, much as Puritans attacked sites in Britain and iconoclasts did elsewhere in Europe.

¹⁵ A name applied in the late eighteenth and early nineteenth centuries to the Ramesseum.

¹⁶ Édouard de Villiers du Terrage (1780–1855), often rendered 'Devilliers' in contemporary accounts.

¹⁷ Sir William Sidney Smith (1764–1840) became one of Britain's great naval figures. As heroic as Nelson, and beloved of his peers, he was described by contemporaries as dashing, resourceful and cool-headed. He rose to prominence at Acre, where he and his squadron virtually saved the Ottoman Empire from Bonaparte, cementing the alliance between Turkey and Britain.

¹⁸ It was here that Bonaparte suggested poisoning the infected troops in hospital, on the grounds that they would be a burden on the return to Egypt and spread further disease. Desgenettes, chief medical officer, flatly refused. Commentators have argued that this was to be a merciful release for the suffering victims, but since Bonaparte did not apparently differentiate between terminal cases and those simply with fever or other curable illness, many conclude that his motives were born more of cold logic than compassion for the suffering.

CHAPTER 5

¹ Some historians relate how the stone was stumbled across in the sand by passing soldiers, without reference to Fort Julien or the renovation works, but this is unlikely and contradicts contemporary reports. Today, Fort Julien bears a commemorative plaque detailing the spot where the

discovery was believed to have been made, currently beneath a turret since built over the area. As corroboration of this practical use of the stone in the foundation, other stele fragments can still be seen mortared into the walls.

[2] The report was dated 2 Fructidor Year VII (19 August 1799) but it appeared in print on 29 Fructidor (15 September).

[3] Also rendered as 'Dhautpool' or 'd'Hautpoul'.

[4] Fort Julien, a small castle of the Sultan Qayt Bey, should not be confused with buildings of similar name in Alexandria. Known to locals as *Borg Rashid* (Tower of Rosetta) it was renamed by the French after the death of one of Bonaparte's aides-de-camp, Adjutant General Julien – often spelt Jullien – who was killed in the first week of the invasion the previous year.

[5] Bouchard's year of birth is often thought to be 1772. This is clarified both by Jean Leclant and in Lagier's 1927 account of the affair: Bouchard was one year too old for the new École Polytechnique, but was sufficiently sought-after that his birthdate was doctored accordingly from 1771 to 1772. His military record, however, remained unchanged, giving his year of birth as 1771. Similar confusion exists concerning the year of his death, sometimes given as 1832 – it seems he died on 5 August 1822 after a long illness. Some commentators also misquote Bouchard's name – it has been given as 'Boussard' and 'Boussart' among others; it has been suggested this misunderstanding originates from the Egypt Expedition itself, where there was a *chef de brigade* called Boussard serving in the Armée de l'Orient.

[6] The first is known in Britain as the Battle of the Nile (1 August 1798).

[7] See footnote by Herold regarding the number of Turkish troops. Bonaparte claimed first it was 9,000 and Sir Sidney Smith, who was present with the Turks, estimated 7,000. Only later did Bonaparte report an enemy force of 18,000.

[8] *La Décade Égyptienne*, vol. 3, pp. 293–4.

[9] Michel-Ange Lancret (1774–1807) a civil engineer from the École Polytechnique, like Bouchard, who also sat his final exams at the Institute in Cairo.

[10] *Précis des séances et des travaux de l'Institut d'Égypte, du 21 messidor an 7 au 21 fructidor an 8 inclusivement*, J.-J. Marcel (Summary of sessions and work of the Institute of Egypt from 21 Messidor, Year 7 [9 July 1799] to 21 Fructidor, Year 8 [15 September 1800]). From Saladin Boustany, ed., *The Journals of Bonaparte in Egypt 1798–1801* (Cairo, 1971).

[11] This was noted and put right in 1987 by Jean-Édouard Goby, in 'Premier Institut d'Egypte. Restitution des comptes rendus des séances, Mémoires

de l'Academie des inscriptions et belles-lettres' [new series, vol. 7, Paris, 1987].

[12] After the Turks landed on the 15th they captured the exposed Aboukir fort overlooking the bay. Menou's command in Rosetta was only a few miles distant, and Bonaparte's army had not yet appeared. See De la Jonquière, *L'Expédition d'Égypte: 1798–1801*, 5 vols (Paris, 1899–1907), vol. 2, p. 350.

[13] More puzzling still, Vivant Denon, who returned to Cairo from Upper Egypt in late July–early August, recorded the victory at Aboukir in some detail, yet casts no further light on the discovery of the Rosetta Stone in his narrative of those weeks even though he personally took a great interest in hieroglyphs. Upon his return to the Institute he says he was besieged by eager colleagues but relates nothing of what they told him; his account was swept up in the events of the Turkish landings at Aboukir Bay and Bonaparte's actions.

[14] Although as governor he would certainly have had a proper house, he was preparing for a campaign against the Turks, and had probably moved his headquarters to a pavilion tent in the garrison encampment.

[15] The Greek was fragmented. The final sentence was later confirmed by the translation of the demotic inscription: 'this decree shall be inscribed on a stele of hard stone in sacred and native and Greek script and set up in each of the first, second and third rank temples beside the image of the ever-living king': trans. R. F. Simpson, in Richard Parkinson, *Cracking Codes: The Rosetta Stone and Decipherment* (London: British Museum Press, 1999).

[16] Thomas Young, in a letter to the father of Egyptologist William Bankes, 1818.

[17] *La chute d'el-Arich', décembre 1799: Journal historique du Capitaine Bouchard*, ed. Gaston Wiet (Éditions de la Revue du Caire, 1945).

[18] Bouchard never equalled his discovery of the stone in later life and ended his days in modest obscurity, having had a varied career.

[19] Original entry in *La Décade philosophique*, reporting on the session of 27 October 1799 of l'Institut national de France, recounting the words of Napoleon Bonaparte: 'On a trouvé dans les fondations de Rosette une plaque sur laquelle étaient gravées ou sculptées trois colonnes, portant trois inscriptions, l'une en hiéroglyphes, l'autre en cophte et la troisième en grec. Les inscriptions cophte et grecque signifient également que sous tel des Ptolémées tous les canaux de l'Égypte ont été nettoyés, et qu'il en a coûté telle somme. Il ne paraît pas douteux que la colonne qui porte les hiéroglyphes ne conti-

enne la même inscription que les deux autres. Voilà donc un moyen d'acquérir quelqu'intelligence de ce langage jusqu'à présent inintelligible (*La Décade philosophique*, 10 brumaire, an VIII: 5 November 1799).

[20] See Paul Strathern, *Napoleon in Egypt* (London: Jonathan Cape, 2007), p. 400.

[21] This action of Bonaparte, apparently deserting his colony in Egypt in pursuit of personal power, was not perceived as such by his men. They believed he should indeed go – they distrusted the Directory government and felt their safety relied on their general. Moiret detected a post-Bonaparte whiff of disapproval for this sudden departure when he wrote in his account that the news 'did not cause the sensation' that readers might have supposed. The army was greatly heartened and looked forward to an early return home. See Moiret, *Memoirs of Napoleon's Egyptian Expedition*, p. 122.

[22] On the night of 23 August he was making his way to a supposed rendezvous with Bonaparte in Rosetta on the 24th – by which time Bonaparte had intended to be sailing for France. Most agree that Bonaparte deliberately arranged this false meeting with Kléber to avoid a confrontation. Judging by Kléber's reaction to the news, this was an unwise move.

[23] The famous Roustain, devoted to Bonaparte.

[24] X.-B. Saintine, J.-J. Marcel and L. Reybaud *et al.*, *Histoire scientifique et militaire de l'expédition française en Égypte*, 10 vols (Paris: A.-J. Denain, 1830–34), vol. 6, pp. 434–5.

[25] Ibid., p. 435.

[26] Ibid., p. 444.

[27] Ibid.

[28] The first two English translations of the Greek, first by Weston, then by Plumptre, differ significantly, and Weston worked on his version from April 1802 to January 1803.

[29] Weston confirms this in his own translation: 'Ftha' (phi, theta, alpha) and not 'Fta' (phi, tau, alpha) as sometimes misquoted. See Appendix.

[30] The French reads literally 'Before the Common Era': *avant l'ère vulgaire.*

[31] Louis Rémi Raige continued to struggle with the translation until his death and Marcel achieved great heights in Arabic and Persian linguistics.

[32] Saintine, Marcel and Reybaud *et al.*, *Histoire scientifique*, vol. 7, p. 316.

CHAPTER 6

[1] See Louis Marie de la Révellière-Lépaux, *Mémoires*, vol. 2 (Paris, 1973), p. 348, cited in Herold, *Bonaparte in Egypt*, p. 341.

[2] *La pierre bilingue de Menouf:* little work other than that by Daressy in 1923 was done on this stele, possibly because it seemed of limited value in light of the Rosetta Stone.

[3] Stone was seen as a 'permanent' material and proclamations made in such a medium inevitably carried royal and/or divine importance; the Greek and demotic would have been meant for the public, but the same message would certainly have been conveyed to the gods by means of sacred hieroglyphs.

[4] Bonaparte's *Correspondance*, 32 vols (Paris, 1858–70), vol. 5, p. 565, cited in Herold, *Bonaparte in Egypt*, p. 324.

[5] It was Poussielgue who had dealt with the Knights of St John on Malta before Bonaparte's attack. He later accused Bonaparte of embezzling two million francs of expedition funds which led to the financial straits inherited by Kléber.

[6] It is this episode which Bouchard recorded in his journals *La chute d'El Arich*. When later the French moved out to parley with the Grand Vizier's troops they had to proceed along an avenue of pikes topped with the severed heads of their countrymen from the fort.

[7] This small oblong island is also sometimes rendered Warth or Warwi.

[8] René-Édouard de Villiers du Terrage, *Journal et souvenirs de l'expédition de l'Égypte 1798–1801* (Paris: Plon et Nourrit, 1899), p. 243.

[9] François Rousseau, *Kléber et Menou en Égypte depuis le départ de Bonaparte (août 1799–septembre 1801)* (Paris: Picard et fils, 1900), p. 299.

[10] Nicholas the Turk actually says he roared 'like an infuriated camel'.

[11] Villiers du Terrage, *Journal et souvenirs*, p. 247.

[12] See Jean Leclant, 'Le Lieutenant Bouchard, l'Institut d'Égypte et la pierre de Rosette', *Société française d'égyptologie*, Bulletin 146, 1999.

[13] Rousseau, *Kléber et Menou en Égypte*, p. 299.

[14] Ibid., p. 301.

[15] Georges Rigault, *Le général Abdallah Menou et la dernière phase de l'expédition d'Égypte (1799–1801)* (Paris: Plon et Nourrit, 1911), p. 39.

[16] Reichardt in Rigault, *Le général Abdallah*, p. 39.

[17] A.-F.-L. Wiesse de Marmont, Duc de Raguse, *Mémoires*, 2 vols (Paris, 1857), vol. 1, p. 410.

[18] He was, however, spared the normally requisite circumcision, owing to his age.

[19] It was also a powerful and diplomatic match. Menou later claimed she was of a high-ranking 'sharif' family and thus descended from Mohammed.

[20] Saintine, Marcel and Reybaud *et al.*, *Histoire scientifique*, vol. 8, p. 90.

[21] Had the stone been abandoned in Alexandria after the collapse of the Convention of El Arish this could not be; however, if true, it explains why so little is mentioned of the artefact until Menou's march north to Alexandria in 1801.

CHAPTER 7

[1] Louis-Antoine Fauvelet de Bourrienne, *Memoirs of Napoleon Bonaparte by Louis Antoine Fauvelet de Bourrienne, his Private Secretary*, ed. R. W. Phipps (1891), ch. 6 (1802).

[2] Lieutenant-General Sir Ralph Abercromby KB (1734–1801).

[3] General Sir John Moore (1761–1809); noted for his humanity, he was involved in the defeat of the Irish republicans in 1798 and stood apart from his peers by refusing to perpetuate the atrocities of a brutal campaign. Later became instrumental in devising the first army training camp in Britain.

[4] As found on another stele, the Tanis Stone, which bears the Decree of Canopus, discovered in 1866.

[5] The stone found by Caristie is today designated Louvre Stele C122 (rather than the 'Caristie Stone') and bears traces of the Canopus Decree.

[6] 'Vaisseaux lestes, tête sans lest,/ Ainsi part l'amiral Gantheaume;/ Il s'en va de Brest à Bertheaume,/ Et revient de Bertheaume à Brest!', quoted in Bourrienne, *Memoirs of Napoleon Bonaparte*.

[7] Lt.-Col. Robert Thomas Wilson (1777–1849) was a cavalry officer under Abercromby in Egypt and author of *History of the British Expedition to Egypt* (London, 1803).

[8] Rigault, *Le général Abdallah Menou*, p. 292.

[9] Bourrienne, *Memoirs of Napoleon Bonaparte*.

[10] Some French accounts suggest 10 a.m.

[11] Édouard de Villiers du Terrage believed it was the 11th, but most agree the 12th.

[12] See the *Journal et souvenirs* of Édouard de Villiers du Terrage, p. 89. These famous words have also been quoted as, 'You are not fit to peel onions in the kitchens of the Republic.'

[13] Saintine, Marcel and Reybaud *et al.*, *Histoire scientifique*, vol. 8, p. 283.

[14] Lieutenant-General Sir John Hely-Hutchinson KB, later Baron Hutchinson, and 2nd Earl of Donoughmore (1757–1832).

[15] Janissaries were special Turkish household troops of the sultan, infantry or cavalry, often armed with the curved *yataghan* sword.

[16] Also rendered in Greek as Lake Mareotis.

[17] He makes no mention of it ever being recovered.

[18] Rigault, *Le général Abdallah Menou*, p. 364.

[19] Villiers du Terrage, *Journal et souvenirs*, pp. 304–5.

[20] Saintine, Marcel and Reybaud *et al.*, *Histoire scientifique*, vol. 8, p. 328.

[21] See Anne Petrides and Jonathan Downs, eds, *Sea-Soldier: The Letters and Journals of Major T. Marmaduke Wybourn, RM, 1797–1813* (Tunbridge Wells: Parapress, 2000), p. 43.

[22] Ibid., p. 42.

[23] Ibid., p. 45.

[24] Ibid., p. 46.

[25] Wilson, *History of the British Expedition to Egypt*, 2nd edn (London: Howorth, 1803), p. 336.

CHAPTER 8

[1] Edward Daniel Clarke (1769–1822).

[2] John Marten Cripps (1780–1853).

[3] Clarke's *Travels* were to make his name throughout Britain and were printed in several editions of numerous volumes between 1810 and 1823.

[4] Cripps had inherited a considerable fortune and decided to continue his education with the renowned polymath and tutor Edward Daniel Clarke of Jesus College, Cambridge. It was largely through funds supplied by Cripps that the great journey was undertaken. At first they were joined by others who later returned to England, exhausted after the initial Scandinavian leg of the expedition. One of these was the Reverend William Otter, one of Clarke's closest friends and correspondents.

[5] A handful of British soldiers under General Sir John Moore escorted a fully armed column of roughly 12,000–15,000 French troops and civilians from Cairo to the Delta. The French happily fraternized with the British in many cases, making no attempt to escape from their situation, overjoyed at the prospect of their return home.

[6] Joseph von Hammer-Purgstall (1774–1856), imperial Austrian diplomat serving in Constantinople in 1799, who came with the British expedition to Egypt in 1801. An oriental scholar and linguist, he translated many great works from Arabic, Persian and Turkish.

[7] The ageing Holy Roman Empire of Habsburg-Austria maintained consulates in both Cairo and Alexandria during the French occupation. Rosetti (also

'Rossetti', 1736–1820) had first travelled to Egypt in about 1780 and had established a special relationship with Murad Bey. He built up a reasonable collection of antiquities in his country house at Bulaq.

[8] There is a full description of this piece in Clarke's *Greek Marbles, Brought from the Shores of the Euxine, Archipelago and the Mediterranean* (Cambridge: the University Press, 1809).

[9] Letter from E. D. Clarke to William Otter, August 1801, in William Otter, *Life and Remains of Edward Daniel Clarke, LL.D.* (London: Dove, 1824), p. 486.

[10] William Richard Hamilton (1777–1859).

[11] Known more correctly today as the Parthenon Marbles.

[12] Clarke, *Travels in Various Countries of Europe, Asia and Africa,* p. 199.

[13] Ibid., p. 276.

[14] Ibid., p. 277.

[15] Ibid.

[16] Letter to Otter, September 1801. See Otter, *Life and Remains of Edward Daniel Clarke*, p. 494.

[17] William Richard Hamilton, *Aegyptiaca, or Remarks on Several Parts of Turkey* (London: Cadell and Davies, 1809), p. 343.

[18] At the time this was done partly with a sense of artistic rescue, but mostly as the act of a conquering power confiscating the chattels of a defeated enemy. Loot or 'war booty' was a motivating factor for men of the rank and file, but loftier than this was the concept of spoils, a long-standing tradition and, usually, an accepted aspect of conquest.

[19] Saintine, Marcel and Reybaud *et al.*, *Histoire scientifique*, vol. 8, p. 416.

[20] Rousseau, *Kléber et Menou en Égypte*, p. 423.

[21] *Archives de la Guerre*, cited in Robert Solé and Dominique Valbelle, *The Rosetta Stone: The Story of Decoding Hieroglyphics*, trans. Steven Randall (London: Profile Books, 2002), p. 33.

[22] A story most likely emanating from his obituary.

[23] Rousseau, *Kléber et Menou en Égypte*, p. 424.

[24] Ibid.

[25] Wilson, *History of the British Expedition to Egypt*, p. 229.

[26] Clarke, *Travels in Various Countries of Europe*, p. 325.

[27] Ibid., p. 327. Just as the savants had needed similar documents from Menou to leave in July, so too did Hamilton, Clarke and Cripps need passports; these were a military necessity, respected by friend and foe alike, to provide the bearer with a warrant for his behaviour in or around the lines, lest he be suspected of desertion or espionage.

[28] Hamilton, *Aegyptiaca*, p. 401.

[29] Clarke, *Travels in Various Countries of Europe*, p. 327.

[30] Ibid.

[31] Ibid.

[32] Ibid., p. 328.

[33] Ibid., p. 330.

CHAPTER 9

[1] Clarke, *Travels in Various Countries of Europe*, p. 329.

[2] Ibid.

[3] Ibid., p. 330.

[4] Ibid., p. 331.

[5] Ibid.

[6] Ibid., p. 333. In an effort to reconcile his general admiration of the French with their behaviour in Egypt, Clarke believed the Armée de l'Orient was composed of nothing but the dregs of the nation and foreign conquests.

[7] Ibid.

[8] Ibid., p. 334.

[9] Ibid., p. 328.

[10] Ibid., p. 334.

[11] Ibid., p. 335.

[12] Ibid., p. 336. The old mosque was discovered in the first weeks of the invasion by Vivant Denon who saw the sarcophagus lying inside, possibly in what he interpreted as an abandoned ruin. It is also possible that this local account had grown in exaggerated horror in the intervening three years since its removal.

[13] E. D. Clarke, *The Tomb of Alexander: A Dissertation on the Sarcophagus Brought from Alexandria and Now in the British Museum* (Cambridge: The University Press, 1805), p. 28.

[14] Hamilton, *Aegyptiaca*, p. 403.

[15] Later Major-General Sir Tomkyns Hilgrove Turner (1766–1843). The 3rd Foot Guards later became the Scots Guards of today.

[16] Hamilton, *Aegyptiaca*, p. 402.

[17] Wilson, *History of the British Expedition to Egypt*, p. 229.

[18] Clarke, *Travels in Various Countries of Europe*, p. 349.

[19] Turner, letter of 30 May 1810, to Society of Antiquaries of London, in

Archaeologia, or Miscellaneous Tract Relating to Antiquity, 16 (Society of Antiquaries of London, 1812), p. 213.

20 Supposedly there were as yet no British soldiers within the city. This was possibly a French sentry.

21 Clarke, *Travels in Various Countries of Europe,* p. 344.

22 Ibid.

23 The direct translation of *'chez'* into English as 'in the house of' or 'at the home of' has caused some difficulty for Anglophone historians, especially with regard to Colonel Turner's account of events.

24 Clarke, letter to Otter, September 1801; Otter, *Life and Remains of Edward Daniel Clarke,* p. 494.

25 Clarke, letter to Otter, September 1801; ibid.

26 Saintine, Marcel and Reybaud *et al., Histoire scientifique,* vol. 8, p. 416.

27 Saintine, Marcel and Reybaud's account is more reliable, written as it was by a number of savants, including Geoffroy Saint-Hilaire, who was, with Savigny, by far more relevant to the protest than Nouet or Redouté. If the latter went on a separate occasion with Fourier, Reybaud makes no mention of it.

28 Saintine, Marcel and Reybaud *et al., Histoire scientifique,* vol. 8, p. 420.

29 Ibid., p. 421.

30 Ibid., p. 422.

31 Ibid.

32 Clarke, *Travels in Various Countries of Europe,* p. 366.

33 Ibid., p. 367.

34 Ibid.

35 Ibid. Trans: 'What do you wish, Monsieur Clarke?'

36 Ibid.

37 Clarke, letter to Otter, September 1801. See Otter, *Life and Remains of Edward Daniel Clarke,* p. 495.

38 Clarke, *Travels in Various Countries of Europe,* p. 369.

39 Clarke wrote retrospectively – Hutchinson was made baron after the campaign.

40 Clarke, *Travels in Various Countries of Europe,* p. 372.

CHAPTER 10

1 Author's italics, Turner, in *Archaeologia,* vol. 16, p. 213.

2 Ibid.

[3] Hamilton, *Aegyptiaca*, p. 402.

[4] In 1803 an account appeared in Colonel Wilson's history of the campaign, but he had not been directly involved and spoke only in general terms: 'Some differences had arisen between General Menou and General Hutchinson relative to the antiquities and collections. General Menou had maintained . . . that the famous stone (called the gem of antiquity by the French, as being the key to the hieroglyphic language) was his private property . . . General Menou at last abandoned the claim to the stone', Wilson, *History of the British Expedition to Egypt*, p. 227.

[5] Clarke, *The Tomb of Alexander*, p. 38.

[6] Ibid.

[7] Clarke, *Travels in Various Countries of Europe*, p. 373. Note he refers to Turner as a general, the rank by which Turner signed his account in May 1810.

[8] At the bottom of page 38 of *The Tomb of Alexander*.

[9] Clarke, *Travels in Various Countries of Europe*, p. 378.

[10] Saintine, Marcel and Reybaud *et al.*, *Histoire scientifique*, vol. 8, p. 422.

[11] It could be possible that Clarke made an error with the dates – in a letter to Otter he referred incorrectly to 'Thursday the 11th' (it was the 10th) – but his *Travels* were more accurate: the correctly dated entry for Sunday the 13th concerns a tour of the Necropolis with one of the younger savants acting as a guide.

[12] Rousseau, *Kléber et Menou en Égypte*, pp. 426–7.

[13] Used to lifting cannon and shot, artillerymen would have been the strongest and most qualified personnel to handle the relic, and a gun-carriage would have been the perfect transport for it.

[14] Clarke, *Travels in Various Countries of Europe*, p. 374.

[15] Ibid., p. 401.

[16] Turner in fact refers to the *Madras* as 'the Admiral', a naval term to distinguish the admiral's flagship in a fleet or squadron and not, as some have mistaken, a vessel named HMS *Admiral*. Upon the departure of Admiral Keith the flag was transferred to Bickerton aboard the *Madras*.

[17] Turner, in *Archaeologia*, vol. 16, p. 214.

[18] Extracts from ship's log, HMS *Madras*, October/November 1801. Admiralty papers ADM 51/1386.

[19] Extract from ship's log, HMS *Madras*, 7 November 1801. ADM 51/1386.

[20] Extract from ship's log, HMS *L'Égyptienne*, 7 November 1801. ADM 51/1378.

[21] *Archaeologia*, vol. 16, p. 214.

[22] Ibid., p. 208.

[23] *Spolia opima*: splendid plunder.

[24] *Archaeologia*, vol. 16, p. 214.

[25] Hamilton, *Aegyptiaca*, p. 20 n.

CHAPTER 11

[1] Clarke, *Travels in Various Countries of Europe*, p. 397.

[2] Ibid., p. 399.

[3] Ibid.

[4] Otter, *Life and Remains of E. D. Clarke*, p. 509.

[5] Clarke, *The Tomb of Alexander*, p. 144.

[6] Petrides and Downs, *Sea-Soldier*, p. 49.

[7] See Dorothy King, *The Elgin Marbles* (London: Hutchinson, 2006).

[8] Clarke, *Travels in Various Countries of Europe*, p. 378.

[9] Otter, *Life and Remains of E. D. Clarke*, p. 508.

[10] Ibid.

[11] *Gentleman's Magazine*, vol. 71, p. 1194: 'thus you do, but not for you'.

[12] Ibid., vol. 72, pp. 726–7, August 1802.

[13] Ibid..

[14] Clarke, *The Tomb of Alexander*, p. 24.

[15] *Gentleman's Magazine*, vol. 72, pp. 726–7.

[16] Ibid., pp. 1106–08.

[17] *Archaeologia*, vol. 16, p. 211.

[18] Thomas Young (1773–1829); Jean-François Champollion (1790–1832).

[19] Silvestre de Sacy (1758–1838).

[20] Johann Åkerblad (1763–1819).

[21] Accounts of Young and Champollion's efforts often suffered from an over-simplified nationalist hagiography, implying a polarized Anglo-French academic conflict which did not begin in earnest until after the publication of their findings in 1819 and 1822 respectively. Without question, both men were giants in their field, their principal aim the decipherment of the Egyptian scripts, whether for scientific or personal gain, and not necessarily for the sake of national pride.

[22] (1778–1867). Known as 'Champollion-Figeac' to distinguish him from Jean-François, who was known as Champollion '*le Jeune*', the Younger.

[23] Both extracts De Sacy to Young, cited in Parkinson, *Cracking Codes*, p. 33.

[24] William John Bankes (1786–1855). His dearest friend, Byron, once described the effervescent and party-loving Bankes as 'the father of all mischief'.

25 On his second journey to Egypt in 1818–19, Bankes employed a former circus strongman-turned excavator, Giovanni Belzoni, to retrieve the obelisk. The operation had an inauspicious start, the 20-foot granite monument plunging to the bottom of the Nile where it lay for two years. It was raised in 1821 and taken to the Bankes estate of Kingston Lacy in Dorset. In 1827 the Duke of Wellington laid its foundation stone and it was erected in 1839 on the pedestal of another obelisk retrieved from Philae. The entire process had taken some twenty years. The obelisk still stands today.

26 Henry Salt (1780–1827) British Consul-General in Cairo and chief architect of British efforts to obtain Egyptian antiquities for the British Museum, at times working with and against the Italian collector Drovetti, who often supplied the French.

27 The hieratic script was a forerunner of demotic, both a cursive, more freeflowing handwritten form of hieroglyphs.

28 Such as 'PH' and 'F' in English.

29 Even in his paper to Dacier, Champollion still believed that pure hieroglyphs were predominantly ideograms, though punctuated with phonetics.

30 From *Miscellaneous Works of the Late Thomas Young*, 3 vols (London: John Murray, 1855); vol. 3: *Hieroglyphical Essays and Correspondence*, ed. J. Leitch, p. 220.

31 *Quarterly Review*, no. 55.

32 Leitch, ed. *Hieroglyphical Essays*, p. 256.

33 *Au Account of Some Recent Discoveries in Hieroglyphical Literature and Egyptian Antiquities Including the Author's Original Alphabet as Extended by Mr Champollion*, 1823.

34 See Parkinson, *Cracking Codes*, p. 34.

35 Ibid., p. 38.

36 From Champollion's *Précis du système hiéroglyphique des anciens égyptiens, par M. Champollion le jeune*, 1824.

37 Saintine, Marcel and Reybaud *et al.*, *Histoire scientifique*, vol. 8, p. 459.

38 Ibid.

39 Plates 52–4.

APPENDIX 1

1 Sacred: hieroglyphs.

2 The middle band on the stone, the demotic inscription, also referred to as the 'enchorial', especially by Young.

3 Weston's guess was inaccurate here: the demotic translation confirms that

the stone was set up only in temples of the first, second and third ranks. The end of the final line should read: 'and third rank temples, beside the image of the ever-living king'.

[4] Plumptre's and Porson's translations, made at roughly the same time, do not bear this valediction. It is remarkable to note that it was this fragmented final sentence that confirmed to Michel-Ange Lancret in Rosetta and the savants in Cairo that the stone bore the same text in three different scripts and, therefore, could serve as the code-key it was later to become.

Appendix 3

[1] 'Never has the world been so pillaged!'

[2] 'We shall see each other up close – up close, I assure you!'

[3] This is Clarke's own footnote.

Bibliography

There is a large amount of contemporary material concerning Bonaparte's Egypt expedition, but not all sources contain references to the Rosetta Stone. Only a few French accounts of the expedition have been translated into English, but this source continues to grow. The most famous, that of Vivant Denon, concerns only the period up to 1799 when the stone was discovered; for information thereafter French accounts tend to vary in detail and emphasis, though the multi-volume history by Saintine, Marcel and Reybaud is possibly the most exhaustive, composed, like the *Description de l'Égypte*, by certain savants of the Institut d'Égypte. Below is a number of works and papers which should provide the best starting-point for research.

CONTEMPORARY SOURCES

Bonaparte, Napoleon, *Correspondence*, 32 vols (Paris, 1858–70).

Bourrienne, Louis-Antoine Fauvelet de, *Memoirs of Napoleon Bonaparte by Louis Antoine Fauvelet de Bourrienne, his Private Secretary*, ed. R. W. Phipps (1891).

Brindle, Rosemary, ed. and trans., Captain Joseph-Marie Moiret, *Memoirs of Napoleon's Egyptian Expedition 1798–1801* (London: Greenhill Books, 2001).

Champollion, Jean-François, *Egyptian Diaries – How One Man Solved the Mysteries of the Nile* (London: Gibson Square Co., 2001).

Clarke, E. D., *The Tomb of Alexander: A Dissertation on the Sarcophagus Brought from Alexandria and Now in the British Museum* (Cambridge, 1805).

———, *Greek Marbles, Brought from the Shores of the Euxine, Archipelago and Mediterranean* (Cambridge: the University Press, 1809).

———, *Travels in Various Countries of Europe, Asia and Africa*, 'Greece, Egypt

251

and the Holy Land', 4th edn, vol. 5, Part II, Section II (London: Cadell and Davies, 1810).

Corbett, Julian S., ed., *The Private Papers of George, Second Earl Spencer First Lord of the Admiralty 1794–1801* (London, 1914).

Denon, Vivant, *Travels in Upper and Lower Egypt and the Campaigns of General Bonaparte*, trans. E. A. Kendal, 1802 (repr. London: Darf Publishers, 1986).

Hamilton, William Richard, *Remarks on Several Parts of Turkey*, vol. 1: *Aegyptiaca* (London: Cadell and Davies, 1809).

Herodotus, *Histories*, trans. Robin Aterfield (Oxford: Oxford University Press, 1998).

Leitch, J. ed., *Hieroglyphical Essays and Correspondence*, vol. 3 of *Miscellaneous Works of the Late Thomas Young*, 3 vols (London: John Murray, 1855).

Malus, E. L., *L'agenda de Malus. Souvenirs de l'expédition d'Egypte, 1798–1801* (Paris, 1892).

Marmont, A.-F.-L., Duc de Raguse, *Mémoires*, 2 vols (Paris, 1857), vol. 1.

Napoleon in Egypt: Al-Jabarti's Chronicle of the French Occupation 1798, trans. Moreh, Shmuel et al., 3rd edn (Princeton, N J: Markus Wiener, 1997).

Nicolas Turc (Nicholas the Turk), Nikula ibn Yussuf al-Turki, *Chronique d'Égypte, 1798–1804*, trans. Gaston Wiet (Cairo: 1950).

Petrides, Anne and Jonathan Downs, eds, *Sea-Soldier, The Letters and Journals of Major T. Marmaduke Wybourn, RM, 1797–1813* (Tunbridge Wells: Parapress, 2000).

Pietro (Domenico di) Dominique de, *Voyage historique en Égypte pendant les campagnes des généraux Bonaparte, Kléber et Menou* (Paris, 1818).

Rigault, Georges, *Le général Abdallah Menou et la dernière phase de l'expédition d'Égypte (1799–1801)* (Paris: Plon et Nourrit, 1911).

Rousseau, François, *Kléber et Menou en Égypte depuis le départ de Bonaparte (août 1799-septembre 1801)*, Documents publiés pour la Société d'histoire contemporaine par M. F. Rousseau (Paris: Picard et fils, 1900).

Saintine, X.-B., J.-J. Marcel and L. Reybaud *et al.*, *Histoire scientifique et militaire de l'expédition française en Égypte*, 10 vols (Paris: A.-J. Dénain, 1830–34).

Tracy, Nicholas, ed., *The Naval Chronicles: The Contemporary Record of the Royal Navy at War* (London: Chatham Publishing, 1998).

Turner, 'An account of the Rosetta Stone, in three languages, which was brought to England in the year 1802', *Archaeologia, or Miscellaneous Tracts Relating to Antiquity*, vol. 16 (Society of Antiquaries of London, 1812).

Villiers du Terrage, René-Édouard de, *Journal et souvenirs de l'expédition d'Égypte*, ed. Marc de Villiers du Terrage (Paris: Plon et Nourrit, 1899).

Wilson, Robert Thomas, *History of the British Expedition to Egypt* (London: C. Howorth, 1803).

MODERN COMMENTARIES

Beaucour, Fenand, Yves Laissus and Chantal Orgogozo, *The Discovery of Egypt: Artists, Travellers and Scientists*, trans. Bambi Ballard (Paris: Flammarion, 1999).

Bierbrier, M. L., 'The Acquisition by the British Museum of Antiquities Discovered During the French Invasion of Egypt', *Studies in Egyptian Antiquities: A Tribute to T. G. H. James*, ed. W. V. Davies, British Museum Occasional Paper No. 123.

Bierman, Irene A., *Napoleon in Egypt* (Reading: Ithaca Press, 2003).

Black, Jeremy, *The English Abroad: The Grand Tour in the Eighteenth Century* (New York: St Martin's Press; Stroud: Alan Sutton, 1992).

Boustany, Saladin, ed., *The Journals of Bonaparte in Egypt 1798–1801* (Cairo, 1971).

Bret, Patrice, 'Le physicien, la pyramide et l'obélisque: problèmes d'archéologie monumentale selon Coutelles', *L'expédition d'Égypte, une entreprise des Lumières, 1798–1801* (Paris: Académie des Sciences, 1999).

Briggs, Asa, and Patricia Clavin, *Modern Europe 1789–Present* (Harlow: Pearson Longman, 2003).

Corbett, Julian S., ed., *The Private Papers of George, Second Earl Spencer First Lord of the Admiralty 1794–1801* (London, 1914).

Crecelius, Daniel, 'Egypt in the Eighteenth Century', *The Cambridge History of Egypt*, ed. Carl F. Petry and M. W. Daly (Cambridge: Cambridge University Press, 1998).

De la Réveillière-Lepaux, Louis-Marie, *Mémoires* (Paris, 1973), vol. 2.

Dykstra, Darrell, 'The French Occupation of Egypt 1798–1801', *The Cambridge History of Egypt*, ed. Carl F. Petry and M. W. Daly (Cambridge: Cambridge University Press, 1998).

Herold, J. Christopher, *Bonaparte in Egypt* (London: Hamish Hamilton, 1962).

Hobsbawm, Eric, *The Age of Revolution 1789–1848* (London: Weidenfeld & Nicolson, 1962; repr. London: Abacus, 2002).

Hoock, Holger, 'The British State and the Anglo-French Wars Over Antiquities, 1798–1858',

The Historical Journal, vol. 50, no. 1 (2007): 49–72.

Iversen, Erik, *The Myth of Egypt and Its Hieroglyphs* (Princeton: Princeton University Press, 1969; repr. 1993).

De la Jonquière, Clément, *l'Expédition d'Égypte: 1798–1801*, 5 vols (Paris, 1899–1907), vol. 2,

King, Dorothy, *The Elgin Marbles* (London: Hutchinson, 2006).

Lagier, Camille, *Autour de la Pierre de Rosette* (Bruxelles: Édition de la Fondation Égyptologique Reine Elisabeth, 1927).

Laissus, Yves, 'La Commission des Sciences et des Arts et l'Institut d'Égypte', *L'expédition d'Égypte, une entreprise des Lumières, 1798–1801* (Paris: Académie des Sciences, 1999).

Leclant, Jean, 'Le Lieutenant Bouchard, l'Institut d'Égypte, et la pierre de Rosette', Bulletin 146, Société française d'égyptologie (Paris, 1999).

Parkinson, Richard, *Cracking Codes: The Rosetta Stone and Decipherment* (London: British Museum Press, 1999).

———, *The Rosetta Stone* (London: British Museum Press, 2005).

Ray, John, *The Rosetta Stone and the Rebirth of Ancient Egypt* (London: Profile Books, 2007).

Robinson, Andrew, *The Story of Writing* (London: Thames and Hudson, 1998).

Russell, Terence M., *The Discovery of Egypt: Vivant Denon's Travels with Napoleon's Army* (Stroud: Sutton Publishing, 2005).

———, *The Napoleonic Survey of Egypt: The Monuments and Customs of Egypt: Selected Engravings and Texts*, 2 vols (Aldershot: Ashgate, 2001).

Shaw, Ian, ed., *The Oxford History of Ancient Egypt* (Oxford and New York: Oxford University Press, 2006).

Solé, Robert, and Dominique Valbelle, *The Rosetta Stone: The Story of the Decoding of Hieroglyphs*, trans. Steven Randall (London: Profile Books, 2002).

Strathern, Paul, *Napoleon in Egypt* (London: Jonathan Cape, 2007).

Sweet, Rosemary, *Antiquaries: The Discovery of the Past in Eighteenth-Century Britain* (London: Hambledon and London, 2004).

Tracy, Nicholas, ed., *The Naval Chronicles: The Contemporary Record of the Royal Navy at War* (London: Chatham Publishing, 1998).

Index